# DESIGN BY COMPETITION

What meanings do buildings and places convey to the people who use and visit them? Too often, design competitions and signature architecture result in costly eyesores that do not work. How can sponsors and clients get more meaningful results? In answer to these questions, Dr. Nasar, supported by riveting studies of competitions and Peter Eisenman's competition-winning design for the Wexner Center at the Ohio State University, suggests the use of prejury evaluation (PJE). Dr. Nasar demonstrates the potential value of this approach, as well as for visual quality programming for many different kinds of environmental design.

These studies, from those specific to the Wexner Center to those of historic significance, point towards a new method for shaping the visual form of buildings, places, and cities. Architects, urban designers and planners, social scientists, clients, government officials, and residents will want to read this thought-provoking book. It will give them a new perspective on the designed environment.

Jack L. Nasar is Professor of City and Regional Planning at the Ohio State University. He has published widely on architectural criticism, environmental aesthetics, and urban design. Dr. Nasar has served as chair of the Environmental Design Research Association, as the Ethel Chattel Visiting Scholar at the University of Sydney, and as Fellow in the American Psychological Association. He has also been a research associate at the Westinghouse National Issues Center and a Lilly Endowment Postdoctoral Fellow.

# ENVIRONMENT AND BEHAVIOR SERIES

**Series Editors**

Irwin Altman    *The University of Utah*
Daniel Stokols    *University of California, Irvine*

**Other Books in the Series**

Edward Krupat    *People in Cities: The Urban Environment and Its Effects*
Irwin Altman and Martin M. Chemers    *Culture and Environment*
Ervin H. Zube    *Environmental Evaluation: Perception and Public Policy*
John D. Cone and Steven C. Hayes    *Environmental Problems/Behavior Solutions*
John Zeisel    *Inquiry by Design: Tools for Environment-Behavior Research*
Ralph B. Taylor    *Human Territorial Functioning: An Empirical, Evolutionary Perspective on Individual and Small Group Territorial Cognitive Behavior*
Stephen Carr, Mark Francis, Leanne G. Rivlin, and Andrew M. Stone    *Public Space*
Paul D. Cherulnik    *Applications of Environment-Behavior Research: Case Studies and Analysis*

# DESIGN BY COMPETITION

MAKING DESIGN COMPETITION WORK

*Jack L. Nasar*

CAMBRIDGE
UNIVERSITY PRESS

PUBLISHED BY THE PRESS SYNDICATE OF THE UNIVERSITY OF CAMBRIDGE
The Pitt Building, Trumpington Street, Cambridge, United Kingdom

CAMBRIDGE UNIVERSITY PRESS
The Edinburgh Building, Cambridge CB2 2RU, UK    http://www.cup.cam.ac.uk
40 West 20th Street, New York, NY 10011-4211, USA  http://www.cup.org
10 Stamford Road, Oakleigh, Melbourne 3166, Australia

First published 1999

Printed in the United States of America

*Typeface* ITC New Baskerville 10/12 pt.    *System* QuarkXpress™    [HT]

*A catalog record for this book is available from the British Library*

*Library of Congress Cataloging-in-Publication Data*

Nasar, Jack L.
    Design by competition : making design competition work  /  Jack L /
Nasar.
        p.   cm. — (Environment and behavior series)
    Includes bibliographical references and index.
        ISBN 0 521 44449-7 (hb)
        1. Wexner Center for the Visual Arts.   2. Architecture.
Modern—20th century—Ohio—Columbus.   3. Eisenman/Trott Architects.
4. Columbus (Ohio)—Buildings, structures, etc.   5. Architecture—
Competitions—United States.   6. Communication in architectural
design—United States.   I. Title.   II. Series.
NA6813.U8CS58   1999
720´.79—dc21                                                  98-44685
                                                                  CIP

ISBN 0 521 44449-7 hardback

*To my daughter Joanna Lynn Nasar*

There was a most ingenious architect who had contrived a new method for building houses, by beginning at the roof and working downwards to the foundation, which he justified to me by the like practice of those two prudent insects the bee and the spider (p. 126). – Gulliver's Travels[273]

Has there ever been another place on earth where so many people of wealth and power have paid for and put up with so much architecture they detested as within they blessed borders today? (p. 3) – Tom Wolfe[311]

# SERIES FOREWORD

In recent decades the relationship between human behavior and the physical environment has attracted researchers from the social sciences – psychology, sociology, geography, and anthropology – and from the environmental-design disciplines – architecture, urban and regional planning, and interior design. What is in many respects a new and exciting field of study has developed rapidly. Its multidisciplinary character has led to stimulation and cross-fertilization, on the one hand, and to confusion and difficulty in communication, on the other. Those involved have diverse intellectual style and goals. Some are concerned with basic and theoretical issues; some, with applied real-world problems of environmental design.

This series offers a common meeting ground. It consists of short books on different topics of interest to all those who analyze environment-behavior links. We hope that the series will provide a useful introduction to the field for students, researchers, and practitioners alike, and will facilitate its evolutionary growth as well.

Our goals are as follows: (1) to represent problems the study of which is relatively well established, with a reasonably substantial body of research and knowledge generated; (2) to recruit authors from a variety of disciplines with a variety of perspectives; (3) to ensure that they not only summarize work on their topic but also set forth a "point of view," if not a theoretical orientation – we want the books not only to serve as texts but also to advance the field intellectually – and (4) to produce books useful to a broad range of students and other readers from different disciplines and with different levels of formal professional training. Course instructors with be able to select different combinations of books to meet their particular curricular needs.

*Irwin Altman*
*Daniel Stokols*

# ACKNOWLEDGMENTS

Though I cannot trace all sources of my ideas, two individuals stand out as important influences. Oscar Newman awakened me to the significance of building milieu to people, the differences in the taste of architects and laypersons, and the idea of evaluating architecture for users after occupancy. Jack Wohlwill brought my attention to principals of aesthetic response and scientific methods of measurement. The book also draws on ideas from Henry Sanoff on the scientific methods applied to architecture and visual quality; Wolfgang Preiser on postoccupancy evaluation; and from several researchers on visual quality, including Daniel Berlyne, Stephen and Rachel Kaplan, and Amos Rapoport.

Some material in this book has appeared elsewhere in different form.[173][182] I thank the many graduate students who worked with me and assisted with the research: Junmo Kang helped with the Post Jury Evaluation; Jahnee Prince helped with the crime and fear studies; Maral Cheterian, Timothy Imeokparia, and Ray Nix helped assemble the data for one of the historiometric inquiries; and Peg Grannis interviewed local architects and gathered data about people's evaluations of competition winners and losers through time. Students in my class on programming and building evaluation helped gather data on the evaluation of the Wexner Center. They included Kari Cassell, Elizabeth Cultice, Mohammad Farhan, Peg Grannis, Michael Giuliani, Junmo Kang, Arif Shahzad Khan, Frank Kretchmar, Dirk Longbrake, Dan Ogle, Jahnee Prince, Cia Rodeman, Larry Rosenthal, Mohamed Tarikel, and Richard Wooten. Kari Cassell did additional work on wayfinding on the Wexner Center site.

Thanks also to Lucy Caswell, William B. Cook, Tom Heretta, Frank Ludden, Al L. Matthews, Patrick Maughan, Jill Morelli, Robert Stearnes, and Susan Wyngaard who provided information about Wexner Center and various buildings on The Ohio State University campus.

Exchange of ideas with my colleagues Bonnie Fisher, Kenneth Pearlman, Burkhard von Rabeneau, Philip Viton, and Gerrald Voss helped shape this work. I am also grateful to City and Regional Planning and the Knowlton School of Architecture at The Ohio State University for giving me the time to work on this book.

I thank the Cambridge University Press editor, Julia Hough, for shepherding me through the publishing process. I am grateful to Kimberly Devlin, Stephan Kaplan, Brenda Lightner, Gary Moore, and Robert Marans for their comments on early material of this book. I am also grateful to Kathryn Anthony, Paul Hekkert, Nick Ingoglia, Sandra Gross, Wolfgang F. E. Preiser, John Simpson, and Paul Young for their comments on early drafts of the whole book. Special thanks go to Irwin Atlman and Dan Stokols whose insightful editorial comments helped me shape this book into its present form.

# TABLE OF CONTENTS

# ILLUSTRATIONS AND TABLES

### Tables

# INTRODUCTION

> My work is not about convenience – it is about art. I am not suggesting
> that people should necessarily live in art – I don't live in art – and I'm
> not suggesting people ought to live in my architecture – Peter
> Eisenman, architect (p. 66)[57]

Budgeted for $16 million, the design for the Wexner Center for the
Visual Arts at The Ohio State University (OSU) ended up costing
almost three times as much. The university architect told me that this
design by Peter Eisenman and Richard Trott had "more than the normal amount of startup problems." Robert Stearns, the first director of
the center, described it as "expensive to operate . . . (with) serious problem in its use."[196] Within six years of the opening, OSU had to spend an
additional $1 million to fix roof leaks. OSU also expects to allocate $5
to $10 million more for a renovation to correct lighting problems inter-
fering with the main function of the facility. The building has had a
flood. Yet, the Wexner Center design resulted from a design competition, in which five teams of internationally known architects submitted
designs, and a panel of experts selected the Eisenman/Trott design as
the best. Critics raved about the design. It won a prestigious award from
*Progressive Architecture* magazine, which also devoted an issue to the
building.

What is going on here? The Wexner Center illustrates a common
phenomenon. The competition-winning building, praised by architects
and critics, does not work; and the citizens, whose tax dollars paid for
much of it, do not like it.

Millions of people experience architecture and competition architecture daily as occupants or passersby. The public nature of architecture
makes it distinct from art, music, literature, or theater, where the audience can freely choose the experience. The public has to live with the
buildings. Architecture and design competition architecture should
agree with and function for the public. Good design can captivate the
viewer, convey meanings about a place, and evoke delight. Too often
competition architecture leaves the typical observer baffled and disappointed. (Signature architecture – buildings by famous architects – has
a similar outcome.) The reaction highlights a split between two kinds of

meanings: the high-brow artistic statement intended for the appreciation of other artists and the everyday meanings seen by the public and occupants.

For thousands of years, elite patrons turned to artists to create public symbols. The patrons decided what was uplifting for the public. Although in the U.S. monarchs or popes no longer make those decisions, we do expect someone to make them. In a democratic society, the decisions should come from the people and for the people. This does not occur for competition architecture and for much public architecture. To encourage freedom in the artistic statement, public clients relinquish responsibility to a competition jury and architect. They accept the prejudice that elite judges should select the design and present it "to the public for its enlightenment." (p. 269).[45]

Architects, like other professionals, value peer evaluations with criteria removed from the interests of the client or public. They see architecture primarily "in sacrosanct terms of art" (p. 36).[58] They give the aesthetic standards of the relatively small audience of their peers priority over popular meanings and function for the end user. For much of the twentieth century, modern architecture rejected historical ornamentation and popular meanings as dishonest and bourgeois. Postmodern architecture came to the forefront briefly with an argument for returning to historical forms, but research shows that the public saw no difference between modern and postmodern designs.[90] [172] Then came deconstructivism with a revived elitist position – the intent to offend the bourgeois sensibility. The public continues to see the resulting buildings as dysfunctional, hostile, and meaningless.[36] [60] This separation of the professional values from those of the public relates to a general phenomenon in academic circles. Theory determines practice, as does deconstructionism in literature, where only professional critics can read certain works or understand their value. Architects, however, have a public responsibility. They require a license to practice. Architecture must consider and have accountability to the public. How can one balance the different perspectives and still get designs that appeal to and work for the public and everyday occupant?

In this book, I present a process for achieving that end. I delve into the importance of meaning and the differences between what appeals to the public and designers. In examining the conflict between these two kinds of meaning, I also touch the broader issue of the clash between democratic and elitist values. In a democracy, design decisions about public architecture should heed citizen reactions. In several studies of Eisenman's competition-winning design for the Wexner Center, I demonstrate and test a democratic method for forecasting meanings conveyed by buildings to the public. This book uses the

Wexner Center competition as a vehicle for presenting my approach to design competitions.

The method – *prejury evaluation (PJE)* – involves the scientific study of popular opinion about design entries prior to the jury deliberations. PJE fits into a broader cyclical and scientific framework for design, that has three phases.[25][48][316] *Programming* develops a detailed and comprehensive document (called the program, specs or brief) that specifies the project requirements. *Design review* analyzes the plan in light of the program and research to make informed predictions about likely outcomes. It tries to catch and correct faults before they occur. For competitions, PJE represents an important part of design review. *Postoccupancy evaluation (POE)* systematically evaluates the functioning of the facility for the occupants and visitors after building completion and occupancy.[156][231] The information from each phase can improve the performance of the existing place. Used as *predesign research (PDR)*, it can also improve future programs and design reviews.[25][48] This book adapts the framework for managing building appearance and meaning to the public. One develops a visual quality plan (or guidelines for appearance); one forecasts likely public meanings through PJE; and one evaluates the appearance of the completed project to the public in a POE.

*Design by Competition* has three parts, each of which adds to the picture. Part One provides a background for understanding design competitions. It introduces a central concern: Preliminary evidence shows competition buildings – highly public entities – as flawed for the occupants and passersby who regularly experience them. Although competitions attract publicity, as did the Wexner Center, publicity does not necessarily translate into a successful building. Architects and juries of experts misjudge public response, tending to focus exclusively on the artistic statement and rejecting popular meanings. Not surprisingly, design competitions and signature architecture often yield controversial buildings, disliked by the public. The increased reliance of public bodies around the world on design competitions and the increased costs associated with them add to the magnitude of this public policy concern. Part One discusses these aspects of competitions. It describes potential pros and cons of competitions and presents examples of competition successes and failures. It concludes with two empirical studies of how well competition architecture has stood the test of time, in the eyes of critics, architects, and nonarchitects.

Part Two narrows to the methods and their application in evaluating the performance of the Wexner Center. It describes the way to develop a visual quality plan (or program) for meaning. It describes a PJE, examining popular reactions to the five Wexner entries, and it evaluates the PJE in postoccupancy studies that look at how well it, as compared to the jury, did in predicting public evaluations of the completed building. Part Two concludes with a comprehensive POE on how well the Wexner Center works for users and its intended purposes.

In the third part of the book, I formulate a model for running competitions. The model includes programming, a series of steps for managing the jury process, and POE. Part Three goes beyond competitions to discuss other ways to achieve a more democratic architecture. It formulates steps clients, communities, and citizens can take to improve the quality of their designed environment.

The text includes some technical details in sidebars. The appendices also offer technical details. The first appendix evaluates the usefulness, accuracy, and generality of the method used in the PJE. The second appendix reprints interviews with the benefactor and the architects competing in the Wexner Center about competitions and the Wexner Center competition. The third appendix present ancillary tables and figures of statistics from the various studies.

I started the research with one question. How well did one jury's choice reflect popular judgments of competition entries? The findings of that study led to another, which in turn led to another, and to the book you hold in your hand. I had no idea where that first study would lead, but each new finding added to a picture of a better way to deliver public buildings. That picture and this book rest on the premise that one can use scientific research to guide decisions about the meanings conveyed by designs. The cyclical process of programming, design review, and postoccupancy evaluation conforms with this view. It makes the details (or design hypotheses) explicit in the program, tests those hypotheses through systematic empirical observation in the design review, and retests them in the POE. This kind of scientific approach can build a knowledge base for evaluating and improving future designs and competitions for the public.

# 1

# THE WEXNER CENTER COMPETITION

Eisenman's competition winning design for the Wexner Center is: one of the most eagerly awaited architectural events of the last decade . . . a remarkable structure – Paul Goldberger, *The New York Times* architectural critic[82]

A masterpiece. – Philip Johnson, architect (comment at Wexner opening ceremony)

An amazing facility. – Stanley Tigerman, architect (comment at Wexner opening ceremony)

The design competition for the Wexner Center had a vague program, *ad hoc* criteria used by a jury weighted toward the arts, and a hands-off position by the client toward the designers. As a client, the university stressed publicity. Although each competition has its idiosyncrasies, the Wexner story illustrate qualities of many competitions.

In autumn 1982, OSU's Board of Trustees authorized the competition and provided $150,000 for it.[193] Richard Miller, a faculty member in the School of Architecture at Ohio State, headed the thirteen-member selection committee that identified the five final teams. Designs from his graduate studio in June 1982 helped spur OSU President Ed Jennings to proceed with a competition. According to Miller, the competition would select "the most fitting architectural form for the center" (p. 22).[153] From a list of eighteen state-approved architects, Miller's committee chose nine Ohio firms. It also chose twenty-seven out-of-state firms, seventeen of which answered the invitation to compete. Each out-of-state firm received instructions to team up with an in-state firm. Nine teams did so and submitted their qualifications and credentials. On January 12, 1983, Miller's committee selected five finalists:

> Eisenman/Robertson (New York) and Trott & Bean (Columbus)
> Arthur Erickson (Vancouver) and Feinkopf, Macioce & Shappa (Columbus)

Michael Graves (Princeton) and Lorenz & Williams Inc. (Dayton)

Kallmann, McKinnell, and Wood (Boston) and Nitschke Associates (Columbus)

Cesar Pelli & Associates (New Haven) and Dalton, van Dijk, Johnson & Partners (Cleveland)

Each finalist already had an international reputation (see sidebar).

---

### THE COMPETITORS

At fifty-one years old, *Peter Eisenman* had designed a handful of houses, but he had built a reputation of architectural theory challenging conventions through his magazine *Oppositions* and through books, lectures, and his Institute for Architecture and Urban Studies. A Fellow of the American Institute of Architects (AIA), he had received the Arnold W. Brunner Memorial Prize in architecture and had held faculty positions at Cambridge University, Cooper Union, Yale University, and, at the time of the competition, Harvard University. He has degrees in architecture from Cornell, Columbia, and Cambridge Universities.

*Arthur Erickson* (age fifty-nine) won the competition for the Simon Frazer University, near Vancouver, twenty years earlier, and had designed the Canadian Pavilion at Expo 1970 in Montreal. An AIA Fellow, he received gold medals from the Royal Architectural Institute in Canada and the presidential award of excellence from the American Society of Landscape Architects. He has a bachelors of architecture from McGill University.

*Michael Graves* (age forty-nine) had designed more than twenty buildings, winning eighteen national design awards. He had won the widely publicized competition for the Humana Tower in Louisville, Kentucky. The Museum of Modern Art in New York City had exhibited his work in seven group shows. A Fellow of the AIA, he won the Rome prize from the American Academy in Rome, the Arnold W. Brunner Memorial prize in architecture, and was named the Interior Designer of the Year. He holds degrees in architecture from the University of Cincinnati and Harvard University and had taught at Princeton for twenty-one years.

*Bernard Michael Kallmann* (age sixty-eight) and *Michael McKinnell* (age forty-eight) had won the national competition for the Boston City Hall in 1962 and several design awards. McKinnell had studied under Kallmann at Columbia University. After the competition, they set up their office with Henry Wood in Boston. They both taught at Harvard University.

*Cesar Pelli* (age fifty-one) had degrees in architecture from University of Tucuman (Argentina) and University of Illinois. He worked for Eero Saarinen and Associates and Gruen Associates before becoming Dean of the Yale School of Architecture and setting up his won office in New Haven. His Pacific Design Center in Los Angeles brought his name to national prominence. An AIA Fellow, he had received the Arnold M. Burnner Memorial Prize. More recently he received the Gold Medal of the AIA, and was named to the top ten list of living American Architects.

---

The university issued a program for the Wexner Center in January 1982.[192] A steering committee of thirty-eight university people met in small groups to develop the initial program. As a participant in these meetings, I noticed that the two facilitators, Jonathan Green (Director of the University Gallery of Fine Art) and Andrew J. Broekema (Dean of the College of the Arts), were interested more in the appearance of a participatory process than in a true participatory process. For example, they disregarded comments by a landscape architect on the importance of the landscape. Green envisioned the site "as a work space and exhibition area for works that range from traditional sculpture to 'earthworks; and land-form art" (p. 19), and envisioned the architecture as "more than functional. It must signify possibility and limitless experience. . . . It must signify to us and future generations a commitment to the broadest notions of experimentation, research and human visual creativity" (p. 20).[89]

The process resulted in a vague program. According to Miller, "neither the program nor the site was proscriptive" (p. 22).[153] Part A of the program described the site and the general characteristics of the building and programs it would house. It allowed the designers to adjust areas and adjacencies. Instead of a specific site, it presented a general territory on the east end of the campus and asked the competitors to choose between two large sites. Part A also indicated some vague goals. It stated that the building should be "an inviting aesthetic statement," "a focal point for the University and the community," "anticipate the directions of the future," "very functional," "dedicated to experimentation and vanguard artistic activity," and "a meeting point for the public and art" (p. 5–6).[192] It gave the designers "the prerogative to review adjacent building" to possibly locate "some of the programmed items into those sites" (p. 5). Part B listed and prioritized spaces along with some minimum descriptions of their characteristics. The description offered little to nothing about the desired character of space and adjacencies,

Figure 1.1. Visual Arts Center entry by Peter Eisenman.
Courtesy of The Ohio State University Archives.

but it did set a project cost of $16 million. The philanthropist Leslie H. Wexner agreed to give a $10 million gift to the university to help build the center.

The five teams visited campus in February 1983 for a briefing. Miller's committee then recommended a final jury to President Jennings. The jury consisted primarily of artists and architects. Heading the jury was the internationally known architect, Henry N. Cobb, Fellow of the AIA (FAIA) (partner in I. M. Pei & Partners and chairman of the Department of Architecture at the Graduate School of Design at Harvard). Other members included Noverre Musson, AIA (an architect from Columbus, Ohio), Jan van der Marck (director of the Center for the Fine Arts, Miami, Florida), Budd Harris (director of the Columbus Museum of Art), Jonathan Green (Director of the University Gallery), Douglas Davis (senior writer in architecture, photography, and contemporary ideas at *Newsweek*), David Black (professor of art, OSU), Barbara Groseclose (associate professor of art history, OSU), and William J. Griffith (assistant vice-president emeritus of Campus Planning and Space Utilization, OSU). The jury, dominated by avant-garde designers and artists, did not adequately represent the eventual consumers and the public.

In April 1983, the five teams submitted their proposals. Figures 1.1 through 1.5 show the final entries by Peter Eisenman; Arthur Erickson; Michael Graves; Kallmann, McKinnell, Wood; and Cesar Pelli.

Figure 1.2. Visual Arts Center entry by Arthur Erickson. Courtesy of Arthur Erickson Architectural Corp.

On April 15, 1983, the jury met to establish its rules and a schedule for their deliberations. Prior to the meeting they received background material "on the historical development of the campus, the campus plan and its objectives and the program" (p. 26).[51] The jury agreed that the entries would be put on display over the weekend, and that each member would go individually, pick up the submission brochures and view the submissions for as long as necessary. On the following Monday morning, they would begin deliberations. They did not set out any specific criteria, but they did agree "to select the best solution to the program of requirements as amended by subsequent communications by the professional advisor to the collaborating architect teams." They decided to base their evaluations on one six-page section of the twenty-four-page program: This short section described the two sites and gave vague and general descriptions of the desired building (p. 26).[51] The jury set aside the specific description of desired facilities and their characteristics as less important. They held all deliberations in private. On the morning of May 29 the jury discussed the entries in the order of

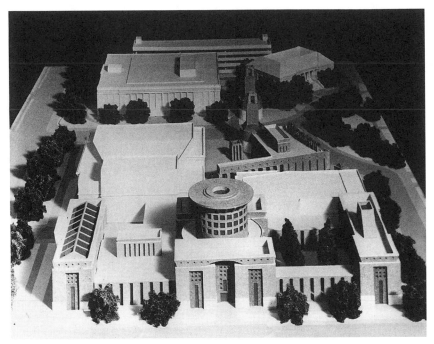

Figure 1.3. Visual Arts Center entry by Michael Graves.
Courtesy of Paschall/Taylor.

their eventual presentation, with each juror presenting an initial
appraisal of each submission. That afternoon each design team gave a
half-hour presentation, followed by a half hour of questions from and
discussion with the jury. On the following morning, the jury met again.
The jurors presented their points of view and then they began a process
of elimination. They had a final round of comments and a vote. That
evening, they wrote the jury report and letter to the university president. The jury indicated a unanimous judgment in favor of one proposal: the Eisenman/Trott design.

In their letter, the jurors indicated that they had selected the design
because it "made the best use of the available site and offers the best
solution to the program requirements" (p. 24).[51] The jury report
echoed some of the vague and metaphorical language found in Part A
of the program. It said:

> This proposal best captured the spirit, dynamism, and open-endeness
> of the new center's programmatic needs . . . It fits a program . . . dedi-
> cated both to experimentation and vanguard artistic activity and to

Figure 1.4. Visual Arts Center entry by Kallmann, McKinnell, and Wood. Courtesy of The Ohio State University.

collecting, scholarship and research. . . . The design solution embodies the notions of participation and accessibility. . . . (It) will offer . . . continuing visual contact with the center's activities. . . . It symbolized collaborative arts activities. . . . It extends the parkscape environment and enhances the pedestrian approach to the university. . . . It provokes speculation and almost relished the idea of uncertainty. . . . The jury feels that the open-ended, accessible and dynamic quality of this

Figure 1.5. Visual Arts Center entry by Cesar Pelli. Courtesy of Cesar Pelli & Associates.

building is its most precious attribute. The recommended solution is adventurous and challenging yet deeply responsive to the campus setting. (pp 24–25).[51]

David Black, a juror who had an abstract sculpture on the site, wrote a separate report. Although he agreed with the decision, describing the design as "very pleasing and adventurous," he expressed concerns that "the present 'long walk' across the Oval from the library be extended as a continued straight walk and vista from the library to High Street and thus remain a main focus of such a plaza" (p. 26).[51] He also questioned the design and placement of a reconstructed historic element (the Old Armory) in the plan.

Publicity took off. An exhibition of the entries appeared at OSU, Harvard University Graduate School of Design, and the American Academy in Rome. Articles appeared in *Progressive Architecture, Architectural Record, Inland Architect,* and *The Architectural Review.* The university contracted Rizzoli to publish an edited collection on it.[17] In January 1985, a little less than three months after the groundbreaking for the new building, *Progressive Architecture* honored the Eisenman design with the top award in its thirty-second Annual Awards Program.[220]

### Opening Ceremonies

Five years later, on November 16, 1989, the Center opened to the public. Several weeks earlier, the university sent out a seventy-page press kit. The press kit came packaged in a specially fabricated box, that slid open along a 12¼ degree angle, representing a generating geometry of the winning design. The kit included the press release and separate articles on the building, the architects, the theory and practice of Eisenman, the genesis of the Wexner Center, and the competition process. It had interviews with Eisenman, with Stearns (Center director), and statements by Jennings (OSU president) and Wexner (the benefactor). OSU invited the press to a separate and private viewing of the facility.

The press kit offered unconditional praise for the competition, the architect, and the design. Jennings described the facility as "extraordinary . . . a pathway into the University . . . (that) links the community and our Columbus campus."[198] He hoped it would serve "as both an example and a powerful symbol of the strengths of this university."[245] Wexner envisioned the Center as opening "an unprecedented cultural era at The Ohio State University and within our community . . . a special place for outstanding students, scholars, visiting artists and critics to converge and examine traditional and contemporary art forms."[199] He wanted it to invigorate "participation in the arts within the University and its community" and to serve as a "magnet for attracting faculty, artists and students."[199] Evaluating the design, he said, "I believe architects Peter Eisenman and Richard Trott skillfully designed the building to accommodate and stimulate creative work."[199] The press release described the architect as "one of the world's most influential and controversial architects" and characterized the design as reflecting the "university's commitment to building an art center that will be forward-looking and innovative" (p. 2).[194] It quoted Eisenman as saying the design "responds sensitively to the history and context of the campus" (p.2).[194] Stearns hoped the facility would allow the presentation of "arts of our time, to reveal the underlying parallels among the many art forms and to offer to the public insights into the future of the arts" (p. 2).[196] He described the design as challenging "conventional thinking about art centers. . . . Anyone who has been working in an exhibition space begins to develop a sixth sense about how to use it. The curators and I don't yet have that sense. No doubt there are possibilities we won't discover till later. I'm more and more convinced as I go through the building how exciting and challenging it is" (p. 2, 12).[196]

The opening ceremonies for the building included leading artists and entertainers, a laser light show, champagne receptions, and a panel of world-famous architects commenting on the building. Rather than having an exhibition in the building, the university made the building the exhibition. Visitors received portable cassette players with a recorded program (developed by the California-based group, Antenna Theater) directing them through the building. The recording described the building as "reason out of control, reason gone crazy, obsessive, mad!"

The morning ceremonies, moderated by the actor Colleen Dewhurst, included performances by the cutting-edge artists J. D. Steel Gospel Singers, the dancer Trisha Brown, the Grammy-award winning Kronos Quartet, and performance artist Laurie Anderson. Barbara Walters provided a video clip. The opening night dinner included Dewhurst, Walters, A. Alfred Taubman, a major real-estate developer and arts patron, and dancer-choreographer Martha Graham.[82] A group of illustrious architects, including Philip Johnson first winner of the Pritzker prize (architecture's equivalent of the Nobel) and Richard Meier, also a Pritzer prize winner, gathered at a public forum to discuss the building. Kurt Forster (Director of the Getty Center for the History of Art and Humanities) moderated the panel. Johnson opened the discussion. Other architects on the panel included Henry N. Cobb, Michael Graves, Stanley Tigerman, and Charles Gwathmey. (Along with Eisenman, Graves, Gwathmey, and Meier were members of a group known among architects as the New York Five). One of the members, John Hejduk, did not attend). Recall that Cobb (a winner of the Arnold W. Brunner Memorial Prize in Architecture) had chaired the competition jury. Graves (FAIA), one of the competitors, had won many design awards, including the Brunner. Tigerman, an architect and educator, had won many awards including the National Interior Architects Award of Excellence. Gwathmey (FAIA), principal of Gwathemy–Siegel Architects, had a Medal of Honor and the Brunner. He had been stranded in New York by a storm, but he rented a Lear Jet to get to the ceremony on time.

Each architect praised the design. Johnson waved off his own comment about the difficulties of finding the front door as minor and proceeded to describe the design as "a masterpiece by a genius." He continued:

> Here in my home state, we have a building that may be one of the turning points in the history of architecture. In this place and on this

day, a new epoch in the history of the world is beginning, and we shall be able to say that we have been present at its origin.

Coming from the person whose book *The International Style*[107] had helped launch modern architecture, this was no small compliment. Tigerman called it "an amazing facility." He said, "I can't think of anything easier to do than to hang art there." Meier said that the design showed Eisenman as "a supremely sophisticated and infinitely subtle orchestrater of space."

### What Is the Design About?

Eisenman challenges the assumptions of architectural practice and the complacency of architects and the public toward their architectural surroundings. He strives to open up the profession. Through his design, writing, lecturing, and studio course throughout the world, he has had a substantial influence on architectural educators and on a new generation of architects. "Eisenman's theories focus on a desire to reject the conventions of architecture. He spurns traditional notions of buildings as responding directly to their functional needs (p. 38).[82] As a leading proponent of deconstructivist architecture, he sought an architecture that "attempts to be disturbing, alienating," (p. 18) and "produce(s) a sense of insecurity" (p. 19).[312] Deconstructivist design tries to transform architecture into an agent of instability. According to Mark Wrigley, the associate curator of the deconstructivist exhibition at The Museum of Modern Art, "This is an architecture of disruption, dislocation, deflection, deviation and distortion" (p. 17).[312] It challenges "the very values of harmony, unity and stability . . . (and strives for) 'impure,' skewed geometric compositions . . . to produce a feeling of unease, of disquiet" (p. 11, 17).[312] Eisenman saw, "this idea of creating uncertainty in space where formerly there was always certainty" as a central idea in the work (p. 3) (Figure 1.6).[195] For the gallery he "wanted to create an edge, where one is not quite sure where one is" (p. 5).[195] The designers also noted that "the campus grid and the city grid differ by $12\frac{1}{4}$ degrees. We have used the Columbus street grid to generate a new pedestrian path into the Oval, a ramped east/west axis" (p. 3–4).[194]

To disrupt the idea of the "ground level as a sacred plane," the site has planters erupting from it; and inside, a long ramp ascends along side the gallery spaces. The design includes reconstructed fragments of the armory, intended as "an analogy to the fragmentation of the past." The Armory, a popular campus building, had burned down in 1958. By peeling and relocating the towers (Figure 1.7), the architects intended "a gesture against literal historicism" telling the viewer, "this is not the

Figure 1.6. View from the entrance lobby to the gallery space. The design as an agent of instability. Photograph by Jack L. Nasar.

real armory. The old is eroded, unveiled, cut away by the present and the future" (p. 3–4).[194] The exterior also has a white scaffolding cutting between two buildings (Figure 1.8). The designers described it as symbolizing "construction in process," because they could not know what a

Figure 1.7. Fragments of the armory peeled and relocated as a gesture against literal historicism. Photograph by Jack L. Nasar.

twenty-first-century art center would look like (p. 3–4).[194] One critic notes that Eisenman sees the idea of a building trying to be beautiful or symbolizing a function as, "limitations . . . not due to any essential aspect of architecture; rather, they constitute a resistance, a received value structure by which the architecture is repressed" (p. 1).[197]

Figure 1.8. White scaffolding symbolizing "construction in progress." Photograph by Jack L. Nasar.

### Media Attention and Awards

The completed building received extensive coverage in the architectural and popular press. Three architectural magazines – *Progressive Architecture, Architecture,* and *Urbanism* – developed special issues on the building. Major newspapers and magazines covered it, weighing in with glowing reviews. Paul Goldberger, the architectural critic for *The New York Times,* described the Center as "one of the most eagerly awaited architectural events of the last decade" (p. 1).[82] He went on to describe it as "a remarkable structure . . . a building of intense brilliantly controlled energy and moments of surprising serenity . . . a building of considerable sensual power" (pp. 1, 38).[82] Writing in *Museum News,* Roger Lewis, architectural critic for the *Washington Post,* mentioned a number of problems, but concluded that the design "succeeded in creating a landmark building . . . a public success" (pp. 34, 37).[136] Catherine Fox, visual arts critic of *The Atlanta Constitution,* described it as "what many consider the architectural event of the year" and as "visually pleasing" (p. 1).[70] In *The Christian Science Monitor,* Laura Van Tuyl described the design as triggering "a surge of emotion here and across the United States" as "prominent architects have flocked to see it" (p. 10).[287] In *Newsweek*, Cathleen McGuigan, called it "crazy, inventive and full of life" (pp. 74–75);[149] and in *Time*, Kurt Anderson described it as "appropriately both grand and zany" (pp. 84–89).[7] In January 1993, the AIA selected the building for its Honor award. "It shrieks at visitors, challenging basic assumptions of what architecture should be," said the AIA (p. 4).[118] In commenting on the Wexner Center design, Eisenman said, "The architecture challenges the notion of how you perceive space, how you relate to art. I can't tell you what to feel about it, though. How you respond to that dislocation and that questioning is up to you, and that's what will determine the success or failure of the building" (p. 4).[118]

The Wexner Center competition proved a publicity coup for the sponsor, the architect, and architecture. It received widespread favorable media attention, helped launch the career of Peter Eisenman as a practicing architect, and it helped launch and legitimize a new direction in architecture – deconstructivism. It demonstrates the publicity possible through a competition. But what happens when the critics leave town? Much of the rest of the book looks at the reality of competition architecture as experienced by users and passersby, and how sponsors could improve the results through a more systematic approach.

# 2

# WHAT DO WE KNOW ABOUT ARCHITECTURAL COMPETITIONS?

In a competition, architects are pressed to do their best work. . . . It is very different working to win than when an architect already has a commission. . . . The client is like the dealer: He cannot lose. He gets a design, models, drawings, and publicity. – Peter Eisenman, architect (author interview)

Quite apart from obvious benefits of opening career possibilities to young or even not so young architects . . . it (a competition) allows one to do what one thinks is right on the basis of a brief, and to be judged by one's peers. It is a vehicle for the exploration of ideas. – Michael McKinnell, architect (author interview)

There's no assurances that the best design is going to be chosen. – Cesar Pelli, architect (p. 207)[8]

You can get a very mixed, mediocre result. . . . I'm not sure that competitions are the best way to select an architect. – Michael Graves, architect (p. 189)[8]

So, in all these (competitions) . . . , the building has been a disappointment to the owners and the public – and the jury escaped unscathed. – Arthur Erickson, architect (author interview)

In the past twenty-five years, the United States and Europe have increasingly used architectural competitions for major buildings. Between 1961 and 1972, the AIA approved 115 architectural competitions,[260] or about 10 a year. By 1986, the number of competitions had grown tenfold to 107 in one year. Although I could not find reliable data on the number of design competitions between 1972 and 1978, I did find numbers for competitions after 1978. *Progressive Architecture* magazine (*PA*) started to list design competitions in 1979. Table 2.1 shows a tally of the listings for each year. *PA* probably did not list every competition each year, but the figures for 1980–1989 show a sevenfold increase from the 1961–72 figures. Between 1980–89, *PA* reported a yearly average of approximately 75 competitions. By 1990–93, that number grew

Table 2.1. *Number of competitions posted in* Progressive Architecture *per year.*

| Year | Number of Competitions |
|------|------------------------|
| 1979 | 7 |
| 1980 | 39 |
| 1981 | 50 |
| 1982 | 59 |
| 1983 | 86 |
| 1984 | 87 |
| 1985 | 87 |
| 1986 | 107 |
| 1987 | 102 |
| 1988 | 79 |
| 1989 | 53 |
| 1990 | 85 |
| 1991 | 64 |
| 1992 | 80 |
| 1993 | 95 |

to 81 per year. A study confirming these findings revealed a tenfold increase in competitions from 1975 to 1985.[8] Approximately 1,500 to 2,000 architects and firms regularly enter competitions.[8]

European countries host even more design competitions.[271][314] For example, in 1980 German law required competitions for all public buildings. Between the 1970s and 1990s, competitions in Germany increased from about 300 to 500 per year. France already had a competition requirement for all large public projects, but in 1986, the requirement expanded to include any public engineering or architectural commission over approximately $177,000. The number of competitions (as reported by the Ordre des Architects) grew to 2,000 per year.

Competition architecture is highly public. The design of buildings and places has a public presence, and competition designs tend to have a greater public presence. Public bodies often sponsor competitions;[4] the resulting buildings often occupy prominent public sites; and public money often pays for them. Because competition architecture often involves large public buildings, it entails a significant public cost. A 1979 report of construction cost of some public competition buildings showed costs of $3 million to $55 million.[260] Adjusted to 1995 dollars, these buildings averaged almost $82 million.[112][286] Approximately 1 percent of this cost,[260] or about $820,000, covered the costs of running the competition. The United States spends approximately $0.5 billion a year on competition architecture. (This figure comes from multiplying the estimated average cost by the average number of competitions posted in *PA*. As such, it underestimates the cost because PA does not list all competitions). Taxpayers pay large amounts for competition architecture. How do design competitions perform for the public? This chapter evaluates design competition architecture. Because competitions stress the architectural statement, the discussion centers on architectural appearance and meaning.

In general, competition can bring out the best in people. When runners compete in a race, they often run faster than they do in practice. Many other athletes show improved performance in competition. Economists see competition in a free market as yielding better products at lower prices. As a method for choosing an architect (see sidebar), design competitions may share the intent of bringing out the best in designers. Do they actually get the best solutions? To answer this, one has to consider the definition of winning. Think of a foot race. The person with the fastest time wins. Imagine a change in the rules so that the first prize goes to the runner with the best form as judged by a panel of experts (as in gymnastics or skating). Then form would take priority. Changing the definition of winning changes the outcome. To win a design competition, designers must get the votes of the jury. The winning design may not be the design that is best for the users and public.

---

### WHAT IS A DESIGN COMPETITION?

In the conventional process for picking a designer, a client might identify potential designers through reputation, then narrow the list, and select one for the job. In a design competition, the client picks a designer based on designs for the specific project. Several designers (sometimes hundreds of them) compete for the commission responding to the same problem according to a set of rules. An independent panel of experts – called a jury – evaluates the entries and selects the winner.

Design competition take different forms. An *open* competition allows any qualified designer to enter. A *limited* competition restricts entries by region or other requirements. An *invited* competition invites a limited a set of designers to enter. A *two-stage* competition uses an open competition to select designers who submit more detailed designs in an invited second stage. Clients typically hire a competition advisor who develops the instructions and criteria for entrants to follow, manages the competition, and recommends the members for the jury.

---

I searched for books or articles that evaluated design competition products. Although many people have written about competitions, none of them critically and systematically evaluates how well the winning solution works for the consumer – the building inhabitants and passerby. Several fine works, such as the *Design Competition Manual*,[186] the *Handbook of Architectural Competitions*,[6] and *Successful Competitions: Planning for Quality, Equity and Useful Results*,[201] offer suggestions for running competitions. Commissioned by competition sponsors, Rizolli press has published several promotional accounts of competitions, including the Southwest Center in Houston,[16] Human Tower in Louisville,[15] Mississauga City Hall in Ontario Canada,[18] and the Wexner Center.[17] Independent observers have also written detailed accounts of individual design competitions – a building at California State Polytechnic Institute-Pamona,[27] Pershing Square in Los Angeles,[21] and the Milwaukee waterfront.[305] Sandra Gunn, a competition sponsor, recorded and published the transcript of the jury deliberation on a competition.[93] Because the accounts end with the jury decision or prior to completion of the building, they do not reveal the success of the project. Other writers offer subjective opinions and excellent descriptive or historical accounts of competitions (sidebar), but these also fail to indicate the success of the project.

People have written more systematic and critical evaluations of competitions, but these accounts overlook the public and eventual building occupants to examine sponsor and designer reactions. Still, the results of these studies (discussed later) suggest that competitions may generate publicity but produce flawed solutions. The evaluation that follows first presents expert opinion and survey results on design competitions; it discusses some competition successes and competition failures; and it presents two scientific studies evaluating design competition architecture through history.

---

## BOOKS ON DESIGN COMPETITIONS

Paul D. Spreiregen's *Design Competitions*[260] has descriptions and drawings of more than 90 competitions and descriptive information on more than 200 competitions from 448 B.C.E. to 1977; Hilde de Haan and Ids Haagsma's *Architects in Competition*[59] provides detailed accounts of 14 major competitions; and Benedikt Taschens' two volume *Architectural Competitions*[274][275] has drawings and descriptions of 48 competitions from 1792 through 1993; in *Winning by Design*,[271] Judith Strong, Competition Director of the Royal Institute of British Architects for ten years, presents case stud-

f nine British competitions. She presents information on the
)f competition and facility, value, promoter, manager, jury, his-
pproach, format, program (or brief), prizes, timetable, win-
pproach, whether it was built and whether it received any
...us; George Wynne's booklet *Winning Designs: The Competitions
Renaissance*[314] has brief accounts of nineteen recent competitions.
A special issue of the *Journal of Architectural and Planning Research* on
design competitions has two articles describing several planning
and urban design competitions in the United States and Great
Britain.[262]

---

### Perspectives on Design Competitions

Some experts praise design competitions as a way to achieve "excellence" in design (p. 5).[260] Others condemn competitions as "unsatisfactory, . . . (and) a waste of people's time and money" (p. 1).[271] The
comments at the start of this chapter by the Wexner Center entrants –
all of whom built their careers on competitions – echo the range of
opinions.

Paul Spreiregen (p. 219) lists several competition benefits,[260] which
can be condensed into three: *discovering unrecognized talent, producing
new solutions,* and *bringing attention to or publicizing architecture.* Two of
these – discovering new talent and publicizing architecture – have more
to do with the architectural profession than with clients or occupants.
Interviews with Wexner Center entrants (Appendix B) and interviews
with twenty-nine architects by Kathryn Anthony[8] about design juries
highlight architect opinion about each benefit (sidebar). Survey
research also points to the perceived publicity value of competitions. A
mail survey of jurors, sponsor representatives, and entrants found that
most (89.5%) agreed that competitions built the public image of the
project. Even more (97.4%) agreed that the competition generated
publicity for the project.[248] In-depth interviews with staff persons for
fifty-one urban design competitions revealed similar results. It showed a
shared belief that the competition captured some media coverage and
that the media gave favorable reports.[4] These favorable responses may
have a bias. According to the investigators, respondents, "intimately
involved with their respective competitions . . . may have viewed other
impressions in an unduly favorable light" (p. 189).[4] The surveys do not
tell whether clients who invest as much time and resources into selecting and working with an architect on a noncompetition building could
get similar publicity.

*[Handwritten margin note: REASONS FOR COMPETITION]*

## ARCHITECT OPINION ON COMPETITION BENEFITS

*General Praise*

"They (competitions) often produce very exciting buildings" (p. 183).[8] – Peter Eisenman

"A valid means for securing work and doing a good building (in Europe)" (p. 203).[8] – Richard Meier, winner of a Pritzker Prize

"Professional juries are certainly a very worthwhile enterprise" (p. 200).[8] – E. Fay Jones, a former apprentice of Frank Lloyd Wright

### *Competitions Discover New Talent*

"Competitions have great potential because they open up opportunities to talented architects that may be young and unrecognized to become recognized" (p. 207).[8] – Cesar Pelli, Wexner Finalist

"It certainly has value in terms of giving the young practitioner that chance to be recognized" (pp. 198–199).[8] – Steven Izenour, AIA National Honor Award Winner

"For younger professionals, it frees them from all constraints" (p. 176).[8] – William Callaway, AIA National Honor Award Winner

"They (competitions) helped enormously in my early practice" (p. 189).[8] – Michael Graves, Wexner Finalist

### *Competitions Produce New Solutions*

In one case "a competition has some value in terms of bringing a variety of new ideas to a given subject" (p. 192).[8] – Donald J. Hackl, a Former President of AIA

"Open competitions flush out new talent and new ideas." – Arthur Erickson, Wexner Finalist (author interview)

"I look at what wins design competition to see what kind of new and inventive use of materials are out there. . . . It's part of an educational process for me" (p. 181).[8] – Larry N. Deutsch, Interior designer and recipient of Merchandise Mart outstanding Achievement in Design in Chicago.

### *Competitions Generate Publicity*

"They (competitions) do a lot of good for architecture in the eyes of the public, when projects are recognized and published" (p. 200).[8] – E. Fay Jones

The interviews with architects also point to dissatisfaction with competitions (sidebar). Architects complain that competitions often fail to get the best solution, lack dialog with the client, exploit architects, or end with unbuilt projects. A reader poll in the magazine *Progressive Architecture (PA)* that drew 700 responses highlighted two of these problems. Most respondents (70%) reported that the best design did not usually win; and most respondents (69%) described competitions as exploitive of architects.[3] Two studies look at the question of unbuilt projects. One study of fourty Royal Institute of British Architects (RIBA) competitions between 1985 and 1994 found 37.5 percent as either abandoned or not built as planned.[271] In a related study, RIBA evaluated English competitions between 1980 and 1984. From press records, survey of briefs, and interviews with sponsors managers and competitors, RIBA determined whether the competition selected a winner, whether the brief or choice of winner caused a controversy, and whether the management and administration went smoothly.[235] Using these three criteria, RIBA concluded that out of sixty-eight competitions, approximately one in five failed. These figures point to costly failures for both sponsors and architects.

Of course, many competitions yield completed projects. My examination of historical case studies of completed competition projects reveals a mixed record of successes and failures. I offer the historical cases with uneasiness, because I view such evidence as inadequate. Still, the case studies highlight some issues.

ARCHITECT OPINION ON COMPETITION
DRAWBACKS

*General Criticism*

"Professional design competitions are questionable" (p. 173).[8] – Carol Ross Barney, a recipient of Distinguished Building Award from Chicago Chapter of the AIA.

"(Considering) the low success rate of competition entries, I don't think it's worth the effort" (p. 176).[8] – William Callaway

"I don't like some professional design juries at all, because I think they are done injudiciously" (p. 184) [8] – Joseph Esherick, recipient of AIA Gold Medal.

"(Though I) never lost a design competition . . . I hate design competitions" (p. 185).[8] – Rodney F. Friedman, architect a whose firm has received more than 160 design awards.

"Can you through the competition process really meet the needs of a client? I have some real questions about that." – Mark Feinknopf, local partner of Arthur Erickson (interview with Grannis)

### Competitions May Not Get the Best Solution

"Professional juries . . . (are) swayed by the look of the presentation rather than the substance of the design" (p. 173).[8] – Joan Blutter, recipient of Designer of the Year Award from the American Society of Interior Designers

"In all these (competitions) . . . the building has been a disappointment to the owners and the public." – Arthur Erickson (author interview)

"You often get a very slanted jury. . . . Many juries tend to judge on a visual basis. . . . What you see . . . are often not interesting places to visit. . . . Concerning practitioners serving as jurors, if they do not agree with the program, they should not serve on the jury. It never happens that way, however; instead they change the program" (p. 179).[8] – Norman R. De Haan, founding national president of the American Society of Interior Designers

"You can get a very mixed, mediocre result" (p. 89).[8] – Michael Graves

"You are really lucky if the jury picks something that satisfies you." – Chuck Nitschke, local partner of Kallmann, Mekinnell, and Wood (interview witih Grannis)

"There's no assurance that the best design is going to be chosen" (p. 207).[8] – Cesar Pelli

### Competitions Lose Dialog with Client

"You're never able to interact with clients" (p. 185).[8] – Rodney F. Friedman

"In t   end (the interview) process is really superior to juries, simply beca   e there is a chance for dialog" (p. 189).[8] – Michael Graves

"The drawback of the competition system is clearly one that eliminates the interchange between the client . . . and the architect." – Michael McKinnell (author interview)

"The most valuable phase of the architectural process is the period of time the architect works with the client to determine what the client needs." – Chuck Nitschke, local partner of Kallmann, McKinnell and Wood (interview with Grannis)

"Competitions distort the design process. A design for a good building is the result of a special type of collaboration of architect with clients and users. This is not possible in a competition. – Cesar Pelli (author interview)

### Competitions Exploit Architects

"The way juries for professional design competitions are conducted today is usury to a great extent. The amount of money lost by well-intentioned architects is frightening and immoral. It takes so much money to win because it seems the ante is increased with each successive competition (p. 189).[8] – Michael Graves

"One of the downsides is the serious abuse of architects. The abuse paradoxically mounts when the competition is an invited one among prestigious architects, because the client . . . knows very well that the architects . . . are known and . . . competing against their peers would engage in greater efforts than if it were an open and anonymous competition." – Michael McKinnell (author interview)

"The . . . drawback is the enormous waste of time and energies of very many architects: Those who do not win. Even in invited competitions, where architects are paid to participate, the amount is never enough to cover costs. . . . Many architects end up very bruised." – Cesar Pelli (author interview)

"They're very expensive. To play to win costs big money. . . . It's a big financial risk. . . . I don't know what that competition cost – $100,000 – but I'm sure it didn't cover the costs." – James Scott (interview with Grannis)

"The general public doesn't really care because they don't understand why architects do all this work for nothing." – Chuck Nitschke, local partner of Kallmann, McKinnell and Wood (interview with Grannis)

"Competitions need enough compensation . . . that people take the thing seriously." – Peter Eisenman (author interview)

### Competitions Result in Unbuilt Projects

"We have been fortunate that the competitions that we have won have been built. In one that we entered but did not win, the final for extension of the Parliament buildings in England, they did not proceed with. – Michael McKinnell (author interview)

"They also need a serious commitment by the owner to build the results. . . . Most competitions do not get built, either because the sponsors do not like the results or they do not have financing in place. Sixty percent of the competitions that I know about or participate in are not serious. They do not get built." – Peter Eisenman (author interview)

---

### Competition Successes

Since the first recorded competition for a war memorial on the Acropolis in Athens (448 BCE),[260] design competitions have yielded some well-known buildings throughout the world. The U.S. Capitol has several prominent competition designs including the White House, Capitol building, Washington Monument, Lincoln Memorial (not strictly a competition, as two architects prepared drawings, and one, Henry Bacon, was chosen),[260] and Vietnam Veteran's Memorial. Other products of competitions in the United States include the Washington Square Arch (New York), Union Station (St. Louis), the New York Public Library, Nebraska State Capitol (Lincoln), Chicago Tribune Building, and the St. Louis Gateway Arch (Figures 2.1–2.3). Elsewhere, competition buildings include the British Houses of Parliament, Paris Opera House, Eiffel Tower, Stockholm Town Hall, and Sydney Opera House.[202] [260] Competitions have shaped the form of many well-known places, such as New York City's Central Park, Philadelphia's Society Hill, Portland's Pioneer Courthouse Square, Rome's Spanish Steps, and Paris's Place de la Concorde.[3] [202] [260] Competitions have also produced plans for St. Petersburg (Russia), Edinburgh (Scotland), and Canberra (Australia).

The building form that one sees as a competition product may not result wholly from the competition. In some cases, it results from a sponsor's personal preference, contacts, or dialogue with an entrant. In others, it results from a detailed program for appearance and a jury supporting that program. Consider some examples, the descriptions of which draw from several sources.[5] [59] [260]

*The White House.* The White House, symbol of the presidency and country, is probably the best-known building in the United States (Figure 2.4). In 1792, Thomas Jefferson suggested a design competition for it, and drafted an advertisement. President Washington, hoping to advance development of the capitol city, agreed to a competition. In March 1792, the commissioners of Federal Buildings announced the

Figure 2.1. Washington Square Arch, 1889–1892, McKim, Mead and White. After construction in wood, a benefit concert raised the money to rebuild it in stone.[260] Photograph by Nick Ingoglia.

competition, offering the winner a prize of $500 or a medal of that value. The announcement called for submissions by July 15. The jury included President George Washington and three commissioners. After several entries came in, Washington contacted James Hoban, an architect from Charleston, North Carolina, whose work he had liked. The

Figure 2.2. The New York Public Library (1897) by Carrere and Hastings,[260] still a popular gathering place. Photograph by Nick Ingoglia.

Commission eventually received eight entries, only two of which came from professionally trained architects, Stephen Hallet of Philadelphia and Hoban. In most competitions, the entrants do not get to interact with the client; but prior to this competition. Hoban met with Washington and then with the commission members to discover their views. No doubt, this gave him an advantage over the other competitors, and a better knowledge of the problem. He won. Yet, the design we see today is largely not his design. It went through extensive changes during its 38-year construction. Washington added ornamentation and enlarged the building footprint. He changed the design from three stories to two stories. Thomas Jefferson and Benjamin H. Latrobe introduced other changes, as did Hoban himself after a fire in 1815. The well-known west wing and oval office did not appear until the twentieth century.

*U.S. Capitol Building* The announcement of the competition for the White House also called for designs for the U.S. Capitol Building.

Figure 2.3. The Gateway Arch (1946–1966), St. Louis, Missouri, by Eero Saarinen and Associates.[260] A symbol of the city, the project took twenty years to complete. Eliel Saarinen, Eero's father had come to the United States after gaining prominence through his second-place entry in the Competition for The Chicago Tribune Building. Photograph by Jack L. Nasar.

Ten people submitted designs. Although one arrived late, the commission did not disqualify it. In a letter dated three days before the July 15 deadline, the physician William Thornton, living in the Virgin Islands, wrote the Commission that he had not heard of the competition in time to meet the deadline, but that he was developing his design. By autumn,

Figure 2.4. The White House (1792), Washington, D.C., by
James Hoban. Photograph by Judy Nasar.

the Commission had rejected all of the designs, but they invited Stephen
Hallet to revise his design. Hallet, who was the one professional among
the entrants, had won second place in the White House competition. Dr.
Thornton, on hearing that the commission had rejected all of the
designs, wrote on November 9 asking if he could submit his design. The
Commission agreed. Later, he discovered that his design would be unac-
ceptable, and he started again. In January 1793, Hallet asked the commission for more time to finish his work, but by the end of the month,
Thornton submitted his design. Praise by both Washington and
Jefferson helped get the approval of the commissioners. They selected
Thornton's design, but put Hallet in charge of construction. Hallet
started to interject his own design. Hoban eventually took over as super-
intendent of construction, and in 1794, Hallet was discharged.
Thornton regained some control when Washington made him a com-
missioner. As with the White House, the original design went through
changes in subsequent years as others worked on it, including Latrobe
(1803–17), Charles Bullfinch (1819–29), Robert Jills (1836–51), and
Thomas Ulstick Walter (1851–65). Walter added the dome in 1850.

Figure 2.5. Eiffel Tower (1886–88), Paris, France, by Gustave Eiffel, Emile Nougier, and Maurice Koechlin. Knowing that Eiffel's design would win, most of the 106 entries copied his design into their site plan. Photograph by Judy Nasar.

*Eiffel Tower* (Figure 2.5). For more than half a century, architects and engineers had tried to break the height limit of 300 meters (about 1,000 feet). In 1884, two years before the announcement of the competition, two engineers in Gustave Eiffel's office had developed the plan for the 300-meter-high iron tower. The drawings went on display at

Paris' Palais de l'industrie, after which Eiffel applied for a patent. On May 1, 1886, when Eduoard Lockroy announced the competition for a "study of the feasibility, location, and shape of an iron tower 300 meters high" (p. 67),[59] he already had Eiffel's tower in mind. He used the competition to advance Eiffel's design. The announcement gave competitors only seventeen days to submit plans. It still attracted 107 entries, most of which used Eiffel's design, the presumed winner, in their plans (p. 68).[59] The jury selected his design, which took approximately two years to build.

*Houses of Parliament.* The success of some competition products – such as the Houses of Parliament – arises in part from explicit guidelines for appearance. In June 1835, Britain announced a competition for the Houses of Parliament. A year and a half earlier, a fire had destroyed the Houses of Parliament and the press called for a new monumental building, worthy of the empire. The announcement offered a maximum of five prizes of 500 pounds each, and an additional prize of 1,000 pounds to the designer of the winning design, if built. Because of many abuses in previous competitions, the committee, made up of members of both houses, "did everything in its power to organize the competition so that no fault could be found" (p. 32).[59] They developed a detailed program. To avoid biases, it specified the number and kind of drawings, and it called for anonymous submissions, with entrants using a motto or pseudonym to identify themselves. This competition had two other notable features. The committee picked a four-person jury made up entirely of former members of Parliament; and the announcement specified the building style: Gothic or Elizabethan. Architects objected, as most of them had turned to the classical Greek and Roman styles. The committee chose Gothic, because of its popularity among the public and its symbol as the national style. Elizabethan, a British style, was offered to give designers some freedom. Three of the four jury members, including the chair, favored Gothic, and one of the three had a personal friendship with the eventual winner. The fourth member had shown support for the Elizabethan style. The competition attracted ninety-seven entries. Charles Barry's Gothic design took first prize. Augustus Welby Pugin, then an unknown architect, had worked on the design for him. The Members of Parliament occupied the building in 1852, though construction continued for eighteen years.

*Vietnam Veterans Memorial.* The Vietnam Veterans Memorial, one of the two most visited memorials in Washington, D.C., stands as another successful design competition product. Like the Houses of Parliament, much of its success rests in the program describing the character of the desired solution. In March 1979, the Vietnam Veteran Jan Scruggs decided to build a memorial to the people who served in Vietnam. "It'll have the name of everyone killed," he told his wife (p.7).[246] A month later, he and another veteran (Bob Doubek) incorporated the nonprofit Vietnam Veterans Memorial Fund (VVMF). By summer, VVMF agreed that the memorial would have the names and take the form of a 'horizontal" and "landscaped solution" in a "spacious garden setting" (p. 49).[246] A year later, President Jimmy Carter signed the legislation giving the memorial two acres on the mall near the Lincoln Memorial.

Frederick Hart, a representational sculptor befriended VVMF, hoping to do the sculpture. Instead, VVMF opted for an open competition as it "fit in with the American spirit of solving problems through fair open contests" (p. 50).[246] In July 1980, Paul D. Spreiregen, FAIA, was hired as the professional advisor. After some disagreement on whether the jury should consist of Vietnam Veterans and their representatives or world-class professionals, the group arrived at a compromise: The jury would consist of professionals screened by the committee for their sensitivity to service in Vietnam. The eight-person jury included landscape architects, critics, and architects, some with personal experience with war and the terrors of fascism. In the spirit of an open contest, the competition announcement invited both professionals and students to enter, requiring them to enter as individuals (anonymously) rather than firms. It called for a design that was "reflective and contemplative in character . . . (that) fit with the neighboring monuments . . . contained all of the names of those who died or were still missing, and . . . made no political statements about the war" (p. xvi).[125] Entrants had to pay a $20 registration fee and the winner would receive a $20,000 prize. By the March 31, 1981, deadline, the competition had drawn 1,421 entries. Over a period of four days the jury narrowed the field to 232, then 39, then 3. They finally unanimously voted for one design (Figure 2.6). Maya Ying Lin, a 20-year-old graduate student at Yale, had won. Frederick Hart finished third. As Lin did not have an architectural license, a local firm (Kent Cooper and William Lecky) served as architect and hired Lin as a student-intern to develop the design. The Veterans supported the design, as did the two commissions whose approval was required to start construction – the Fine Arts Commission and the National Capital Planning Commission. The proposed solution also drew favorable popular reactions. The editor of a magazine for marines reported "wide acceptance among our 30,000 readers" for the design (pp. 97–98).[246] A fund raiser reported that "in over 500 industry contacts," he had received only "two negative comments about the design" (p. 98).[246]

Figure 2.6. Vietnam Veteran's Memorial (1980–81), Washington, D. C., by Maya Ying Lin. Lin, a 20-year old Yale graduate student won this competition, which attracted 1,421 entries.[246] Photograph by Sheldon Nasar.

However, the Texas billionaire Ross Perot, who earlier had donated money to VVMF, did not like it. He wanted a flag and something representational. Some veterans, including Hart, joined his campaign against it. In January 1982, James Watt, President Reagan's Secretary of the Interior, bowed to conservative political pressure and put the project on indefinite hold. A year later, a compromise was struck to include a statue and a flag, and in March construction started. Hart had played his politics well. When the panel met to select a sculptor, they chose him. Though he had lost the competition, he got in the back door.

In its first two years, the memorial attracted more than five million people. Maya Lin's design, not the flag and sculpture (added in 1983 and 1984), draws the crowds. Anyone observing visitors crying, touching names, or leaving flowers cannot doubt the emotional power of her design. Much of that power goes back to the program and its call for the names, a landscaped solution, and a horizontal form.

### Competition Failures

From the thousands of competition throughout history, we may recognize a few enduring products. We are less likely to have extensive objective information on flaws, because getting that information requires systematic study. Still, research does point to general problems with competitions and some specific examples of competition failures.

The winning design may end up flawed from the public's standpoint because of a vague or ignored program and the exclusion of the public and users from the process. Rather than selecting buildings that fit the local context, jurors often select the design that "stands out" (p. 22).[135] One review of juries in architecture concluded that professional design competitions have closed juries and evaluation criteria often "intentionally written in vague language . . . to encourage a wide variety of interpretations among solutions;" and the winner "frequently breaks some rules" (pp. 140–41).[8] Even if a professional jury agrees on a set of criteria, they may not heed them when judging the designs.[202] Furthermore, the jury's report may convey a misleadingly favorable judgment of the winning design. Because the comments become part of a ceremony for the winner, the jury tends to stress "the positive" (p. 143).[8] According to one study, jury reports tend to gloss over likely disagreements to convey the appearance of unanimous support for the winner.[99]

Competitions exclude the public and users from the process. A mail survey of competition entrants, jurors, and sponsors found that two-thirds of them recognized limited opportunities for eventual users of the project to participate, and 81 percent of them believed the public had little involvement.[248] The *PA* magazine poll echoed these findings.[31] Approximately 75 percent of the architects responding reported adverse effects on the solution due to the lack of client consultation in competitions. Though the survey results may suffer from some biases, they still suggest widespread dissatisfaction with competitions from within the profession.

The German system for competitions has received praise as "exemplary, efficient and successful," but a review of the competition in Germany concluded that "competitions do not always work well for the end users" (p. 39).[116] It states that the users, "normally have little opportunity to influence the brief and design decisions – and yet their needs are hardly known, let alone emphasized" (p. 39).[116]

*CHDC National Housing Design Awards Program.* In 1981, the Canadian Housing Design Council (CHDC) contracted Jacqueline Vischer and Clare Cooper Marcus to evaluate the CHDC national housing design awards program.[291] Though these awards, unlike design competitions, went to completed projects, they share with design competitions the reliance on a jury of experts. Vischer and Cooper evaluated five projects in Vancouver, three award winners and three nonwinners. They found that residents disagreed with the jury. Although both groups had similar criteria, they had diametrically different evaluations of the projects. The residents' ranking reversed the jury's ranking of the schemes. Had this been a competition with the jurors selecting one design to build, they would have chosen the one least agreeable to the residents.

*Brasilia.* In 1956 the Brazil's President Juscelino Kubitschek staged an open competition for the design of Brasilia, a new capital. From the 26 entrants, the jury selected a design by Lúcio Costa as "a work of art" (p. 143).[65] One juror dissented saying that the jury decided "in haste and without sufficient study of the entries" (p. 121).[65] Costa had only submitted "five cards containing a few freehand sketches and a brief statement" (p. 143) and apologized for "the sketchy manner in which I am submitting the idea" (p. 145).[65] The scheme, carried out by Costa, Oscar Niemeyer (a member of the jury, who along with Costa assumed control of design decisions), and Israel Pinhiero de Silva (engineer) held closely to Costa's concept. In treating city design as geometry and a piece of art, the design may have given the president a symbol, but it does not work. The government had to bribe people to move there, in part from its isolation and unlivability.[29]

Analysis of Brasilia shows a monumental design devoid of human scale, habitability, social richness, and vitality.[108] [130] In holding to an ideology about how people should live and how places should look, Costa disregarded local culture, individuality, and patterns of life. James Holston's anthropological analysis of Brasilia found that residents complained about the absence of the social life they expect to find in public places.[108] They described Brasilia as lacking "the bustle of street life . . . there are no people in the streets" (p. 105). The city lacks "street corners . . . curbs, sidewalks . . . with shops and residences, squares and streets themselves" (p. 105). This led to the replacement of the chance encounter in public arena with formal home visits. Residents rejected the anti-street nature of the plan. They reversed the design for a shopping center to make it usable.[36] Occupants "refused the proposed garden entrances of commercial units and converted the service backs into store fronts" (p. 139),[108] but the absence of real streets left these commercial streets isolated. Planned sterile supermarkets replace the vital outdoor markets common in other Brazilian cities (pp. 168–69).[65] Though on paper the plan segregated functions (work, residence, recreation) into separate sectors, the buildings in each sector look alike: freestanding monuments. The uniformity has led to the feeling of an "overwhelming sense of monotony . . . that Brazilienses experience in the city" (p. 153).[165] Residents dislike the similar appearances of their places of work and residence. Because of the abstract basis for the plan, "even long-term residents regularly have difficulty finding the location of a place" (p. 149).[165] The plan also removed the social spaces from residences, leading residents to complain about the isolation. Holston found residents saying that the designs did not function as a neighborhood. They complain of the loss of community, friendship, and sociality from the design. The inside of the unit removes customary family socializing spaces, leading residents to feel uncomfortable with them and describe them as "cold," and "antifamily." (pp. 181–82). Residents rejected the plans and where possible "countered them with opposing interpretations." (p. 308) Just as they put shop entrances on the curb, they rejected the "transparent facade of the apartment blocks . . . by demanding a return to an opaque wall" (p. 309). Others, who could afford it, moved out and "created their own neighborhoods of individual houses" outside of the residential sector (p. 309). Whether they stayed or left, residents rejected the design. Although Costa treated traffic movement as central to the plan, the commercial districts and government center lack adequate parking (p. 173).[65] Brasilia has "phenomenally high" transportation costs (p. 160). Although planned as an economically integrated community, Brasilia ended up with a more extreme and spatially segregated split of the rich and poor than other cities (p. 179).[65] The jury's choice of "a monumental plan" (p. 142)[65] substituted "art for life (pp. 372–73).[115] Other monumental failures occurred in the United States.

*Boston City Hall.* In 1962, Boston held an open competition for a City Hall, which attracted 256 entries. The winning design by Kallmann, McKinnell and Knowles ended up as a costly building that met with public contempt.[260] The design was part of a movement called Brutalism, in that it left concrete exposed and rough. As a critic, echoing public opinion, noted thirteen years later: "Many Bostonians, unfamiliar with the articles of faith of modern architecture, . . . consider this building a grandiose, extravagant and ultimately distasteful work." (p. 10).[36] An analysis of the plaza in front of the building found it as "one of Boston's most monumental and least-used public open spaces . . . (fulfilling) architectural rather than human needs, as many of the most basic aspects of comfort have been ignored" (p. 88).[45]

*Boston's Copley Square.* The Copley Square went through two design competitions. The first, in 1960 by Sasaki–Walker & Associates, resulted in a design that had angular concrete forms and poor-quality

Figure 2.7. Copley Square (1960), Boston, Massachusetts, by Sasaki–Walker & Associates.[260] Photograph by Lena Sorensen.

materials, seen by many Bostonians as "antithetical to the graceful land-mark buildings that surrounded it" (p. 340).[45] Corporate neighbors became concerned when part of the space became "a hangout for street people" (p. 341). A wall by a fountain eight feet below the adjacent street gave the street people a hiding place from passersby. The city and corporations ran a second competition and shared the $5 million cost of redevelopment (Figure 2.7). After reconstruction, the "initial reviews have not been favorable, and Copley Square may yet become a monument to the liabilities of competitions as vehicles for designing important spaces" (p. 342).[45] A public plaza in New York ran into a different problem.

*Tilted Arc.* In 1979, a panel of experts chose the sculptor Richard Serra to create a work for the Federal Plaza in New York. In 1981, his design received approval by a General Services Administration (GSA) design review panel. GSA had funded the work under a program setting aside $1/2$ to 1 percent of building costs for art. The sculpture cost $175,000. Tilted Arc, a 12-foot by 112-foot Cor-Ten steel wall tilting toward the federal building and courthouse, cuts across the plaza, blocking the view and access between the buildings and the street. The public outcry against it included a petition signed by 1,300 workers in the buildings demanding its removal. Serra claimed that any relocation would destroy his art. In a public hearing, major artists came to testify on his behalf. Office workers and others attacked Tilted Arc, calling it, among other things, a "rusted piece of junk" (p. 93).[270] After a trial and appeal, GSA removed it.

*National Gallery in Trafalgar Square.* Another competition was stopped prior to construction because of public opposition: England's competition for an addition to the National Gallery in London's Trafalgar Square. After seeing the winning entry, Prince Charles, with much popular agreement, described the winning design as "a monstrous carbuncle" (p. 7).[46] He wrote that he received nearly 5,000 letters, out of which 99 percent agreed with his position on architecture. The winning design did not proceed.

*Florida A & M Architecture Building.* Florida A & M university held a competition for an architecture building. The building, designed by Clements/Rumpel Associates, opened in 1985 to a favorable review in *Progressive Architecture.* The sponsors "got more than they asked for" (p. 74).[69] A year later a systematic evaluation of the building by Craig Zimring, Jean Wineman, and Mim Kantrowitz and Associates suggested that the sponsors may have gotten a bit less.[303] The evaluation team interviewed students, faculty and administrators; they observed the character of the facility and its use; and they examined change orders. Considering this information, they evaluated the building in relation to six goals stated in the competition program. Figure 2.8 shows a section through the building with notes from the evaluation.

The evaluation revealed a seriously flawed design.[303] The program called for "a comfortable state-of-the-art HVAC system that demonstrates energy conservation" (p. 115). The evaluation found that building failed to achieve this goal. "The lack of ventilation . . . has resulted in cries of outrage from architecture students" (p. 116). Faculty, students and staff also complained about its thermal comfort. Because the design does not allow them to control the heat level mechanically or through opening windows, "some students have taken the situation into their own hands by dismantling the computer-operated ventilation panels and opening them manually" (p. 116). Temperature varies noticeably from one side to the other of the studio space. The cooling/ventilation system leads to excess humidity. Because of this, students complain that drawings left out "bubble and curl" (p. 116). The building rains on their drawings.

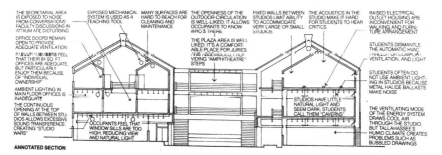

THE SECRETARIAL AREA IS EXPOSED TO NOISE FROM CONVERSATIONS; FACULTY DISCUSSIONS IN ATRIUM ARE DISTURBING

OFFICE DOORS REMAIN OPEN TO PROVIDE ADEQUATE VENTILATION

FACULTY MEMBERS FEEL THAT THEIR 84 SQ. FT. OFFICES ARE ADEQUATE, BUT PARTICULARLY ENJOY THEM BECAUSE OF "INDIVIDUAL OWNERSHIP"

AMBIENT LIGHTING IN MAIN FLOOR OFFICES IS INADEQUATE

THE CONTINUOUS OPENING AT THE TOP OF WALLS BETWEEN STUDIOS ALLOWS EXCESSIVE SOUND TRANSFERENCE; CREATING "STUDIO WARS"

EXPOSED MECHANICAL SYSTEM IS USED AS A TEACHING TOOL

OCCUPANTS FEEL THAT WINDOW SILLS ARE TOO HIGH, REDUCING VIEW AND NATURAL LIGHT

MANY SURFACES ARE HARD TO REACH FOR CLEANING AND MAINTENANCE

THE OPENNESS OF THE OUTDOOR CIRCULATION IS WELL-LIKED: IT ALLOWS OCCUPANTS TO KNOW WHO'S THERE

THE PLAZA AREA IS WELL LIKED: IT'S A COMFORT-ABLE PLACE FOR JURIES AND PROVIDING "AMPHITHEATRE" STEPS

FIXED WALLS BETWEEN STUDIOS LIMIT ABILITY TO ACCOMMODATE VERY LARGE OR SMALL STUDIOS

THE ACOUSTICS IN THE STUDIO MAKE IT HARD FOR STUDENTS TO HEAR CRITICS

STUDIOS HAVE LITTLE NATURAL LIGHT AND SEEM DARK, STUDENTS CALL THEM "CAVERNS"

RAISED ELECTRICAL OUTLET HOUSING ARE INCONVENIENT FOR WALKING AND FURNI-TURE ARRANGEMENT

STUDENTS DISMANTLE THE AUTOMATIC HVAC FOR COMFORT VENTILATION, AND LIGHT

STUDENTS OFTEN DO NOT USE AMBIENT LIGHT-ING IN STUDIOS BECAUSE METAL HALIDE BALLASTS MAKE NOISE

THE VENTILATING MODE OF THE ENERGY SYSTEM DRAWS COOL AIR THROUGH THE STUDIO, BUT TALLAHASSEE'S HUMID CLIMATE CREATES PROBLEMS SUCH AS BUBBLED DRAWINGS

**ANNOTATED SECTION**

Figure 2.8. Florida A & M School of Architecture (1985) by Clements/Rumpel Associates. Courtesy of *Architecture.*

The program called for the design to "provide security in a building open 24 hours" (p. 115). The completed building only partially achieved this goal. The open plan, nighttime lighting, and clustering of functions enable students to "look out for each other," but high windowsills "reduce direct visual contact with the outside" (p. 117).

The program also called for an "image that would be advanced, yet humanly scaled and inviting." The evaluation found the completed design only partially achieved this goal. Though architecture students and faculty felt "proud of the new building" (p. 115), it leaks, has problems with cracks and durability of materials, and has maintenance problems leading to a buildup of dust. All of these problems detract from its image.

The program called for a "flexible and efficient" building (p. 117) "increasing building use . . . and promoting social interaction among student and faculty" (p. 115). The building had mixed results on these goals. The evaluation found that the plan facilitated movement in and out, and yielded a heavily used and well-liked gallery space, but it lacks flexibility, not allowing the scheduling of classes much larger or smaller than 20 students. Instead of increasing faculty–student interaction, the plan reduced it. The placement of faculty office in a separate wing received both good and bad evaluations from faculty and uniformly negative evaluations from students. Graduate student must "go up three floors to converse with most of their professors" (p. 117). Students also report that they feel isolated from one another due to the arrangement of the studios.

Finally, the program called for "effective workspace (p. 115). The evaluation found mixed results on this goal. Faculty liked private offices, but the studios fell short of expectations. "Even on bright sunny days, the studios are dim: Students refer to them as 'caverns'" (p. 117).

In sum, the evaluation showed that the competition's winning design met one goal (increasing building use), had mixed results on three (image, effective work space, and security), and failed to meet two (increased social interaction and energy efficiency).

### Systematic Evaluations of Competitions Over Time

The evidence points to possible successes and failures from competitions. The Wexner Center example and survey research highlight the publicity possible through competitions. If accompanied by a good program and sympathetic jury, competitions may lead to popular successes. However, because they tend to cut the dialogue between client, users, public, and architect, they may lead to flawed designs. Recall the second competition for Copley Square. Even though it had a good program, the resulting design proved unsatisfactory. The competition process excluded the public.[45]

The current knowledge of competition successes and failures rests largely on anecdotal evidence. Those who support or oppose competitions can selectively marshal anecdotes to bolster their point of view. We cannot build a knowledge base for design on a shaky foundation of such opinions. Because design competition products can affect city form and the daily experience of millions of people, we need a better basis for evaluating their merits. As the scientist Carl Sagan noted, no argument by anecdote "no matter how sincere, no matter how deeply felt, no matter how exemplary the lives of the attesting citizens – carries much weight" (p. 180).[240]

I attempted to go beyond anecdotes on individual buildings. Following methods pioneered by the psychologists Colin Martindale and Dean Simonton,[147][253][254] I conducted two studies on many competitions over time to see whether they deliver masterpieces that stand the test of time (sidebar). In one study, I derived a list of architectural masterpieces and examined how many resulted from competitions. In the other, I looked at architect and popular reactions to competition winning and competition losing designs through history.

---

A SCIENTIFIC APPROACH TO HISTORY

The approach, called *historiometric inquiry*, represents the intersection of psychology, science, and history.[254] Following the scientific method, it (1) defines and samples the "unit of statistical analysis," (2) sets up measures for "the crucial variables under investigation," (3) calculates "relationships among these variables;" and (4) uses "statistical analyses to tease out the most probable causal connections" (p. 8).[253] It makes the process explicit so that others can critique the work, replicate it, and extend it, thus contributing to knowledge. The approach differs from the earlier anecdotal approaches in its attempt to uncover general laws without an emphasis on singular events.

Historiometric inquiry also provide a validity check. For building meaning, cross sectional findings may only reveal short-term preferences. Historiometry adds the time dimension. If the historiometric results converge with these cross-sectional findings, it would increase our confidence in the accuracy of the findings.

---

### *Do Competitions Yield Architectural Masterpieces?*

In the first study, I wanted to find out the degree to which design competitions produced architectural masterpieces. Using buildings and places as the unit of analysis, I defined masterpiece as buildings or places that have stood the test of time. They are not just a whim of passing fashion but a lasting achievement. To develop an objective measure for masterpieces, I looked at the frequency of citation of buildings by architectural experts. I assumed that the buildings most frequently cited represent masterpieces. They have stood the test of time. I constructed a list of masterpieces in two ways. First, I looked at five widely used encyclopedias: *Americana*,[138] *Britannica*,[150] *Collier's*,[96] *Compton's*,[84] and *World Book*.[114] Encyclopedias choose experts on architecture to write the sections on architecture. In each encyclopedia, I tallied the buildings cited. I did not count the amount of text devoted to each entry, because research shows that the frequency of citation correlates with it.[253] I also tallied the amount of space devoted to images of each building. The list of masterpieces came to fifty-eight. It included fifty-two buildings cited in at least three of the five encyclopedias and six additional buildings with high amounts of space devoted to their graphic depiction. Because encyclopedias may devote less space to newer buildings, I supplemented the list for twentieth-century buildings with two other sources. One source tallied citations for buildings between World War I and II in forty-seven books on architecture.[266] The other source tallied citations for buildings from 1945 to 1977 C.E. in forty nine books on architecture.[267] The two sources listed fifty-six buildings – twenty-five from between the wars and thirty-one afterward. From the two lists, I chose the buildings cited in at least half of the references for the respective period: This identified ten newer buildings as masterpieces – three from 1930 to 1945 C.E. and seven from 1945 to 1978 C.E. As four of the buildings had already appeared in the encyclopedia listing, the final list had sixty-four architectural masterpieces. It included buildings from around the world and from thousands of years ago through the twentieth century (Table 2.2). It had nineteen buildings from more than 1,000 years ago, thirteen buildings more than 500 years ago, eight from more than 200 years ago, six from more than 100 years ago, and nine from more than 50 years ago. Still referred to today, these buildings have stood the test of time.

From the sixty-four masterpieces, I sought to determine how many resulted from design competitions. This involved an extensive and detailed readings by my student Maral Chetterian and myself on the history of each masterpiece to find which ones resulted from competitions. That search revealed that only two resulted from competitions: the Paris Opera House, the British Houses of Parliament. The Chicago Tribune building also resulted from a competition, but the praise went to the losing designs by the modernists Eiliel Saarinen and Walter Gropius, not to the winning design by James Mead Howells and Raymond M. Hood. Portions of three other buildings resulted from competitions: the Cathedral of Florence, St. Peters in Rome, and the eastern wall of the Louvre. In each case, most of the building did not result from the competition. The design and construction of the Cathedral of Florence took place over 168 years with five architects. The competition portion, the dome (1420–34 C.E.) by Brunelleschi, occupied less than ten percent of this time.[160] For St. Peters, Bramante won the competition sponsored by Pope Julilus, but many notable Roman architects, including Michelangelo, designed most of the building. Most of the Louvre did not result from the competition. It was built over a 332-year period with designs by nine architects. Only the eastern facade (1667–74 C.E.) resulted from Louis XIV picking Claude Perrault after considering several designs.[160] In the 1980s, another competition produced an addition to the Louvre, but the encyclopedias did not mention it. Nevertheless, if one counts the Brunelleschi's dome, Bramante's work, and Perrault's wall each as one-fourth of their masterpiece building, the results indicate that less than five percent (3 out of 64) of the masterpieces result from competitions.

Although the findings suggest that competitions may not yield masterpieces, the numbers allow only tentative inferences. To make sense of the less-than-five-percent number, one would need more information: the proportion of buildings (or major public buildings) that result from competitions, the proportion of leading architects of their time who avoided competitions, and the proportion of competition winners in their early versus late careers. With that information, one could con-

Table 2.2. *Rankings of building fame by frequency of citation.*

| Building (year completed) | If shown graphically, Mean Percent of Page for Image |
|---|---|
| *Cited in all five encyclopedias* | |
| Hagia Sophia, Constantinople (532) | 0.376 |
| Pantheon, Rome (118) | 0.314 |
| Paris Opera House (1861) | |
| St. Peter's, Rome (started 150) | 0.462 |
| *Cited in four encyclopedias* | |
| Amon-ra, Karnak (1786) | |
| Angkor Wat, Cambodia (1100) | |
| Basilica of Constantine, Italy (313) | 0.200 |
| Baths of Caracalla, Italy (217) | |
| Bauhaus, Germany (1925) | 0.180 |
| Chateau at Fountainebleau, France (1494) | |
| Crystal Palace, London (1851) | |
| Home Insurance Building, Chicago (1883) | |
| Illinois Institute of Technology, Chicago (1939) | |
| Notre Dame, Paris (1163) | 0.166 |
| Palace of Versaille, France (1678) | 0.150 |
| Pantheon, Paris, (1792) | |
| St. Paul's Cathedral, London (1710) | |
| Taj Mahal, Agra (1653) | |
| Villa Rotunda, Italy (1550) | 0.256 |
| Wainright Building, St. Louis (1891) | |
| *Cited in three encyclopedias* | |
| AEG Turbine Factory, Berlin (1909) | |
| Audience Hall of Xerxes, Persia (begun 518 B.C.E.) | |
| Biblotheque St. Geneviene, Paris (1850) | |
| Cathedral of Florence, Italy (1462) | |
| Chateau de Maisons-Laffitte, France (1642) | |
| Chateau of Chambord, France (1547) | |
| Church of San Lorenzo, Italy (1460) | |
| Church of San Marco, Italy (1085) | |
| Cloth Hall, Belgium (1304) | |
| Ctesiphon, Bagdad (579) | |
| Forbidden City of Peking, China (1644) | |
| House of Vetti, Pompeii (79) | 0.184 |
| Houses of Parliament, London (1868) | |
| Luxembourg Palace (1651) | |
| Marche de la Madeleine, Paris (1824) | |
| Marshall Field Warehouse, Chicago (1885) | |
| Medici Palace, Florence (1444) | |
| Monastry of Horyuji, Japan (772) | 0.15 |
| Palace of Sargon II, Assyria (750) | |

*(Table 2.2 continues)*

Table 2.2. *(Continued)*

| Building (year completed) | If shown graphically, Mean Percent of Page for Image |
|---|---|
| *Cited in three encyclopedias* (continued) | |
| Palas of Minos, Crete (1800 B.C.E.) | |
| Palazzo Rucella, Florence (1451) | |
| Parson Capen House, Massachusetts (1683) | |
| Parthenon, Greece (447 B.C.E.) | 0.223 |
| Pazzi Chapel, Florence (1446) | |
| Pyramids of Giza, Egypt (2680 B.C.E.) | |
| Seagrams Building, New York (1958) | |
| St. Sernine, Toulouse (1506) | 0.166 |
| St. Etienne, France (1062) | |
| Tower of Babel, Mesopatamia (500 B.C.E.) | |
| TWA Terminal, New York (1960) | |
| Villa Savoye, Italy (1929) | |
| Woolworth Building, New York (1913) | |
| *Cited in fewer than three encyclopedia but encyclopedia shows image* | |
| Arch of Constantine, Rome (312) | 0.200 |
| Basilica of San Ambrogio, Italy (1128) | 0.200 |
| Salisbury Cathedral, England (1258) | 0.200 |
| Lever House, New York (1952) | 0.176 |
| Robie House, Chicago (1909) | 0.176 |
| Louvre, Paris (1878) | 0.15 |

| Building Completed Between World Wars | Number of References Citing |
|---|---|
| Falling Water, (Kaufmann House), Pennsylvania (1938) | 31 |
| Johnson Wax Administration, Wisconsin (1936) | 27 |
| Philadelphia Savings Fund, Pennsylvania, (1932) | 23 |

| Buildings Completed 1945–1978 | Number of References Citing |
|---|---|
| Lever House, New York (1952) | 33 (already cited above) |
| Illinois Institute of Technology, Chicago (1954) | 32 (already cited above) |
| Guggenheim Museum, New York (1956) | 29 |
| Lake Shore Apartments, Chicago (1951) | 28 |
| General Motors Technical Institute, Detroit (1956) | 27 |
| Seagrams Building, New York (1958) | 27 (already cited above) |
| TWA Terminal, New York (1962) | 27 (already cited above) |

struct expected values to interpret the meaning of the number found here. Still the results suggest that most competitions do not produce masterpieces.

### *The Merits of Jury Decisions: A Comparison of Competition Winning and Losing Designs Over Time (with Peg Grannis)*

A hallmark of science involves multiple-testing of hypotheses through different methods. Each method may have unique biases, but if several methods converge on the same finding, one can have more confidence in the accuracy of the findings. With this in mind, I conducted a second test on competitions over time. I examined the responses of present-day observers to competition winners and losers through history. This study grew from a pilot study of student responses to award-winning designs and nonaward-winning designs over time.[185] The pilot study had fifty students (half of whom were architecture majors) rate their preference for award-winning designs and nonaward-winning designs from 1930 through 1990. More often than not, nonaward-winning buildings outscored the award-winning ones. Architecture students reported higher preferences for the nonaward buildings than the award-winning buildings. The nonarchitects gave neutral to negative scores for both. The results suggested that the magazine award jury choices did not stand the test of time.

Would similar findings occur for adult judgments of competition winners and losers? Perhaps competition juries do a better job than magazine juries. Perhaps adults would respond differently from students. Perhaps the judgments of preference, or what people like and dislike, missed judgments of what makes a good design. For example, some readers might like to read pulp fiction, even though they feel it is not great literature. Similarly, observers might like a design, even though they realize it is not a good or great design. In the second study, I considered adult preference and judgments of good design.

Along with Peg Grannis, I selected competitions from 1882 through 1986 C.E. (see sidebar). Note that the AIA had set out its first set of guidelines for running architectural competitions in 1870.[6] For the 104-year period, we constructed a sample of fifty designs by pairing each of twenty-five competition-winning designs with a losing design from the same competition (Appendix C, Table C.1). This yielded five pairs of competition winners and losers from each of five time periods: 1882–1916, 1921–1929, 1930–1947, 1950–1967, and 1981–1987. Each winner and loser had comparable views and presentation media (Figure 2.9). The sample included some famous competitions – the

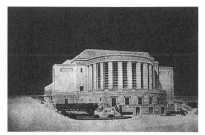

Figure 2.9. Examples of competition winning designs paired with a losing entry. *Note:* For the top pair, the picture on the right was the winner. The winner is on the left for the bottom pair.

Reichstag (1882), Helinski Station (1903), Stockholm Town Hall (1903), *Chicago Tribune* (1922), and Humana Building (1982). It had fourteen different building types. To allow comparisons within a building type across time, we used at least one example of one building type – single-family house – in each time period. A recent review of architecture competitions over forty years found that their criteria "reflected the accepted architectural values of the times" (p. 11).[314]

Fifty practicing architects and fifty other professionals (from more than 21 nonarchitectural professions) evaluated the designs (see sidebar). The 100 respondents came from 42 firms. Respondents in each group were on average forty-two years old with approximately sixteen years of practice (Appendix C, Table C.2). Reflecting the actual professions, the architects had a higher proportion of males than did the nonarchitects.

---

DEVELOPING THE SAMPLE OF COMPETITION
WINNERS AND LOSERS

To develop this sample, we searched journals and books for competitions for images showing competition winners and losers.

The search uncovered ninety competitions with published images of both winners and losers. Experimental controls reduced the sample to fifty usable competitions from 1882 through 1987: Because variations in mode of presentation (drawing, model, photo of completed building) or viewing angle might affect response, we retained only those instances with similar modes of presentation and similar viewing angles for the winner and at least one loser.

We initially sought five examples from each decade from 1880 through 1990, but only two decades (1921–30 and 1981–90) had an adequate number of paired winners and losers. Therefore, we combined four competitions from 1882 through 1903 with one from 1916 to get a thirty-four-year category (1882–1916). Because we found few competitions from the Depression through World War II, we joined two competitions from 1930 and 1931 with three competitions from 1946–47 to create a twenty-seven-year category. We also joined three competitions from 1956 with two competitions from 1965 and 1967 to make up an eleven-year category. The resulting sample had several kinds of drawings and models.

Because building type may influence appraisals, we tried to match building types in each time period. The samples did not have enough building types to match each building type over the five periods, but we did match one building type – single-family house – in each time period. This allowed for longitudinal comparisons of responses over time to this one building type.

## THE SAMPLE OF RESPONDENTS

To obtain the sample, we selected at random and contacted twenty-one architecture firms in Columbus, Ohio. We also contacted twenty-one nonarchitectural professional offices nearby the architecture firms. In each group, 90.4 percent of the firms agreed to participate. We interviewed between one and eight persons per firm, although most firms (92%) had fewer than five participants.

The nonarchitects included people in the fields of engineering, accounting, marketing, management, communications, teaching, school administration, insurance, nursing, radiology, counseling, federal investigation, writing, pharmacy, ministry, social work, optometry, loan processing, banking, and firefighting.

---

The survey had respondents select which building in each pair they *liked* better, which one they felt was the *better design*, and which, if any, of the buildings they *recognized* (see sidebar). It also asked them for their sex, year of birth, and years in practice. Statistical tests revealed consistent responses on the preference and better design ratings for the full sample and for the architects and nonarchitects taken separately. This evidence of consensus supported the use of the composite scores. To find whether recognition of a design may have biased responses, we examined building recognition. The results showed that recognition did not affect judgments of preference or better design.

---

## DESCRIPTION OF THE SURVEY

In a booklet, photographs of each winner were placed in a plastic folder next to the loser of the same competition. To lessen possible order effects, the order of presentation of the building pairs was varied and for each pair the location of winner and loser was switched. Half the time a winner appeared on the left and half the time it appeared on the right. The interview matched these arrangements of the cards across the architects and nonarchitects. Each respondent saw only one pair at a time, made the ratings, and turned the page.

The instructions assured respondents of anonymity and confidentiality. It asked them to look at each pair of buildings and select the one they liked more. It asked them to select the building they see as a better design. It also had them circle the space corresponding to any building they recognized. Half of the respondents in each group received the "preference" questions first. Half received the "better design" questions first. Respondents repeated the judgments tasks for all twenty-five building pairs, after which they answered questions about their gender, year of birth, profession, and years of work in the profession.

### Reliability

Cronbach alpha reliability tests revealed high inter-observer reliability scores on liking (alpha = 0.89) and better design (alpha = 0.85). They also show high inter-observer reliability scores for the nonarchitects on liking (alpha = 0.93) and better design (alpha = 0.82), and acceptable inter-observer reliability scores among the architects for preference (alpha = 0.79) and better design (alpha = 0.73). The lower reliability among the architects may reflect different design philosophies among the professionals.

### Testing for Effects of Building Recognition

The analysis examined potential biases from building recognition. It tallied the number of respondents indicating that they recognized a building. For all but three competitions, fewer than 5

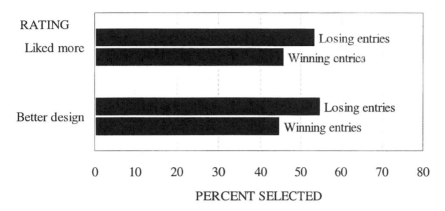

Figure 2.10. Percentage of choices of winning or losing entries as more liked ($N$ = 2496) or the better design ($N$ = 2495). *Note:* Liking: $\chi^2$ (1, 2496) = 27.08, $p$ < .01; Better design: $\chi^2$ (1,2465) = 17.18, $p$ < .01.

---

percent of the sample said they recognized a building. For the *Chicago Tribune* Tower competition (1922), ten respondents said they recognized the winner and eight said they recognized the loser; for the Harding Memorial (1925), ten respondents claimed to recognize the loser; for the Human Tower competition (1982), twelve respondents said they recognized the loser, and four said they recognized the winner, and an additional thirteen claimed to recognize both. Inspection of responses to the recognized buildings suggested that the small number of recognitions did not skew judgments of preference or better design. Dropping responses to "recognized" buildings did not change the pattern of results, so we report the results from the full sample.

---

Did the respondents evaluate the winning entries more favorably than the losing entries? No. They favored the *losing* entries! Remember that if competition juries make the correct choices, one should expect to find the respondents picking more winning entries than losing entries. They did not. For both preference and better design, they chose more losers (55%) than winners as preferred and as the better designs. Although the number may not appear large, it indicates statistically significant differences in favor of losing entries (Figure 2.10; and Appendix C Table C.3). Similar numbers would happen by chance in less than 1 in 1 million times. Analysis of the responses of the architects

PERCENT LIKED

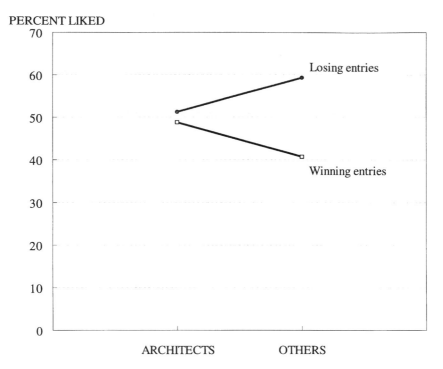

Figure 2.11. Architect and nonarchitect *preferences. Note:* Though nonarchitects selected more losing entries as liked than did architects, both groups liked more losing entries than winning ones [$\chi^2$ (1, $N = 2496$) = 16.56, $p < .001$].

and nonarchitects separately confirmed the pattern. Although the nonarchitects had larger differences than the architects, more members of each group selected losing entries than winning entries as preferred and as better designs (Figures 2.11 and 2.12). The pattern also held for responses to each time period. For all but one time period, respondents chose more competition losers than winners as both preferred and the better designs. Five of these differences achieved statistical significance: For liking, respondents picked more losing entries (approximately 60 percent) than winning ones in 1882–1916, 1930–47, and 1981–87. Similar numbers would happen by chance less than one in 1,000 times for the first and last period and less than 1 in 50 times for the middle period. For better design, respondents picked more losing entries (63 percent) than winners in 1882–1916 and more losing entries (57 percent) than winners in 1981–1987. Similar numbers would happen by

PERCENT
JUDGED BETTER
DESIGN

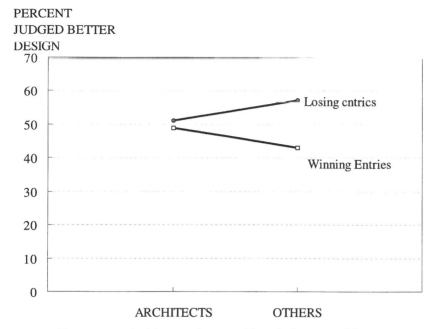

Figure 2.12. Architect and nonarchitect judgments of *better design. Note:* Though nonarchitects selected more losing entries as better designs than did architects, both groups judged more losing entries than winning ones as the better designs [$\chi^2$ (1, $N$ = 2495) = 9.17, $p$ < .01].

chance less than one in 1,000 times and less than one in 100 times respectively.

The results for the houses agree with the results for the full sample of buildings (Appendix C, Table C.6). Respondents gave higher scores to the losing entries. They picked as preferred and better designs approximately twice as many losing entries than winning entries in 1882–1916 and 1981–87. For 1930–47, which included two house competitions, respondents gave significantly lower scores to the losing entry in one of them. The pattern also held for architects and nonarchitects over time. For each group, the losing house designs outscored the winning ones. The nonarchitects exhibited significant differences in preferences for winners and losers in four time periods. In three periods they preferred more losers (63%) to winners: 1882–1916 (60%), 1930–47 (64%), and 1981–87 (72%). The architects had one significant difference in preference between winners and losers: For

1882–1916, they preferred more losers (60%) to winners. Each of these differences would happen by chance less than 1 in 1,000 times. For ratings of better design a similar pattern emerged. The nonarchitects had two significant differences between winners and losers and the architects had one. In each case, they had selected more losers than winners as the better designs (nonarchitects: 1882–1916, 64%; 1981–87, 64%; architects: 1882–1916, 60%). These differences would happen by chance less than 1 in 1,000 times. (See sidebar for more detailed results).

---

DETAILED RESULTS

Although the nonarchitects chose a significantly higher proportion of losers to winners as preferred (59%) and as better designs (57%) than did the architects (preferred: 51%; better design: 51%), each group chose more losers than winners. The group × choice interactions achieved statistical significance.

For all but one time period, respondents preferred more losers than winners (Appendix C Table C.4). The three time periods with significant differences showed preferences for more losers than winners. For better design, respondents chose more losers than winners as better designs in all but one time period. In the two periods with significant differences, they chose more losing than winning entries as better designs.

Scores on houses echoed these scores. The contingency coefficient showed that scores across the five time periods for houses and for all competitions (house responses removed) correlated for Like at $r = .29$ ($p < .001$) but not for Better Design at $r = 6.28$, $p > .10$). For single-family houses, the results also point to more favorable responses to losers than winners over time. More respondents chose losing than winning entries as liked in three of the six comparisons. Two of the three significant differences and one marginally significant difference represented more of the respondents selecting losing entries as preferred. For judgments of the better design, four of the six periods have more respondents choosing losing entries as the better designs. Two of the three significant differences reflect higher numbers choosing losing entries as the better designs.

For preference, the nonarchitects chose more losers than winners in four of the five time periods, three at a statistically significant level. The one period for which they chose more winners than losers (1950–67) also achieved statistical significance. The architects chose more winners than losers in three periods and more losers than winners in two, but the only difference that achieved statistical significance (1892–1916) showed them preferring significantly more losers than winners.

The judgments of better design echo the preference responses. The nonarchitects chose significantly more losers than winners as better designs for the earliest period and for the most recent period. The architects did so for the earliest period. For the remaining periods, differences did not achieve statistical significance.

The results also confirm the familiar pattern of differences in meaning for architects and nonarchitects. Their scores had low correlations with one another. For liking and better design, the correlations ($r = .05$ and $r = .06$, respectively) did not achieve statistical significance. Though both groups favored losing designs, they did so with different intensity. The groups also differed in the strength and direction of response in four of the five periods (Appendix C, Table C.5). The nonarchitects chose a significantly higher proportion of losing entries than did the architects in three periods, and the architects chose a significantly higher proportion of losing entries than did the nonarchtitects in one period. For 1921–29 and 1930–47, more architects chose winners and more nonarchitects chose losers as preferred and as the better design. For 1950–67, this pattern reversed. More architects chose losers and more nonarchitects chose winners as preferred. For 1980–87, more architects chose winners and more nonarchitects chose losers as preferred, but more architects and nonarchitects chose losers than winners as better designs, though the effect was more pronounced among the nonarchitects.

---

### Related Findings

Some critics and architects deplore the reliance on public opinion as pandering to the public and yielding mediocre designs. For example, the architect Le Corbusier claimed that the public needed reeducation. The architect Philip Johnson commented on the vulgarity of popular tastes in architecture, and asked whether architects should take these tastes seriously.[107] According to this view, designers lead popular tastes, such that the unfavorable popular meanings will change to favorable meanings in the future.[141] This *avant-garde* view of art may seem compelling, but the evidence of the current studies contradicts it. Research also shows that the public has maintained a strong and enduring dissatisfaction with much of twentieth architecture. In spite of changes in preferred style among the professionals, the public has maintained a preference for "popular" over "high" style designs.[60 101 224] As the architect Brent Brolin noted:

> After fifty years of indoctrination, the majority of the public remains indifferent or hostile to the modern aesthetic. The predicted universal acceptance of modern architecture has never happened (p. 8).[36]

The public did not follow the lead of the architects.

Other evidence contradicts the avant-garde view. The public used to flock to see Leonardo's paintings, "as if they were attending a festival" (p. 56).[36] Consider also the case of the Eiffel Tower. At the time of the competition, Eiffel had already established a reputation for his designs "greatly admired by the public" (p. 67).[59] When construction started on the project, it was the artistic community, not the public, who denounced the design. Three hundred prominent artists signed a 'Protestation contre la Tour de M. Eiffel' published in the daily newspaper *Le Temps* (p. 65).[59] They complained about the design as a "dishonor to Paris," "barbaric," and a "stupefying dream" (p. 883).[264] [110] The public liked it immediately, and have continued to do so.[66] Also, think of the British Houses of Parliament, another well-liked symbol that has stood the test of time. At the time of the competition, architects objected to the Gothic style, which the public liked.[59] Beyond this anecdotal evidence, a series of scientific studies of reactions to the Transamerica Tower in San Francisco confirm the stability of popular preferences and contradicts the avant-garde theory of art.

As with the Eiffel Tower, experts initially disliked the Transamerica design (Figure 2.13). They judged it as likely to have negative effects "on the city and immediate area" (p. 179).[113] The San Francisco architect and researcher Arthur Stamps reported surveys of public reactions two years, eighteen years, and twenty-three years after construction.[264] The results showed that the early public reactions remained stable over time. The public initially liked the building and they continue to do so.

For the Eiffel Tower and Transamerica, the unenlightened reaction came from the experts, not the pubic. Other research confirms the stability of public preferences over time. In 1986 and 1992, *The San Francisco Examiner* published a poll of the most liked and least liked buildings in San Francisco.[142] [143] Stamps supplemented the newspaper polls with a smaller study in which he had forty-two people rate the twenty buildings from the earlier surveys.[264] Comparing the results of the three polls, he found strong correlations between the ranking of the buildings, with the Transamerica Tower near the top of each list.

### Summary

Earlier in this chapter I asked whether design competitions get the best design solutions. If, as Peter Eisenman said (Appendix B), "signature architecture is a long-term proposition," the evidence suggests that they have not. Interviews with architects revealed mixed opinions on the merits of competitions. My informal look at some competitions pointed to mixed results. Some competition successes may have arisen from fac-

Figure 2.13. Popular evaluations of Transamerica Tower in San Francisco showed stability over time and contradicted the early negative appraisals of the design by experts. Photograph by Arthur E. Stamps, III.

tors other than the competition itself. The search for an answer pointed to the need for systematic inquiry (or postoccupancy evaluation information), and this led to the two scientific studies evaluating the performance of competitions over time. The results suggested that competition juries may not select lasting masterpieces. One study found that competitions seldom produced masterpieces; and the other found that architects and nonarchitects favored losing entries to winning entries in competitions over time. These findings and other scientific studies contradict the avant-garde theory of art, in which architects, as seen through the competition juries, lead public taste. Appraisals of popular preferences and meanings emerge as better indicators of long-term reactions.

My discussion of design competitions has emphasized appearance and meaning. I did this because meaning and appearance takes priority in design competitions, but I do not mean to imply that good design is only about meaning. It must satisfy other goals as well. As Vitruvius noted approximately two thousand years ago, good design should have beauty (*venustas*) or a "pleasing" appearance, but it should also have convenience (*utilitas*) and durability (*firmitas*) (p. 12).[292] Convenience implies "no hindrance to use;" and durability implies a solid "foundation," "solid ground," and firm "materials" (p. 12).[292] The design program, the management of the jury and postoccupancy evaluation should address these requirements as well as appearance.

# 3

# MEANING MATTERS

The aesthetic is the only important thing about building. – Robert Sterns, architect (p. 98)[58]

I'm interested in architecture as a work of art. – Frank Gehry, architect (p. 98)[58]

(Competition juries) lose sight of the objective and . . . get caught up in the image. – Charles Gwathmey, architect (p. 191)[8]

Usually the whole purpose is to make the outcome something entirely different . . . unexpected. – Joseph Esherick, architect (p. 185)[8]

The final pick is always subjective . . . affected by . . . momentary fashions. – Cesar Pelli, architect (p. 207)[8]

I recall walking through an unfamiliar city. It was a pleasant morning, I was enjoying the new scenery, and I felt good. After a while, I noticed that the character of the environment had changed, and that change led me to feel that I might be entering an unsafe area. I do not recall what features led to my feeling or whether it was accurate, but it led me to change directions to avoid this area. Appearances effect human experience. Visual features, noticed but not always within our awareness, convey meanings. They influence our assessment of places, our feelings, thoughts and behavior. They may attract or repel us from an area. In our houses, commercial buildings, offices and main streets, we care about the meaning of the front (or public) elevation.[297]

To get the desired meanings, one should not relegate decisions on meaning to the ad hoc discretionary judgments of a jury. One needs to develop and monitor a visual plan. The plan, or *visual quality program*, should specify guidelines for appearance. Design review should test the entries against the guidelines. Postoccupancy evaluation should evaluate the completed design against them. The method at the center of this book – *prejury evaluation* – offers a rigorous and systematic way to evaluate likely popular meanings as part of design review. It takes a scientific approach to measuring meaning. This chapter lays the foundation for the method.

### Approaches to Developing Guidelines for Appearance (Meaning)

How does one arrive at and test guidelines for appearance? Though people often think of decisions on appearance as subjective and a matter of taste, research discussed throughout this book indicates strong and consistent commonalties in popular evaluations of building appearance. These shared evaluations can become the basis for appearance guidelines. Efforts to develop guidelines for appearance have come from two kinds of inquiry: architectural history (or theory) and scientific.

### Historiography and Architectural Theory (Speculative Aesthetics)

Two subdisciplines of architectural history try to draw patterns from the historical record: historiography and architectural theory.[254] *Historiography* attempts to establish and convey facts to the reader. It stresses the particulars such as persons, buildings, dates, and places. *Architectural theory*[129] (or *speculative aesthetics*)[92] attempts to support conclusions from an analysis of patterns. It tries to build an argument for the author's particular aesthetics. Through profiling a select set of designs or designers, the author argues for how things *ought to be*, rather than describing *how they are*.

To argue for a particular theory or present an interesting narrative, architectural historians and theorists choose facts, arrange them, and chose which facts to emphasize. This subjectivity makes the facts and inferences questionable. The argument stands less on objective criteria than on its subjective persuasiveness and ideology.[253] We cannot build a knowledge base for design on a shaky foundation of such opinions.

The traditional approaches to architectural history and theory also tend to focus on an unrepresentative and limited set of monumental buildings and architect "hero" figures. Buildings occupy less than two percent of the built environment; monumental buildings occupy less; and architectural heroes differ from most architects and others who shape the built environment.[227] The traditional approaches also stress architecture as an artifact and art, overlooking its durability, convenience, and pleasantness to the layperson.[227] An art object need not have durability or convenience, nor does it have to appeal to most viewers. The artistic merit rests more on the artistic statement as seen by other artists and critics, whose views differ from those of the public.[60][90]

### The Scientific Approach

We need to move "from an art history metaphor to a science metaphor" (p. 58).[227] This does not imply a call to drop historical (or philosophical) inquiry. It argues for the applied value of the special kind of knowledge obtained through science. Through reason, objectivity, and empirical evidence, science builds a knowledge base to guide future actions. It can provide the basis for guidelines on building appearance.

The meaning of a building or place depends on individuals' experience of it. To develop guidelines for appearance, one needs to know what people think and feel about places. Answers to this kind of question come from the social sciences. Like the hard sciences, social science relies on systematic empirical observation to test a claim. Investigators examine hypotheses in a systematic way, attempting to avoid biases. They define *constructs* of theoretical interest for study. (The constructs are the things they want to measure). They develop observable indicators to measure the constructs. (This rests on the assumption that although measures may be imperfect, one can develop measures for all constructs of interest.) They examine the relations among the constructs, and use statistical analyses to determine causal connections or associations between the constructs.[117] [253] Two kinds of relations serve as hypotheses. One set of hypotheses has to do with the relations between observable indicators and constructs. Scientists consider whether the measures are accurate and consistent indicators of the constructs. Another set of hypotheses have to do with the relations among constructs. Scientists consider whether one construct causes another construct for a certain condition and population. Although social science may address deeply felt beliefs and values and may not use the technical equipment of the "hard" sciences, the methods allow one to develop scientific tests of seemingly qualitative phenomena such as meaning.

The resulting scientific knowledge is substantially different from ordinary knowledge.[117] On the surface, they may look alike, because they both rely on observation to put together and evaluate explanations. At a deeper level, they differ. Scientific knowledge differs not so much in what scientists do, but in how they do it. Scientists try to construct hypotheses to allow them to interpret experimental data unambiguously. They take a skeptical position toward the hypothesis, looking for biases to judge the relative value of various explanations. Good science does not involve seeking to prove a hypothesis or theory. It involves ruling out rival hypotheses and evaluating the degree to which the data agree with a hypothesis.

Although ordinary observers may also look for biases, they do so to a lesser degree. Their observations have biases that tend to support the beliefs or naive hypotheses. Research suggests that individuals may unknowingly seek and give more weight to confirmations of their beliefs or wishes, ignore inconsistencies in beliefs, rely on opinions of authorities or peer groups – neither of which may be accurate – and have biased observations or inaccurate recall of past experiences.[117] The scientist, aware of the research on biases, uses that information in the design and evaluation of a study. Scientists may still have biases and a vested interest in a finding, but the structure of scientific inquiry makes science "self-correcting, progressive, and cumulative" (p. 64).[227] By making the details of their work – the questions, assumptions, and methods – explicit and public, scientists leave the findings open to independent testing that can confirm or falsify the results.

The general model presented in this book also has its roots in the scientific approach. Programming, managing the jury process, and POE each use a scientific approach, and as an integrated set, they also follow the scientific approach. The program specifies a set of hypotheses about the building performance. Once scientists have hypotheses, they may test them first in a controlled simulated condition. For example, they may first test a new medication on rats. In my model, the pre-jury evaluation (design review and management of the jury process) is a test of the hypotheses in simulated conditions. Scientists then test the hypothesis in the real condition. They may try the new medication on humans. In my model, postoccupancy evaluation serves as the retest of the hypotheses in the real condition. Just as the scientific approach has led to advances in medicine and other sciences, it can advance our knowledge about building meaning. It can also suggest guidelines for appearance.

> When it come to *knowing* (at the cognitive level) and being able to communicate and use such knowledge, the thing we call science is by far the best, most elegant, most powerful and most successful way so far developed to achieve *well-founded, reliable knowledge* (p. 60).[227]

### Shared Meanings

The designed environment is a channel of nonverbal communication.[228] Meaning arises from an interaction between persons and the environment. It involves the subjective experience of observers in relation to physical form. Through interacting with the environment, humans infer meanings and develop preferences.

Persons may experience rapid emotional responses to features of form, such as shape, proportion, scale, or complexity.[92][129][307][315] These responses capture *formal* meaning.[129] A person may also experience slower emotional responses associated with mental processing.[120][132] These responses capture *symbolic* meanings. They arise from associations and inferences about the form.[157] In one kind of symbolic meaning, people make judgments about place identity, perhaps recognizing a building as a church, an office, or a particular style. Such judgments of identity are *denotative* meanings. In another kind of symbolic meaning, people make inferences about the quality and character of the place and its users. These evaluative appraisals are *connotative* meanings.

Because denotative and connotative meanings involve subjective experience, they may vary across people. Research confirms such variation associated with previous experience,[259] adaptation level,[236][310] disposition,[80] taste group,[141] and cognitive set.[134] The presence of individual differences does not rule out shared meanings across various groups.[184] Science recognizes individual differences, but it tries to bring order to the apparent disorder by finding agreement or universal principles. Although individuals may not completely share meanings with one another, they have much in common. Their shared physical reality, biology, culture, and experience would lead to some agreement on environmental meaning. Acknowledging possible individual differences, science can look for the areas of substantial agreement.[139] It can find the shared meanings that represent consensus among many people.

Research confirms strong agreement on evaluative meanings. In 1876, the German psychologist Gustave Fechner conducted the first published scientific studies of preference for visual form.[67] His report demonstrated the potential for scientific research to quantify visual preferences and revealed shared preferences. In the past thirty years, psychologists have renewed the empirical search for principles underlying environmental preferences and meaning. Their findings demonstrate strong and consistent commonalties in preferences and meanings associated with the visual characteristics of places.[39][42][106][120][124][168][173] Knowledge of such collective meanings has particular relevance for public designs such as competitions, which many people experience. One can use knowledge about public meanings to program and evaluate designs for the well-being of the public.

### Meaning versus Aesthetics

I use terms such as *meaning* and *appearance* to describe what others may call "aesthetics." I avoid the term *aesthetics*, because it may create some misleading inferences.[229] As long as aesthetics is linked to art, people may view decisions on it as part of the artists' realm – subjective, qualitative, and not scientifically measurable. *Aesthetics* also implies a focus on the design as an object or sculptural form independent of the observer. Although architects and juries may view a design in this way, my view goes beyond artistic properties to include the human experience of it.[1] In referring to meaning, I am not referring to the transcendent experience of beauty, the subjective experience independent of the material world,[214] or to sublime experience of beauty in the arts.[250] I am referring to the less extreme feelings that ordinary people experience regularly in relation to the physical environment.[306] This conforms with Thomas Aquinas's view of aesthetics as "that which pleases when seen" (p. 46).[13] Replacing "aesthetics" with meaning and appearance reflects the psychological and scientific approach of measuring how humans experience the visual features of the environment.[283][307]

### Does Meaning Matter?

Research shows that people care about visual quality or meanings of their environment. For example, several studies of housing found *appearance* as a major predictor of residential satisfaction[131][295] and as a major factor in people's evaluation of the quality of urban environments.[44] Other research shows appearance as the major factor in people's response to architecture.[101][109] Making meanings is a key part of our lives. It probably played a role in survival. To survive, our predecessors had to notice and identify things around them, and they had to evaluate their potential for harm or gain. Survival depended on assigning meanings.[120][283]

Many people mistakenly treat appearance as a trivial concern. Yet, John Stuart Mills, an advocate of Jeremy Benthan's utilitarian philosophy, argued against the distortion of the concept to reject "or the neglect . . . beauty." He argued against treating utility as superior (pp. 406–407).[154] Appearance has value in itself and in its effect on function. It can affect the appeal of a place. In theory, people would rather go to and spend time in likable places and avoid disturbing ones.[151] Research confirms that they do.[282] Beyond that, different activities and purposes benefit from different kinds of appearance. Some purposes may call for a friendly appearance; others may call for something else. A setting for entertainment, such as Times Square or Las Vegas, may benefit from an exciting appearance. Places for healing may require a relaxing appearance. Knowledge of the visual features associated with the desired meanings can identify appearance guidelines to fit the purpose.

Design competition buildings, more than most buildings, involve "public meanings." They often use public money, a prominent site visible from public rights-of-way, and public land. For example, the Wexner Center occupies a conspicuous public site. Located on a land-grant university campus, it faces a major street at the traditional front door to that campus. Approximately 40 percent of the project costs involved money from the State of Ohio. Maintenance and operating costs also involve state money. One may not notice or care about the appearance of privately funded designs on private property and not visible to others. However, when a building (or sculpture) uses public money or land, serves a public or quasi-public agency, or is visible from public rights-of-way, it becomes public and answerable to the public.[137] For buildings, the part extending from "the exterior . . . outward" stands as a quasi-public entity (p. 8).[252] Unlike art, literature, music or theater, where the viewer can choose what to experience, public architecture imposes itself on the passerby. One can see recognition of this in public policy on visual quality. U.S. federal and state courts treat building exteriors as public entities and grant aesthetics alone as an adequate basis for design controls.[209] Communities use various techniques to control appearance, and most U.S. communities use design review to control appearance.[137] Aesthetics and related terms such as *beauty, compatibility* and *harmony* appear in federal, state, and local planning guidelines. The National Environmental Policy Act and the Coastal Zone Management Act mandate consideration of aesthetic variables.[50] [187]

### Outsider versus Insider Meanings

Design competitions tend to seek an aesthetic statement and publicity. To get a functional building, one could develop a comprehensive program, evaluate the work of various architects on related projects, interview architects, and work with one through the design process. Clients opt for a competition to get publicity and an artistic statement. A supporter of competitions notes among the benefits of competitions that "new design forms can result," and "accepted norms are tested as well as challenged" (p. 218).[260] Within the context of a competition, sponsors can improve the chances of getting a better product and conveying the desired meanings, if they use an adequate program for appearance and a more systematic and inclusive design review process than typically occurs in competitions. This might prevent some of the arbitrariness of jury decisions, and the neglect of popular meanings, convenience, and durability for high art solutions.

People may evaluate places in one of two ways: as participants or as indifferent outside observers. Competitions, with invited jurors of outside experts, tend to favor the perspective of the outsider. For outsiders, appearance becomes the top priority. In a series of studies, the urban designer Sidney Brower showed that outsiders view places differently from insiders.[37] Other studies agree. Although outsiders, architects, and the architectural press praised a feasibility study for a development, residents hated it, describing it as a "prison," "concentration camp," "depressing," and "claustrophobic" (p. 232).[228] Through prejury evaluation (PJE), clients can supplement the outside perspective with information on inside popular meanings.

Research confirms that architects and juries stress appearance. Interviews with fifty staff persons for urban design competitions found that respondents judged the competition as a success, even though almost half of the programs had major omissions or errors.[4] The favorable assessments rested primarily on perception of the publicity. A survey of jurors, sponsors' representatives, and entrants in competitions found that most of them thought the jurors did not judge the project on function – how well it follows the program.[248] This poll also found that half of the respondents reported that many entrants do not receive fair consideration and that two-thirds of the respondents did not believe the best designs won. A *Progressive Architecture* reader poll produced similar results.[31] Most respondents (70%) indicated that the best design did not usually win; most of them (75%) characterized the jury as spending too little time to evaluate the entries; and most of them (59%) described jurors as biased and not conscientious. One-third of them reported that the quality of presentation counted too much in decisions. A content analysis of leading professional architectural magazines revealed that most of the text dealt with speculations about form and most of the graphics stressed form – views of buildings from unrealistic perspectives and devoid of life.[161] A study of an awards jury for housing found that unlike the residents, who emphasized livability, the jury focused on appearance.[291]

For an example of the emphasis on appearance, consider the jury comments on the winning design for the Sydney Opera House in Australia (Figure 3.1). After reviewing 220 entries, the jurors unanimously selected the design by the thirty-eight-year-old Danish Architect, Jörn Utzon. In explaining their choice, they stressed the "original" and "creative" form, saying virtually nothing about practical concerns. Although they admitted that the drawings were "simple to the point of being diagrammatic" (p. 96), they praised the design for its appearance: "The great merit of this building is the unity of its structural expression . . . a striking architectural composition. It is difficult to think of a better silhouette for this peninsula" (pp. 96–97).[219]

Figure 3.1. Sydney Opera House (1956–73), Sydney, Australia by Jörn Utzon – Visually successful, functionally flawed. Photograph by Jack L. Nasar.

In this case, the jury may have made an accurate judgment of the design's appearance, though the choice probably had more to do with the similarity of the design to the work of the jury chair, Eero Saarinen. (Research discussed throughout this book indicates that expert judgments on meaning tend to be inaccurate). The Opera House attracts more than 2 million visitors a year and has become a symbol of Sydney and Australia. Yet, a focus on appearance to the outsider can overlook critical aspects of convenience and durability. While outsiders see a striking form, the client and day-to-day users encounter serious problems. It took Utzon and his structural engineer Ove Arup five years to figure out a way to build the roof for the Sydney Opera House. Three years later, when Utzon had yet to put anything on paper for the interior, a newly elected government appointed a supervisory state architect. Utzon resigned in protest. To his surprise, the government accepted his resignation. It took fourteen years to build. Scheduled to cost $7 million (Australian), the project cost escalated to almost fifteen times as much ($102 million). To pay the extra cost, the government held a lottery. The government pays $4 million a year just to maintain and operate the building, and several years ago, they allocated an additional $58 million for a seven-year maintenance program. The Opera House requires a 40 percent government subsidy to break even. The building is sinking. Leaks in the roof threaten the structure. The interior is disorienting. The audience must climb hundreds of narrow steps, only to descend again to their seats. From its opening, performers complained about the design. The stage and pit are too small. Such problems of convenience and durability do not seem unexpected for a design selected principally for a sketch of the shape of its roof.

For centuries, architects have considered themselves artists. Several theorists argue that twentieth-century architects moved toward the avant-garde and art for the sake of art.[30] [36] They have sloughed off skill areas, such as civil engineering, structural engineering, and site planning for design or art.[233] Interviews with several notable architects, including Louis Kahn, I. M. Pei, Richard Meier, Gio Ponti, John M. Johansen, Edward Durrell Stone, and Philip Johnson confirm that they tend to see architecture primarily as art (p. 48).[30] For example, the architect Paul Rudolf says, "If an architect is not an artist, he should not be an architect." Other interviews confirm that most architects feel protective of the artistic value of their work, focusing on high style, symbolism, and form for its own sake.[57] One survey of architects found almost universal agreement (98%) about art and creativity as the distinctive feature of architecture.[30] Architects' comments on competitions also show their emphasis on appearances. In Kathryn Anthony's book on design juries,[8] I examined interviews with architects for their comments on design competition juries. Fourteen designers commented on what makes a winning entry in a competition, Most of them (90%) mentioned appearance, citing such things as "exciting building," "aesthetics and character," "style," and "symbols." Some of their comments about juries and competitions (italics added) illustrate the priority they give to appearance or image:

> What tends to happen is that you lose sight of the objective *and you get caught up in the image* – Charles Gwathmey (p. 191).
>
> Many juries tend to judge *on a visual basis* rarely in three dimensions. What you see on the cover of design magazines are often not interesting places to visit. . . . They just have this great idea for a dish pan but the competition is for a tea kettle. But if it's the most gorgeous dish pan they've ever seen, some jury will give the award to the dish pan – Norman R. Dehaan (p. 179).
>
> I think that with modern design competitions, the objective is to *produce the unexpected.* I'm all for innovation, but not for innovation at all costs – Joseph Esherick (p. 184).
>
> The final pick is always subjective. It's what's in the mind of the jurors, and is affected by personal preferences and *momentary fashions* – Cesar Pelli (p. 207).

> At first *we went through every one in about ten seconds.* That's awfully fast. But by the time we started getting into it, we realized that we could see whether or not there was any merit in a project in even less time. We actually got it down to about five seconds – Martha Schwartz (p. 211).

My interviews with finalists for the Wexner Center Competition (Appendix C), all of who have entered and won many competitions, confirm the impression that appearance sways juries. Cesar Pelli, who said he had served on more than twelve juries, said that the architects choose "according to their stylistic preferences . . . the architects look primarily at the looks of the buildings." Arthur Erickson said juries look for a "memorable new direction in architecture," and Michael McKinnell described competitions as "a vehicle for the exploration of ideas."

If the decision rests on appearance, then sponsors and the public may want to ensure that the jury hunches about the meaning conveyed by the appearance are accurate. Too often, juries use ad hoc unverbalized criteria, rather than holding to criteria specified in the program. A taped transcript of a jury's deliberations highlights the importance assigned to appearance and the potentially inexact approach juries use to arrive at a decision.[93] Steven and Gordon Gunn sponsored a competition for a hotel. The jury, consisting of the Gunns and five eminent designers – Bill Lacy, Paul Frieberg, Ralph Knowles, Charles Moore, and Moshe Safdie – judged the 129 submissions in three days. They began by eliminating entries. Many of their comments did not include a reason. They simple said things like, "out" or "retain this one." Where they give reasons, they made quick judgments based on appearance rather than on technical or functional criteria.

> Entry 1
> Safdie: Members of the Jury. Is there anyone who would like to retain scheme number one?
> Gunn: No
>
> Entry 2
> Safdie: Is there anyone here who wishes to keep scheme number two?
> Moore: Absolutely not.
>
> Entry 3
> Safdie: Entry number three? No one for three (Rejected) (p. 32).[93]

And so it went.

Other comments suggest the emphasis on appearance:[93]

> Frieberg: It's a pedestrian scheme . . . a competent job, but for a competition it's boring.

Safdie: I think this is a series of different languages on the same site
        plan (p. 33).
Moore: It's ugly but it has character (p. 34).
Lacy: It's getting brutal now, that's what I like, blood. [said with gusto
        and humor] (p. 35).
Frieberg: It's absolutely beautiful, it's vertical (p. 37)

After they eliminated 105 entries, an architect on the jury asked the
Gunns, "What kind of hotel would work here?" (p. 149)[93] For the first
time, the jury considered the land use plan, that showed the density
allowable on the site. Before they knew about function and code, the
designers on the jury had eliminated 81 percent of the entries.

Looking at the final twenty-four entries, two jurors commented on
the jury's emphasis on form. Friedberg says, "I don't know that in any
of these schemes *that we have been dealing with anything more than the formal aspects of them*" (italics added), to which Knowles responds, "I think
that is right" (p. 66).[93] None of the other jurors questioned the conclusion that their decisions had dealt only with form. I went through the
written transcript of comments, counting the reported reasons for
eliminating entries. My count confirmed the accuracy of this conclusion. The jury dropped most entries for reasons having to do with
appearance. (A $\chi^2$ test revealed that they dropped significantly more
for appearances than for other reasons, $p < .01$). Occasionally they did
mention the site plan or function, commenting on such things as
buffering traffic, view to the sun, views into enclosed spaces instead of
outdoors, what people will do in a recreation core, and the orientation
of tennis courts, but most of their comments refer to appearance and
meaning. The jury went on to group the twenty-four entries into
generic form or style groups: "Chateau," "Crescent," "Hilltown,"
"Downhill finger," and "Castle" (p. 54).[93] Unfortunately, the book did
not report the discussion of the five to retain, because it took place out
of range of the microphone. Still, the transcript shows that the jury
acted primarily on the basis of appearance.

### Whose Meanings?

Who should make the decisions about public appearance? In the first
reported competition, the Council of Athens took a democratic
approach. It put the designs for the war memorial on display for ten
days, after which the citizens of Athens voted to select the winner.[59]
Such a democratic approach makes sense for a democracy. Public
designs must consider public meanings – the meanings shared by large
numbers of people. Yet, many people believe that public art and architecture "is to be selected by an elite of qualified judges and then pre-

sented to the public for its enlightenment (p. 269).[45] This belief receives support from design professionals. The AIA recommends that competitions use a jury dominated by architects, stating that "experience indicates that a majority of jury members in architectural competitions should be architectural professionals with substantial knowledge and skill" (p. 15).[6] The United Kingdom traditionally required an architect-only jury, and many European countries and the international system require that the competition jury have a majority of architectural professionals.[271] RIBA recommends a jury of four with at least two architects, because such a jury can visualize the finished buildings from drawings and evaluate the technical, economic, and construction viability of the design.[235] Other professionals, such as engineers and contractors, probably have better qualifications to make such evaluations.

A jury dominated by architects may scoff at popular values as "vulgar." Observers from within and outside the design professions have noted the scorn many designers have for popular values and the negative consequences that result.[29][76][189][241][311] Architects continue to condemn the aesthetic and social values of single-family suburban development, yet it remains the most popular form of housing in the country.[36] In one case, architects evaluated an area a slum, though residents maintained it well.[344] The architects disliked the materials used by the residents in making renovations. Commenting on competitions, Frank Lloyd Wright described the architecture as "an average upon an average by averages in behalf of the averages" and went on to describe them as democratic "if mediocrity is the democratic ideal in architecture" (pp. 176–77).[72] Traditional architectural theory suggests that many architects produce buildings as art for the pleasure of their peers, regardless of how well buildings work for the users.[228] Research confirms substantial differences between architects and the public in their evaluations of building appearance and meaning: Architects like what the public dislikes.[60][90][172] For example, the appearance of the Pruitt Igoe housing project appealed to architects, but held negative connotations to the residents.[189] Louis Kahn's Richards Research Laboratories had a host of serious problems thwarting use for occupants and the client, which led the client to forbid him designing another building on campus. Yet architects continue to revere the building and Kahn. A survey of architects found him rated second as "your architectural heroes/heroines of the past."[221] Another study showed Kahn among the top five architects in the eyes of critics.[215] The Museum of Modern Art gave a show on Richards Laboratories, one of twelve shows on a building in the museum's history.[95]

A study of designer and resident reactions to the British new town of Milton Keynes found that the two groups held opposite evaluations:

The residents liked the features of the town and the design professionals did not.[28] Rapoport reports a feasibility study for a development, praised by the architects and architectural press but disliked by the residents, who described it as a "prison," "concentration camp," "depressing," and "claustrophobic." (p. 232)[228] One study had architects and other professionals evaluate forty home exteriors.[60] The architects often most liked the homes that the public liked least, and visa versa. Each group saw different meanings in the same physical forms. In design competitions, the lack of contact between the designer and the public may heighten these differences.

The differences in meaning take on greater importance in light of the importance of visual quality and meaning to people.[131] Humans naturally notice things and draw meanings from them. This ability may have a basis in evolution.[120] [205] [283] Studies consistently find meaning and appearance as a central component of human responses to buildings, community, neighborhood, and houses.[44] [101] [109] For example, a study of public housing found that residents identified physical appearance as a chief concern.[24] A study of residents in squatter housing improved the exterior appearance (meaning) of their new units before dealing with serious security threats and problems of insulation.[177]

Architectural meaning matters on a day-to-day basis to people. It also matters to designers, but they have different views from the public who experience the design. The elite standards of the profession may be acceptable for private objects, but public entities should reflect a more democratic process. For meaningful buildings, the building delivery process must respect the "public" meaning conveyed by competition designs. It can do this in each phase of the cyclical design process. The program can use the latest scientific predesign research to specify appearance guidelines; the prejury evaluation, by scientifically examining the public meanings, can guide the jury decision; and the postoccupancy evaluation can assess the meanings and derive ways to improve it. Using Wexner Center as an example, the next chapters demonstrate the steps in the model.

# 4

## MANAGING MEANING THROUGH VISUAL QUALITY PROGRAMMING

(In a competition), the client is often stuck with something that he or she does not want, because the client has no input in the process.
– Peter Eisenman, architect (author interview)

Can we forecast the likely meanings of a building or place to the public? Competition juries try to do that, though they look at the artistic meanings conveyed to their peers. The details of a design might change with design development and construction, but such changes would occur for any winning entry. Just as design juries implicitly forecast likely reactions to designs, research can explicitly derive the likely popular reactions to designs. Sponsors can apply scientific methods or findings on meanings to establish appearance guidelines or to evaluate design entries.

For competition juries, the evaluations arise from the inner subjective criteria of the "experts." My approach replaces inner subjective criteria with a public set of scientifically based criteria for evaluating the entries. By looking at empirical findings on environmental appearance and meaning, one can start to understand the practical implications for design and develop a *visual quality program*. One can also derive appearance guidelines from the scientific study for the specific situation – *visual quality programming (VQP)*. As with *architectural* (or *facility*) *programming*, in VQP one investigates, develops, gathers, and organizes information.[243] The visual quality program specifies appearance guidelines for the entries to satisfy and for the jury to use in judging the entries. By using scientific research, it should more accurately predict eventual public meanings than would judgments by a jury of outsiders and design experts. This chapter discusses scientifically based appearance guidelines and discusses a method for visual quality programming.

### Appearance Guidelines

In spite of individual differences, many people have shared meanings and these can serve as a basis for appearance guidelines. To set relevant

75

guidelines, one must first know what emotional meanings and what features of the visual environment stand out in human experience. Then, one can consider the relation between the prominent features and the prominent dimensions of response. First consider emotional meanings.

### Emotional Meanings

When people look at a building or place, they may judge how much they like it or how pleasant it looks. These kinds of judgments refer to feelings of *pure evaluation*. People may also judge how arousing and active or sleepy and dead a place looks. These judgments refer to feelings of *arousal* (or activity). The combination of evaluation and arousal yields two other aspects of emotional meaning: *exciting* and *relaxing*. If one judges a place as exciting or boring, the judgment refers to its level of excitement. If one judges a place as relaxing or distressing, or safe or unsafe, the judgments refer to its level of relaxation. Excitement and relaxation have different mixes of evaluation and arousal. *Exciting* places are more pleasant and arousing than boring ones. *Relaxing* places are more pleasant but less arousing than distressing ones.

Research confirms preference, arousal, excitement and relaxing as the prominent dimensions of human emotional response to buildings and places (sidebar).[237] This finding has received confirmation in studies using a variety of research strategies and measures.[236] People may also infer social meanings, such as status, from environmental cues.[228] Of the various meanings, preference has particular importance, because measures of it yield a composite of the various evaluative and social meanings.[85]

---

### DIMENSIONS OF EMOTIONAL MEANING

Early research into emotional meaning uncovered three dimensions of meaning – evaluation, potency, and activity.[100] [206] These early studies overlooked response to the physical environment. Newer research examined emotional meanings of the physical environment,[42] [101] [128] but these studies suffered from biases that clouded the interpretation of the findings. They used verbal scales and factor analysis, the results of which depend in part on the scales used. They also combined ratings of visual features and emotional response, confounding the interpretation of dimensions of each. The psychologists Jim Russell and Larry Ward initiated a program of research that overcame these problems.[237] They used verbal and nonverbal approaches to examine dimensions of emotional meaning for the physical environment.[236] The nonverbal approach involved having respondents judge the similarity between scenes. Using multidimensional scaling analysis, they mapped the scenes in conceptual similarity space. Then, they fit emotional appraisals to the space. Their results showed pleasantness and arousal (or activity) as two independent dimensions of emotional meaning. Potency did not emerge as important. Combinations of pleasantness and arousal yielded excitement and relaxing. Subsequent research confirmed the generality of the dimensions for appraisals of urban scenes.[97 170]

---

### Environmental Features

Six features stand out in human perception and evaluation of the physical environment: diversity (visual richness), order, openness, naturalness, upkeep, historical significance, and livable space. *Diversity* (visual richness) refers to the number of noticeably different elements in a scene. It refers to complexity without negative content such as clutter and disorder.[120 307] *Order* refers to the degree to which a building looks organized and the degree to which it and its parts are compatible. *Openness* refers to the openness and definition of the vista. *Naturalness* refers to the perceived prominence of vegetation and water. *Upkeep* refers to the perceived maintenance and cleanliness of a place. *Historical significance* refers to the perception that a place has historical significance or a traditional style. *Livable space* refers to the presence of people. Theory and research indicate that people prefer moderate diversity and they prefer order, openness, naturalness, upkeep, historical significance, and livable space.

*Diversity (Visual Richness).* Theories suggest that people should feel increases in interest (excitement) from increases in diversity and should prefer moderate levels of diversity (sidebar). What does the research show?

---

THEORIES ON DIVERSITY

According to one theory, evaluation depends on arousal.[26 144 307] Variables such as diversity, novelty or atypicality, produce uncertainty and arousal, which, in turn, affects preference. These theories predict that interest increases with arousal and that preference peaks at a moderate level of arousal (Figure 4.1). Similarly, interest

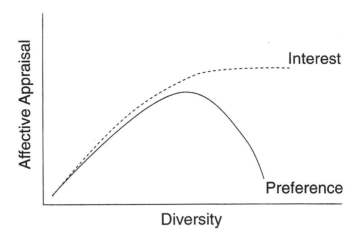

Figure 4.1. Predicted effect of diversity on interest and preference.

should increase with diversity and preference should peak for a moderate level of diversity.

Another theory replaces arousal with information processing.[120] This theory argues that because people must find their way through the environment, cues that help people make sense of the surrounding become important. People should like places that make sense and offer involvement. Features that increase involvement include diversity and the promise of further information ahead. Features that help people make sense of a place include coherence and legibility. This theory states that people should like coherence and legibility for their contribution to making sense. They should like diversity and mystery for their contribution to involvement. Both theories arrive at similar conclusions: People should like coherence and moderate levels of diversity.

It confirms a difference between what people view as interesting and what they view as preferred. As predicted by theory, research consistently finds interest associated with increases in diversity (and related variables such as ornamentation, atypicality, and information).[120 164 204 307] For example, a study of onsite responses to twenty buildings in Toronto found increases in interest associated with increases in the diversity of the building exteriors.[203] A study that systematically manipulated the diversity of commercial signs found excitement and desire to visit associated with increases in sign diversity.[165]

The findings for *preference*, though less consistent than those for interest, show that people prefer moderate diversity over low or high diversity (see sidebar). For example, a study of a variety of scenes found preference highest for a moderate level of diversity.[306] Controlled investigations show similar results. One study had people evaluate movies of trips through scale-model streets varying in diversity.[307] Another had merchants and shoppers evaluate color photographs of model retail streets varying in signscape diversity.[165] Both studies found that preference was highest for moderate diversity.

Research has also examined novelty and atypicality. Observers see something as novel or atypical if it has a discrepancy from what they expect relative to previous experience. As such, these variables, like diversity, can increase arousal or involvement. Several studies confirm that these variables evoke interest but that ordinary people prefer relatively low levels of them.[60 103 164 222 223 224] Artists and architects have been found to favor higher levels of novelty or atypicality.[26 223 224 256 293]

---

BIASES IN STUDIES OF PREFERENCE FOR
ENVIRONMENTAL DIVERSITY

Research has found increases in preference associated with increases in the diversity of natural scenes.[122 306] Studies of buildings and urban scenes have also found preference to increase with diversity.[60 103 163 164] Although these findings do not show the expected downturn in preference, they may suffer from several kinds of flaws. Some studies did not have scenes with high enough diversity to get the downturn in preference for high diversity. Some studies left content (such as land-use) uncontrolled, or they examined preference across content categories. Because diversity and preference vary across content categories,[122 103 104 306] effects attributed to diversity may result from the content associated with diversity. Some studies suffer from ratings biases, because they did not separate ratings of diversity and preference. Independent ratings remove this bias and obtain different results.[120] Finally, most studies did not test for the nonlinear relationship between diversity and preference.

---

*Order.* Theory suggests that people should prefer coherence and order (sidebar). Most studies show increases in *preference* associated with increases in order and related variables, such as unity, coherence, clarity, compatibility, and legibility.[120 169 203 204] Several studies also show ordering variables such as legibility, identifiability, and coherence as important predictors of preference.[120] This preference for order and related variables has held in a variety of contexts. It has shown stability for many respondents and places,[174] U.S. and Japanese street scenes,[164] house exteriors,[60] building exteriors in Toronto,[203] architectural exteriors from around the world,[204] signs,[165] buildings in relation to neighboring buildings,[91] and buildings in relation to their natural settings.[308] Research also shows that people dislike environmental disorder such as dilapidation and litter.[163] [174] Features that may contribute to order include repetition, uniform texture, distinctive elements, identifiabilitly,[120] focal point,[283] low contrast (in the color, size, texture, and shape of elements or between objects and their background), and replication of facade features.[91] [165] [308]

Familiarity may also contribute to order; and research shows that people prefer the familiar.[37] [43] [103] [162] [259] For example, one study had people rate their own front yards and ones that looked like their own. People rated their own yards more favorable.[208] Research also shows increases in preference related to increases in frequency of exposure and familiarity.[32] [158] [159] The findings that people like both familiarity and novelty may appear contradictory, but they agree with the models for diversity and order: Novelty catches the observer's attention and arousal; and familiarity helps the observer make sense of it. Thus, designs that offer order, familiarity, and related features should evoke pleasurable responses, and that pleasure could be heightened through a combination of order and familiarity with moderate complexity or atypicality.

*Openness.* Theory suggests that people should like open vistas, because such views would allow them to see and predict what might occur.[10] A completely unrestricted open view, however, would not have enough diversity to evoke involvement or arousal. Thus, people should prefer open but defined spaces and spatial diversity.[78] [109] [169] [227] An early study found openness or constriction of streets as the most important part of the pedestrian's experience.[140] Studies of natural scenes show preferences for moderate and defined openness to either wide open or blocked views.[120] Although some studies of built places suggest a preference for more space,[163] [164] the scenes in the studies all had spatial boundaries. Studies of built space indicate that people favor prefer defined openness, shallower spaces, low-rise over high-rise buildings, and lower building obtrusiveness.[78] [106] [111]

A related spatial variable deals with the arrangement of space: the promise of information ahead. A deflected vista (or curved path) is an example. Research shows ample evidence of preference for deflected vistas during the day.[120] After dark, this changes. In theory, darkness would make people feel more vulnerable, leading them to dislike hidden information ahead. It could conceal danger. Studies confirm that places of concealment ahead evoke fear, especially in conditions of perceived social danger.[105] [178] [189] [181] Sensitive design can provide the mystery desired during daylight and the visibility desired after dark.

*Naturalness.* Natural features differ in form from built ones,[309] and people notice the difference. They do so in response to many kinds of scenes: familiar and unfamiliar,[103] [104] rural, natural, and urban,[78] [120] housing,[169] and other land uses.[103] [104] Natural and built features also convey different meanings. People tend to judge built features (such as poles, wires, signs, vehicles, and intense uses) unfavorably and natural features favorably. This pattern of response has emerged in many contexts, including residential environments,[145] multi-family developments,[53] planned residential environments,[131] and other land uses.[54] For example, in studies asking residents and visitors in several cities to tell what they like and dislike about the appearance of their cities and neighborhoods, the respondents often mention natural features (such as vegetation, water and mountains) among their likes and built features (such as poles, wires, signs, vehicles and industry) among their dislikes.[174] Other work has had people respond directly to a variety of scenes. It has also found preference associated with naturalness and decreases in the prominence of built features.[103] [104] [163] [164] Studies of specific features have confirmed the more general findings. When the landscape architect Donald Appleyard studied effects of traffic in San Francisco, he found a variety of negative effects associated with traffic in residential areas.[11] Similar negative responses to traffic emerged in other research.[54] [131] [166] Research found that the removal of utility poles, overhead wires, billboards and signs from photographs of roadside scenes produced increases in preference for the scenes.[304] A study of retail signs found that reductions in sign size and contrast enhanced the perceived pleasantness of retail scenes for both shoppers and merchants.[165] A study of the fittingness of built structures to the natural surroundings found that preference increased with decreases in size and increases in the compatibility of the built structure.[308] The preference for the addition of nature and for natural over built scenes has amassed consistent empirical support. Research has shown that people prefer natural over fabricated scenes,[122] [306] naturalness within built settings,[39] and increases in naturalness or reductions in the visibility of buildings.[163] [164] [277] Water, particularly moving water, enhances scenic quality.[213] [283] [301]

Naturalness may have other effects. People may gravitate toward it. A study of commuters faced with a choice of a natural parkway and a built-up expressway found that more of them used the parkway, even though it was out of their way.[282] Naturalness may also have calming and restorative effects.[121] A study of hospital patients found that patients with a view of trees had faster postoperative recovery, fewer negative evaluations by nurses, and fewer doses of narcotic painkillers than did other patients.[284] Prison inmates with a view of farmland had fewer sick calls than inmates with a view to the prison yard.[155] Individuals viewing videotapes of nature showed more rapid stress recovery than did those viewing tapes of urban scenes.[285] People walking through natural as opposed to constructed environments showed restoration on verbal, behavioral, and physiological measures.[98] For design, the research indicates that lessening the prominence of built elements and strengthening the prominence of natural elements should improve the perceived appearance of places.

*Upkeep.* Upkeep has also emerged as prominent feature that people notice.[103] [104] [168] [171] [173] In an early study, the architect–planner Kevin Lynch asked people to describe their city. In Jersey City, he found that people said they disliked it because it looked "old," "dirty," and "drab" (p. 50).[139] My research on Knoxville and Chattanooga found that residents and visitors often cited dilapidation as a reason they disliked areas; and they cited cleanliness as a reason for their preferences.[174] Other research agrees. A study relating evaluative responses (preference, interest, and safety) to visual features of residential scenes found upkeep as a principal predictor of evaluative response.[169] Studies on fear of crime and crime show that increases in each relate to dilapidation, absence of care and other physical incivilities.[189] [276]

*Historical Significance (and Styles).* Styles have distinct formal features,[191] and people recognize styles by such features. For example, research finds that people perceive two styles of architecture as different and as having distinct features from one another.[63] Other work confirms differences in formal features of "high" and "popular" styles and differences in evaluations of them.[60] [288] Respondents use consistent categories for sorting modern, postmodern and transitional styles.[90] Other research uncovered clusters of perceived home styles, each with distinct physical characteristics.[119] With common formal organization of styles, computer algorithms can generate a style such as a Frank Lloyd Wright prairie house or a Palladian home.[268] In agreement with the idea that style conveys meaning, research finds that observers looking at building exteriors make accurate connotative inferences about building interiors and inhabitants.[47] [239] They can even accurately gauge characteristics of the original residents of an older community.[49] Evaluative meanings dif-

Figure 4.2. A popular style preferred by many Americans. Photograph by Jack L. Nasar.

fer across styles. People favor vernacular over high style designs.[60][300] Across four U.S. cities, three different sets of housing stimuli and response measures, several studies converge on the desirability of popular over high styles (Figure 4.2).[172] Architects differ from the public. They use different criteria in styles,[90] in their descriptions and in their evaluations of popular and high styles.[60] Unlike the public, architects tend to favor the high styles.

Though building type (such as home, school, store, stadium) may moderate meanings associated with a style,[103][152][183][280][281] popular preference for vernacular over high styles remains stable across many classes of building. The preference may reflect a favorable response to historical content. Research shows that people in several cities prefer buildings and places that look historical.[174] A study on the design of city halls, found that people preferred historical designs to modern ones.[133] When The Ohio State University tore down a historic structure to replace it, the alumni drove the university to recreate the character of the old building. In a subsequent survey of alumni, the replica and another historical building, Orton Hall, emerged as the two most liked campus buildings.[212] Historical and vernacular forms should evoke favorable responses.

*Livable Space.* As social animals, people enjoy watching one another. William Whyte used stop-action photography of plazas in New York City to discover what made some successful and others unsuccessful. From analysis of the patterns of use, he concluded that people were attracted to places – called *livable spaces* – that had a view of other people.[301] Other research confirms that the presence of people increases preference for scenes.[166][278] Though the presence of people may appear to be a social feature, designs can affect it. As Whyte noted, the design can create livable gathering places or dead places.[201] Places to sit with views of others tend to attract people, as does food and activity. Entry steps in front of buildings represent a natural gathering place. Designs having such features should attract use, making them more appealing.

### Applying the Findings

The review points to commonalties in people's responses to prominent scene features (diversity, order, openness, naturalness, upkeep, historical significance, and livable space). In developing appearance guidelines, one should bear in mind that people can derive satisfaction from places for different reasons. For some places, such as homes, people may prefer a lower arousal or promise of information. They want rest and relaxation.[26][251] For other places, such as places of entertainment, people may want a boost in arousal or promise of information. They go there for excitement.[26][251] For other places, they may seek a mix of excitement and relaxation. Guidelines for appearance should first consider the desired goal, and then apply research-based criteria to help achieve it. Tables 4.1 through 4.3 and Figures 4.3 and 4.4 show lists of research-based criteria for different emotional meanings. Treat the criteria less as final answers than as hypotheses to use, test, and refine. The guidelines need not restrict the designer's creativity. Rather than specifying "the" solution, the guidelines provide a framework within which designers can operate. Each designer can create an infinite number of solutions that fit the guidelines. Many designers value such guidelines as a source of creativity. Appropriately used, appearance guidelines should not create uniformity or boredom. Because different meanings apply to different places and purposes, the guidelines should lead to variation across space, creating variety and interest.

Competition clients could include the desired meanings and a list of desired visual features in the design program, provided to the competitors. They could also give the jury the list of features for judging the entries for likely popular meanings. As an alternative, the client could score the entries relative to the desired visual features. To demonstrate

Table 4.1. *Criteria for pleasantness.*

To achieve PLEASANTNESS
   Increase natural or soft elements (such as foliage and water)
   Decrease prominence of built elements and visual nuisances
      (such as billboards, poles and wires, intense land uses, and traffic)
   Increased coherence (order, compatibility, legibility)
   Provide moderate variety, novelty, or atypicality
   Provide defined open space, deflected vistas
   Use familiar, popular, or historic styles and elements
   Provide livable space

Table 4.2. *Criteria for excitement.*

To achieve EXCITEMENT
   Increase obtrusive built or hard elements (such as billboards, poles
      and wires, intense land uses, and traffic)
   Decrease the coherence, order, compatibility, and legibility
   Increase diversity, novelty, or atypicality
   Provide livable space

Table 4.3. *Criteria for relaxation.*

To achieve RELAXATION
   Increase natural or soft elements (such as foliage and water)
   Increase coherence, order, compatibility, and legibility
   Use familiar elements, historical elements, and popular styles

the latter approach, I scored the five Wexner Center entries relative to the research findings on preference, the most encompassing evaluative meaning. I judged each entry for order (coherence and compatibility), diversity, familiar (popular or historic styles), naturalness, open space, and livable space. Table 4.4 shows the results. The evaluation suggested that the public would most like the designs by Arthur Erickson and by Kallmann, McKinnell and Wood. The evaluation represents one person's subjective appraisal. If clients followed this approach, they could have more confidence in the results through having several impartial observes making the judgment.

Figure 4.3. A scene satisfying criteria for pleasantness. Photograph by Jack L. Nasar.

Figure 4.4. A scene satisfying criteria for relaxation. Photograph by Jack L. Nasar.

Table 4.4. *Preferred features scored for each of the five Wexner entries.*

| Preferred Feature | Designers | | | | |
| --- | --- | --- | --- | --- | --- |
| | Erickson | Kallmann | Graves | Pelli | Eisenman |
| Moderate facade diversity[a] | + | − | − | − | − |
| Order (coherence, compatibility)[a] | ++ | + | + | + | −− |
| Openness | + | + | − | − | − |
| Naturalness, unobtrusive building | + | +− | − | − | +− |
| Popular style | + | − | + | +− | − |
| Livable space | + | − | − | − | − |
| **LIKELY EVALUATION** | ++ | +− | − | −− | −− |

[a] I emphasized facade diversity and order because laypersons tend to notice it more than the massing and spatial configuration.[91]

### Conducting a Visual Quality Program

Because different building purposes, contexts and desired meanings may require special treatment, sponsors may want to use *visual quality programming (VQP)* to uncover guidelines for appearance and meaning. VQP entails several methodological choices. These involve trade-offs between the need to establish causal relationships, the need for the results to apply to the situation, and the practical concerns of costs, resources, and time. Researchers refer to the first as *internal validity*, the second as *external validity* and the third as *practicality*. For any project, one tries to balance the three for the goals of the project.

In designing a method, one faces at least four methodological choices, outlined here and shown in Table 4.5. (Readers interested in more detail should see texts on research methods and reviews on research on visual quality).[117 171 307] Different choices apply to different situations and purposes. Whether that involves exploring what is going on, demonstrating a hypothesis, refuting alternative hypotheses, or replicating a study, each purpose calls for a different research design. For application, the study conditions should approximate the real conditions, while minimizing loss of control. The right column of Table 4.5 shows one set of choices that can satisfy these goals. VQP should seek a sample of respondents representative of the individuals who will eventually experience the completed facility. A *random sample*, in which one selects at random from a list of people who might experience the building, can gain the desired representativeness. The VQP should also seek a high response rate from the people contacted, because nonresponses

Table 4.5. *Possible research choices for a visual quality program.*

| Method Question | Choice |
| --- | --- |
| Who to interview? | Random sample of those who might experience the building |
| How to interview? | Drop-and-leave questionnaire |
| How to present the environment? | Color photographs or slides of scenes |
| What kind of response to get? | Rank order judgments of scenes for preference, excitement, calmingness, activity, and status |

make inferences from the sample to the full population less certain. A *drop-and-retrieve questionnaire* can get a high response rate efficiently. An interviewer visits the households, leaves the survey with the respondent, and tells that person that they will return shortly for the completed survey. VQP should seek a realistic simulation of the designs (sidebar). Eye-level *color photographs* have proven an effective simulation. Research shows that responses to them accurately reflect responses to the real places.[263] Furthermore, research shows that scanned images, manipulated on a computer and printed as photographs or slides, produce products indistinguishable from color slides and photos of real environments.[290] For VQP, one can use such manipulated photographs effectively. Finally, VQP should seek realistic responses efficiently. Research shows that having people *rank order* scenes is an efficient way to get consistent responses that should generalize to other responses.

---

APPROACHES TO PRESENTATION OF SCENES

To establish visual quality guidelines, one might sample places for evaluation. Sampling scenes can vary in the degree of control over scene selection and environmental variables. A controlled approach might systematically manipulate a scene along variables of interest. A less controlled approach might select real scenes that vary on the variable of interest. A more naturalistic approach might select scenes at random. In moving toward random selection, the sample may gain in its representativeness of real places but lose control and the ability to establish cause. In moving toward controlled selection, the sample may gain control but lose representativeness and generalizability.

Do you have to trade off control for generality? No. Image processing technology can serve as a viable alternative. With it, you can sample a wide variety of real environments, scan them, and digitally alter them on a computer to control extraneous variables. The resulting scenes could have both the realism needed for generalizing the results and the experimental control needed to establish cause.[290]

In sum, to develop appearance guidelines, clients can follow one of two courses. They can refer to existing scientific findings, or they can develop situation specific guidelines through VQP. In addition to programming future designs, they can use the guidelines to evaluate existing designs. Beyond answering immediate questions about meanings, VQP can become part of a database for the future. This would allow sponsors and others to combine results from several studies to build a firmer knowledge base for guiding future decisions. For a competition, sponsors can present the VQP guidelines to entrants to use in developing their designs and to jurors to use in evaluating the entries. To ensure that the winning design captures the desired popular meanings, the client should use prejury evaluation.

# 5

## POPULAR EVALUATIONS OF THE WEXNER CENTER ENTRIES

Dade County . . . sent construction workers with heavy equipment to rip out . . . a large ugly wad of metal set in the concrete. . . . It turns out . . . it was Public Art . . . purchased by experts who are not spending their own money. . . . The money, of course, comes from taxpayers, who . . . would not buy the crashed-spaceship style of art that the experts select for them.[22]

Prejury evaluation (PJE) directly studies the popular meanings conveyed by a design or designs. It should take place before the jury deliberations so that the client and jury can use the findings in evaluating the entries. It can build on a visual quality program or it can stand alone. For Wexner, the jury had already made their decision. Along with my student Junmo Kang, I conducted the PJE to demonstrate and test the idea. To predict likely public evaluations of the completed building, we asked people for their reactions to the competition entries. We treated the jury's public report about their rationale for choosing the Eisenman design as if it represented the desired meanings for the Wexner Center. The report centered on various meanings the jury expected the public to see in the winning entry. It stated that the jury had selected the Eisenman design as the winner because, more than the others, it:

- Embodies the notions of participation and accessibility
- Serves as a magnet and focal point
- Is adventurous and challenging
- [Is] responsive to the campus setting
- Takes particular advantage of the site
- Enhances the pedestrian approach to the university
- Provokes speculation and almost relishes the idea of uncertainty
- [Is] dynamic
- [Is] accessible

- Extends the parkscape environment
- Acknowledg[es] the importance of the landscape (pp. 24–25)[51]

Each statement implies a meaning to the public, some more explicitly than others. For example, the statement that the design "serves as a magnet and focal point" implies that the public would experience the completed building as a magnet and focal point. They would feel attracted to it, gather there, and notice it. Eisenman also described his design as a magnet and center of activity, when he said, "students and visitors on their way to and from classes or the stadium will be drawn into the new Center for the Visual Arts en route. The Center will become a focus of interest and activity within the campus" (pp. 4).[194]

If the winning design embodies the jury-defined meanings, the public should evaluate it on those criteria more favorably than the other entries. We used the comments by the jury as the basis for evaluating the perceived meanings of the entries. We systematically examined public reactions to the designs in terms of the jury's speculations about public meanings. Carrying out the research after the announcement of the winner, but before the start of construction, we wondered if the public would agree or not with the jury's appraisal of the Eisenman design.

The sample included a cross-section of 65 local residents and students, faculty and alumni of The Ohio State University. Interviewers showed each person a set of photographs of the original drawings and models for each entry. The survey included the eleven items from the jury statement. To them, we added four items that represent the salient aspects of emotional appraisals of the environment – pleasant, exciting, calming, and active. Each respondent ranked each entry on each item. For example, for the item "embodies participation and accessibility," respondents placed the five entries in order for how well they achieved that objective. They could score entries as equal in rank. From the rankings, we assigned each entry a score from one to five, where one stood for the worst score and five stood for the best. (The next chapter and Appendix A give a more detailed description and evaluation of the method.)

Did the jury choose the design that fit their stated criteria? Would a cross section of the public (potential users) make the same choice? We compared the evaluations of the entries at several levels of detail. All of the comparisons confirmed unfavorable impressions of the winning entry and more favorable impressions of the designs by Erickson, and, to a lesser extent, Kallmann, McKinell and Wood. We first analyzed the degree to which individuals and groups had similar patterns of response. Finding strong consensus (See Appendix A, and Appendix C, Table C.7), we examined the combined scores of the full sample.

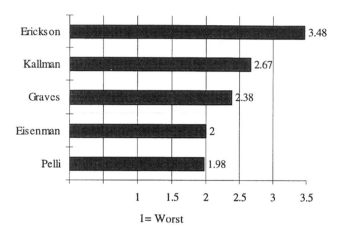

Figure 5.1. Composite public evaluations of the five Wexner entries on the eleven-item scale. *Note.* Kruskall Wallis $\chi^2$ (4, $N = 65$) = 4.448, $p < .01$).

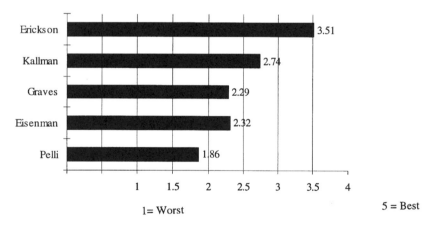

Figure 5.2. Composite public evaluations of the five entries on the fifteen-item scale. *Note.* Kruskall Wallis $\chi^2$ (4, $N = 65$) = 51.32, $p < .01$.

To evaluate the entries for the jury meanings alone, we tallied composite scores on the eleven jury items (Figure 5.1). The analysis showed that people ranked Erickson first, Kallmann second, Graves third, *Eisenman fourth,* and Pelli last. A similar pattern of differences emerged for the broader fifteen-item composite (Figure 5.2). The public ranked

Erickson first, Kallmann second, Graves and Eisenman tied for third, and Pelli last. The two sets of differences achieved statistical significance.

For a finer grained look at the meanings, one can consider responses to sets of related scales. A statistical procedure, called *principal component actor analysis*, finds sets of items related to one another (side bar). Such sets are called factors. Using this procedure, we found three sets of interrelated items. Through examining the items in each set, we label one set (or factor) *livability*, another *campuslike*, and the third *novelty*. One can then compare the scores for the entries on each factor (Figure 5.3). Our comparisons showed that the Erickson entry ranked first on all three factors. Kallmann ranked second on all three factors. Graves ranked third on two and fourth on one. *The winning entry ranked fourth* on two factors and third on one. Pelli ranked last on all three factors.

---

PRINCIPAL COMPONENT FACTOR
ANALYSIS RESULTS

We used principal component analysis to condense the data, and then compared scores on the resulting factors. A three-factor varimax solution (eigenvalues over 1.0) accounted for 56 percent of the variance. An elbow in the scree values at three dimensions indicated the three factor solution as adequate.

The statements with substantial loading on the first factor include: "embodies the notions of participation and accessibility," "is good use of site," "enhances pedestrian approach to university," "is accessible," "acknowledges the importance of landscape," "pleasant," and "relaxing." This factor seems to combine concern for pedestrian access and pleasantness. We labeled it *livability*. The statements with substantial loading on the second factor include, "serves as magnet and focal point," "responds to campus setting," "extends the parkscape environment," and "activity." This factor seems to combine concerns for both a landmark building and the park-like setting of the campus. We labeled it *campus-like*. The statements that load on the third factor include "is adventurous and challenging," "is dynamic" and "exciting." We labeled this factor as *novelty*. One statement, "provokes speculation and uncertainty," did not have a substantial loading on any of the factors.

---

For a more detailed look at meaning, one can also examine the scores of the entries on each scale separately. Our analysis showed that fourteen of the fifteen items produced significant differences among the entries (Appendix C, Table C.8). Focusing on those fourteen items,

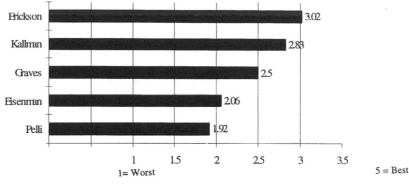

Livability (embodies participation and accessibility, from 1 = Worst to 5 = Best)

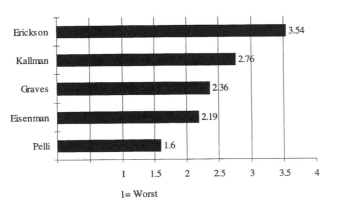

Campuslike (responds to campus setting, from 1 = Worst to 5 = Best)

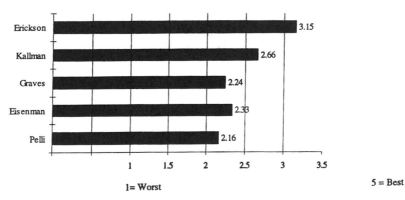

Novelty (is adventurous and challenging, from 1 = Worst to 5 = Best)

Figure 5.3. Mean rank scores on each factor. The scores are calculated for the scale with the highest loading on each factor.

94

we found that Erickson had the best scores, scoring best on every one. Kallmann ranked second, scoring second on eleven and third on three. Each other entry achieved only one second-place ranking as its highest ranking. Overall, Graves ranked third, *Eisenman fourth,* and Pelli fifth.

### Use of the Results

The analysis showed strong consensus across items and respondents. It converged on the relatively favorable meanings conveyed by the Erickson design, and the Kallmann design and the unfavorable meanings conveyed by the winning Eisenman design. For Wexner, the results raise questions about why the jury chose the Eisenman design in the first place. Could the jury have had some other reason for selecting it? I could not find a reasonable one. I wondered whether they had given weight to uniqueness, as they described the winning design as "adventurous and challenging," "dynamic," provoking "speculation and . . . uncertainty." For these meanings, the PJE gave higher scores to Erickson or Kallmann. I wondered whether they had integrated technical properties of the entries into their assessments. For Wexner, it seems unlikely, because the jury report did not refer to such criteria, and a subsequent evaluation of the technical performance (Chapter 7) reveals a seriously flawed design. I wondered whether the jury statement was a rationale for feelings that they could not express in words. If so, the winning entry should have scored well on the nonjury items that capture important dimensions of evaluative meaning. It did not. Finally, I wondered whether the jury made the written statement *por la galleria* – a justification for a political or personal decision. This perspective agrees with many architects opinions about juries. Surveys reveal that many architects feel that competition juries fail to pick the best design and that jurors are unconscientious and biased in their decisions.[31] [248] If so, the jury undermined the stated competition goal of the competition.

---

HANDLING DIFFERENCES

This study found consensus among respondents and consistent findings at the various levels of detail. If a PJE turns up differences across items or groups, the client has several options. One could simply present the information to the jury, but this leaves the interpretation as ambiguous. One could instruct the jury to give more weight to certain groups or items deemed more important. This still leaves the interpretation as vague. To deal more systematically with differences in groups and items, one should use multiple-objective, multiple-criteria decision-making procedures.[126] These procedures apply weights to the various groups and items to come up with a weighted score. The jury could receive this score for each entry.

---

The findings point to a conflict between the jury choice and the scientific study of popular choices. The public ranked the winning entry toward the bottom of the five entries. Similar results may apply to other competitions. The preferences of juries dominated by outsiders and by architects and artists may conflict with popular preferences. Recall that research confirms differences in evaluation between outsiders or visitors and insiders or users and residents.[37] Similar patterns of differences apply to architects (outsiders) and the public (insiders). Observers from within and outside the design professions have noted the disregard many architects hold for popular values and the negative consequences that result.[29] [76] Many studies confirm such differences between architects and others. Research shows that architects differ from others in what they notice in buildings, how the evaluate buildings, and what meanings they infer from them.[60] [90] [172] Architects' evaluation of the atypical differs from that of the public.[223] [224] [302] They value novelty, atypicality, excitement, and potency more and comfort less than does the public.[60] [101] [222] Architects view and evaluate styles differently from the public.[302] [172] They attend less to facade and more to massing and site organization than does the public.[91] Architects like best designs that the public likes least, and visa versa;[60] and they misjudge public preferences and aspirations.[90] [172] One recent movement in architecture called *postmodernism* sought solutions conveying favorable meanings to the public. Research suggests that designers misjudge those meanings. One study showing photos of modern and postmodern buildings to the public found that respondents did not differentiate between the two styles. Respondents disliked both of them.[90] Another study asked architects to guess public meanings conveyed by six different house styles. It found that the architects misjudged the public meanings.[172] Recall the evaluation of the Canadian Housing Design Council design awards program.[291] The design awards jury had the judgments opposite to those of the residents. A study of an *architectural-award-winning* Federal Building in Ann Arbor, Michigan, found that the occupants and public disagreed with professionals on the effectiveness and aesthetics of the building. The users rated its architectural quality as poor.[146] Thus, competition juries composed primarily of visitors and architects would likely miss popular values and aspirations. The studies of competitions over time

(Chapter 3) suggest that their judgments do not lead public or expert tastes in the future. In contrast, research shows high correlations between initial public preferences and subsequent public responses to completed buildings.[264] [265]

Given the potential conflict between the judgments of outside professionals and those of the public and building users, we should heed the conclusion from the Ann Arbor study. "If in the future, informed judgments about the quality of architecture are to be made, the sentiment of . . . user groups needs to be considered" (pp. 665, 667).[146] VQP and PJE offer a way to do that. Had the Wexner jury had an explicit set of visual quality guidelines and had the PJE occurred prior to their deliberations, the results could have guided their deliberations. Although the jury might not choose the public's first choice, they should weigh the information against other information. Their final report should explain their rationale.

Before applying PJEs, one should have more information on their relative accuracy. How well do the popular and jury evaluations of the entries apply to the completed building? The next chapter looks at this question. It reports a series of postoccupancy evaluations of the meanings conveyed by the completed Wexner design.

# 6

# POPULAR EVALUATIONS OF
# THE COMPLETED BUILDING

I've heard that (people) hate the building . . . and if they don't like it, it is for very good reasons. It is because in that building is an aesthetic of "not like" in a certain way. – Peter Eisenman (pp. 289–90)[83]

Because the PJE took place before construction, it forecasts likely responses to the building. To gauge its accuracy or the accuracy of the jury choice, we need to examine responses to the completed building. This chapter looks at the meanings conveyed by the completed building. It also serves as an example of an appearance POE.

I examined meanings in three ways: a mail survey, on-site interviews, and comparisons to other campus buildings. Although each approach may have biases, the use of multiple methods offsets the potential biases (sidebar). Convergent findings across the methods increase confidence that the findings did not result from biases, but instead accurately reflect public feelings about the design.[41]

---

## BIASES IN DIFFERENT SURVEYS

In a mail survey, those who agree to participate may differ from the nonparticipants. The mail survey may draw a higher level of response from people with strong feelings, negative or positive, about the design, and this could skew the results. Because I do not know what distinguished nonparticipants from participants, I cannot determine whether or in what way the mail survey skewed results. The mail survey may have another potential bias. Responses depend on respondent's recall of the building. Potential distortions in memory might make such responses different from direct responses to the actual building. Although the survey respondents reported familiarity with the building, this does not guarantee the accuracy of their recall.

The on-site survey eliminated these bias. It obtained participation before respondents knew the specific survey topic; it obtained a high rate of participation; and it obtained on-site responses to the building. The on-site survey may have opened up a different bias. Because it interviewed people on the site, the results may not represent responses of people elsewhere. The mail survey did not have this bias because it tapped a broader sample of the campus community.

Both approaches gauge responses to the Wexner Center only. Without comparative data for other buildings, the meaning of the scores remains uncertain. A neutral rating could imply a relatively unfavorable evaluation, if other buildings receive higher scores; or it could imply a relatively favorable evaluation if other buildings receive lower scores. To clarify the meaning of the Wexner scores, I also obtained on-site responses to other campus buildings.

---

### Mail Survey

A diverse sample of ninety-two members of the OSU faculty and staff responded to a mail survey, which asked for their reactions to the design and for their background and demographic data (sidebar). Most respondents reported that they had experienced the building regularly.

---

MAIL SURVEY SAMPLE

I sent the survey to 500 individuals selected at random from the university directory of faculty and staff. The written instructions assured them of anonymity and confidentiality and the instructions asked them to return the survey at no cost through campus mail. Only 18.4 percent responded. The sample had respondents from fifty-one departments from anatomy to zoology, including five each from chemistry, English, journalism, and math, and one or two participants from each of the others (Appendix C, Table C.9). Ten people described themselves as designers. Most of the sample consisted of faculty and staff between 25 and 54 years old. It had more males than females (reflecting the make up of the directory), and it had individuals with varied amounts of experience with the campus and the Wexner Center. Most respondents reported passing by the Center at least once a week and entering once or more.

THE SURVEY

The questionnaire requested background and demographic data, and had respondents rate the design. It asked them to report their age, gender, position, years on campus, department or major, how often they walked by the Wexner Center, and how often they walked inside. It gauged their reactions to the design with one open-ended question about what they thought of the design. It also had eleven seven-point items. Six reflect the jury's statements about the merits of the design, and four reflect the important dimensions of emotional meaning. To boost response rate, I shortened the survey by dropping five items with lower factor loadings in the PJE. I added a question about "goodness-of-example" to get at the possible process underlying preferences. The item measures the amount of discrepancy from each person's knowledge structure.[77] Recall that research suggests a relation between the amount of discrepancy and preference.[224] Using the item, I could see whether the relationship applied to the Wexner entries. The instrument had the poles and orders of items assigned at random to lessen potential biases from order effects and response set.

---

How did they feel about the completed building? Confirming the findings from the PJE, the mail survey revealed unfavorable evaluations (Appendix C, Table C.10). Respondents judged the completed building as fairly atypical and they rated it unfavorably for *livability* and *suitability to the campus*.

As with the PJE, I condensed the mail survey data into related sets of items. The analysis yielded two groupings that accounted for most of the variance: *aesthetic value* and *atypicality* (sidebar). I then looked at the building score on each factor. The completed building had a low score on *aesthetic value* and a moderately high score on *atypicality*.

---

MAIL SURVEY FACTORS

The two-factor solution from the principal component factor analysis accounted for 70.4 percent of the variance. Each factor had eigen values over 1.0. The elbow in the scree values at two dimensions indicated little improvement from adding additional factors. Several items fit (or had substantial loadings on) the first factor. They included: good use of site, pleasantness, responds to campus setting, adventurous and challenging, embodies participation and accessibility, active, calming, dynamic, exciting, serves as a magnet and focal point, and calming. These items came from all three PJE factors. This factor might represent *aesthetic value*, a combination of pleasure, excitement and calmness. The second factor had two items: atypicality and calmness (negatively). It may reflect *atypicality* (discrepancy from a schema) or novelty.

Individual items showed high variances: 2.26 for calming, 3.52 for participation/accessibility, 3.53 for active, 3.83 for dynamic,

3.83 for pleasant, 4.49 for magnet/focal point, 4.55 for responds to campus setting, 4.86 for exciting, and 5.10 for adventurous/challenging, 5.58 for good use of site.

---

At first glance, this suggests an atypical design neutral in pleasantness, but high variances in responses for each item pointed to possible disagreements within the sample. Counts of responses to the open-ended question about what respondents thought of the design confirmed a split. Of the 85 persons expressing clear opinions, most gave negative appraisals. They described it in such terms as "awful," "an eyesore," "highly nauseating," "worst art gallery I've ever seen," "stinks," "doesn't fit campus," "a waste of $44 million," "I hate it." Fewer people described it favorably. They described it in such terms as "I like it," "great," "'inspired," "excellent," and "nice." Although I did not test for it, the favorable publicity surrounding the competition and the building may have swayed some people.

A subsequent test revealed that the differences reflect differences between designers and nondesigners in the sample. The nondesigners gave lower scores than did the designers (Appendix C, Table C.11). Compared to the designers, the nondesigners gave the design lower scores for good use of the site, pleasant, responsive to the campus setting, active, and magnet or focal point. Each of these differences achieved statistical significance. The nondesigners also judged the design lower on five other scales (dynamic, calming, adventurous or challenging, exciting, and embodying participation), though the differences did not achieve statistical significance. The groups did not differ in their judgments of the typicality of the building. Both groups judged it as atypical.

I examined the consistency of response. The comparison between other groups in the sample revealed some minor differences in response, but agreement on the neutral to negative appraisals of the building (sidebar). I compared responses by position, years on campus, age, and gender. The results showed some minor differences in response between the faculty, graduate students, and staff and between other sociodemographic groups that likely relate to educational differences. Still, most group means revealed unfavorable evaluation of the building (Appendix C, Table C.12).

---

GROUP COMPARISONS

For *livability* and *campus-like*, faculty reported the most favorable responses; students gave less favorable responses; and staff gave the least favorable responses. For judgments of *adventurousness and challenging*, faculty gave the most favorable responses, followed by staff and then students. Only one score, the faculty rating of *adventurousness and challenging*, indicates a favorable evaluation. The rest are neutral to negative ratings. Males gave higher ratings than did females for *adventurous and challenging* and *responsive to the campus setting*. As the faculty had a higher percentage of males and the staff had a higher percentage of female, this sex difference may reflect an artifact of the education differences between these two groups. Comparisons by age revealed a significant difference on *responsiveness to the campus setting*: the youngest group (under 30) and the 40–49 group responded least favorably, the oldest group (over 49) responding most favorably, and the 30–39 group responded in between. These age differences probably reflect an artifact of difference between faculty, staff, and students. The youngest group had a relatively small proportion of faculty and a high proportion of staff and students; the 40–49 group had the highest proportion of staff; and the oldest group had the highest proportion of faculty.

In sum, the mail survey on the completed building confirmed the PJE predictions of negative evaluations. Although groups differed somewhat in their ratings of the building, they shared neutral to negative evaluations of it. Because people tend to respond toward the positive end of scales, the scores suggest an unfavorable evaluation. The findings also contradict the jury speculations about the success of the design.

### On-Site Survey

The on-site evaluation used the same form and questions as the mail survey. Between September and November 1990, interviewers contacted ninety individuals nearby the Wexner Center and had them fill out a survey about their reactions to the building. Sampling took place during the morning, afternoon, late afternoon, and night. At several locations around the Wexner Center site, the interviewers took a position and stopped the first passerby (or sitter), asking them to participate. People did not know that the study dealt with the Wexner Center until they had agreed to participate. Interviewers handed them the instructions and interview to complete, assured them of confidentiality and anonymity, and asked them to complete the survey and return it. The interviewer proceeded to the next passerby of the opposite gender and asked for participation. Respondents completed the form themselves and returned it on-site. After obtaining five interviews, the interviewer moved to a different location and repeated the procedure.

I again condensed the data into sets of related items. The results replicated the factors of the mail survey (sidebar): *aesthetic value* and *atypicality*. The mail survey and on-site surveys had similar scores. The on-site survey showed neutral ratings except for judgments of atypicality, which were slightly higher. On-site respondents did report slightly higher scores than did mail respondents on four of the eleven scales – embodying participation and accessibility, pleasantness, dynamic, and calming (Appendix C, Table C.13) – but the scores remained in the neutral range.

---

FACTOR ANALYSIS FOR ON-SITE RESPONSE

The principal component factor analysis pointed to a two factor solution. Eigen values exceeded 1.0 and the solution accounted for 59 percent of the variance. An elbow in the scree values at two factors indicated little gain from additional factors. Items with substantial loading on the first factor include pleasant, good use of site, embodies participation and accessibility, adventurous and challenging, dynamic, serves as a magnet and focal point, exciting, active, responds to campus setting. I labeled this mix of pleasure and excitement *aesthetic value*. Items with substantial loading on the second factor include atypicality and calming (negatively). I labeled this mix of atypicality and distressingness *atypicality*.

---

For the on-site sample, comparisons across sociodemographic groups produced no significant differences by gender, age, years on campus, or position (graduate versus undergraduate student) on the index items. The on-site sample differed from the mail group on several sociodemographic and experiential dimensions (sidebar). Compared to the mail group, it had more students and fewer members of the faculty and staff; they were younger; they had spent fewer years on campus; and they reported passing by Wexner more often. Each of these differences achieved statistical significance. With the position and age differences in mind, I ran a matched comparison between students in each group. In this comparison, all but one of the differences in response disappeared. The on-site respondents gave significantly more favorable responses to one item – responsiveness to campus. Still, the on-site score for this item remained in the neutral to negative range.

STATISTICAL COMPARISONS

When compared to the mail sample for type of respondent (student, faculty, or staff), the on-site sample differed at a statistically significant level ($\chi^2$ = 140.00, 2 df, $p$<.001). It also differed at a statistically significant level for age ($F$ = 210.17, 1 df, $p$ <.01), years on campus ($F$ = 61.65, 1 df, $p$ <.01), and frequency passing by Wexner Center ($F$ = 4.49, 1 df, $p$ <.05). The on-site score for *responsiveness to campus setting* emerged as significantly different from the mail survey response ($F$ = 4.07, 1 df, $p$ <.05), though still in the neutral range ($\bar{x}$ = 3.87).

The results suggest that the PJE findings did generalize to the completed building. The completed building received neutral to negative evaluations that remained stable for the on-site survey and mail survey. Favorable biases in the use of rating scales suggest a more negative evaluation. The convergent findings also suggest an absence of serious bias resulting from the two kinds of methods. To get a better understanding of the meaning of the scores, I compared the on-site responses to Wexner to on-site responses to four other campus buildings.

### Comparisons to Other Campus Buildings

As did the Wexner on-site interviews, interviews for reactions to other buildings took place in Autumn 1990. Rotating from site to site, interviewers used the same procedures as those at Wexner to obtain fifteen interviews per site. The on-site survey for the other buildings used the same form and items as did the Wexner interviews, but the questions referred to the building in view.

I selected buildings to represent a variety of buildings on campus. The sample includes three new buildings, one adaptive reuse, and one older building. One new building, the Celeste Chemistry Laboratory, looks simple and modern (Figure 6.1). Another, the James Cancer Center, looks more varied with some historical references (Figure 6.2). A third, Enarson Hall, represents a renovation and adaptive reuse of an older building (Figure 6.3). The fourth, the Main Library, is an old campus landmark, located on the axis of the main open space on campus (Figure 6.4). The buildings also vary in height, from two to eleven stories. Recall that the review of the scientific findings (Chapter 4) indicated lower evaluations associated with higher buildings and buildings with signs of decay. I intentionally chose two high-rise buildings and one older building with signs of decay to make for a more conservative com-

Figures 6.1. Celeste Chemistry Laboratory. Photograph by
Jack L. Nasar.

parison to Wexner. Compared to taller and older buildings, the low rise
and newer qualities of Wexner should elicit more favorable evaluations.
If Wexner fails to score better than these buildings, it becomes clearer
that its scores represent negative evaluations.

Respondents at the other sites and the respondents to Wexner
reported similar ages and frequency of walking by the building rated.
The Wexner respondents differed from the others in reporting entering the building less and having spent fewer years on campus
(Appendix C, Table C.14).

Figures 6.2. James Cancer Center. Photograph by Jack L. Nasar.

How did the responses to Wexner and the other buildings compare? The comparison of the Wexner on-site scores to the *combined* on-site scores for the other buildings confirmed judgments of Wexner as unpleasant and atypical. Wexner received lower scores on pleasantness, responsiveness to the campus setting, good use of site, and calmingness. It scored as less typical, and more dynamic, exciting, and adventurous or challenging than the others. It did not differ from the other buildings in creating a magnet and focal point, or embodying participation and accessibility (Appendix C, Table C.15).

Figures 6.3. Enarson Hall. Photograph by Jack L. Nasar.

How did Wexner compare to each of the other buildings separately? It scored poorly in these tests (Appendix C, Table C.16). The buildings had significantly different scores on each factor from the PJE. For *campus-like*, Wexner had the lowest score of all of the buildings, scoring significantly lower than three of the four buildings. For *livability*, it had the third lowest score; though this achieved significance (marginal level) for one building. For *novelty*, Wexner scored higher than all four buildings, though this achieved statistical significance for two comparisons – the Celeste chemistry Laboratory and the Library. The buildings also differed significantly on the on-site indices. Wexner had the lowest score for *aesthetic appreciation* and the highest score for *atypicality*. These differences achieved statistical significance for one building on aesthetic appreciation and three buildings on atypicality.

### Ad Hoc Comparisons to Two Other Buildings

I ran two additional comparisons to Wexner. As part of comprehensive POEs on two new buildings at OSU, I obtained evaluations of their appearance. In 1995, students and I evaluated a Math Tower designed by Philip Johnson (Figure 6.5).[176] We interviewed thirty passerbys for their impressions of its appearance. In 1996, students and I evaluated

Figures 6.4. Main Library. Photograph by Jack L. Nasar.

the Newman and Wolfrom Chemistry Laboratory (Figure 6.6).[175] We asked eighty-six passerbys for their impressions of its appearance. In each case, some scales repeated or approximated those used on Wexner. Although I did these evaluations to develop appearance guidelines for the two buildings and for future campus buildings, the results have bearing on the Wexner findings. Keep in mind that these POEs took place several years after the Wexner studies and did not use the same forms or scales. As a result, the comparisons to Wexner lack the control of the earlier studies. Still, the results agree with the earlier

Figure 6.5. Math Tower. Photograph by Jack L. Nasar.

comparisons. The scores revealed that respondents rated the Math
Tower and the Chemistry Laboratory as significantly more pleasant and
as a significantly better fit to the campus than Wexner (Appendix C,
Table C.17).

Figure 6.6. Newman and Wolfrom Chemistry Laboratory Addition. Photograph by Jack L. Nasar.

### Summing It Up

Taking place over a six-year period, the studies of the completed building confirm the validity of the PJE and suggest possible drawbacks in decisions by a jury dominated by outsiders, architects and artists. For Wexner, the jury's stated opinion about the design meanings did not stand. The mail survey, the on-site responses, and the comparisons to other buildings indicate that the public view the Wexner Center design unfavorably and that they did so on the criteria cited by the jury as their reasons for picking the Eisenman design. On the jury's criteria, the public rated the completed building as having neutral to negative meanings. On the same criteria, they evaluated other campus buildings more favorably. Public evaluations of the entries contradicted the jury conjectures and served as a better guide to subsequent building meanings. The public response to the entries accurately predicted subsequent popular meanings of the completed building. People consistently responded more favorably to other buildings on campus.

The results point to a process underlying the differences in meaning for the jury and the public. The public, designers and jury agreed on the design as *atypical*. They had a shared image of a good example of an arts center and they judged the Eisenman design as discrepant from it. The jury and public differed in their response to the discrepancy. In agreement with earlier findings, the public did not like a large discrepancy from their image of the typical while the jury favored such a discrepancy.[222][224][300] Yet, the jury did not choose the Kallmann, McKinnell, and Wood design judged as more discrepant in the PJE. If designers favor a higher level of discrepancy, knowledge of this difference may help them as jurors to select solutions more fitting to the public.

Architecture involves more than meanings and appearance. A successful building should also work technically and functionally for the inhabitants. A more complete analysis goes beyond meaning to examine comprehensively the workings of a completed project. Because competition juries tend to stress the architectural statement over durability and function, it seems likely that the resulting buildings will have technical and functional flaws. To determine whether this is true, I conducted a systematic postoccupancy evaluation, reported in the next chapter.

# 7

## WORKING IN A WORK OF ART:
## A POSTOCCUPANCY
## EVALUATION OF THE
## WEXNER CENTER

For all the publicity the building brings, its design also poses serious problems in its use. – 1991 Annual Report Wexner Center for the Arts [200]

When critics praised the Wexner Center before its opening and occupancy, and months before it hosted an exhibition, they lacked a basis for judging its technical and functional merits. Yet, they concluded that it worked well. Paul Goldberger of *The New York Times* wrote: "How does the building work? Surprisingly well" (p. 38).[82] In *Newsweek* the critic Cathleen McGuigan wrote, "Does the Wexner Center work? In its handsome theaters, yes" (p. 75).[149] Kurt Anderson of *Time* simply said, "and it works" (p. 84).[7] Such evaluations often miss the true functioning of a facility. Recall the example of critically praised projects like Boston City Hall, Brasilia, Tilted Arc, and the Florida A & M Architecture School that did not work (Chapter 2). What happens after the critics leave town?

Here's what the critics wrote about Wexner several years after it opened. Michael Kimmelman, the art critic for *The New York Times,* wrote that it "may be a tour de force of architectural theory . . . but it is also a spectacular failure as a place to see paintings and sculptures" (p. C15).[127] He cited poor lighting, inadequate enclosure, distractions (such as air vents), the ramp (occupying nearly a quarter of the building), inadequate space for viewers to step back to view the art, and works lost in rooms or hidden by columns. In the *Chicago Tribune,* Blair Kamin called the design a "functional flop," noting that carpenters had to "regularly construct extra walls and ceiling when art exhibitions open" (p. 4);[118] and Roger Lewis, architectural critic for *The Washington Post*, referred to widespread criticism of the building, "some aesthetic, some practical" (p. 37).[136] These appraisals may also have flaws, as they do not reflect comprehensive and systematic evaluations.

### The Wexner Center POE

To understand how well the Wexner Center worked, I conducted a postoccupancy evaluation (POE). This kind of evaluation differs from the informal feelings of designers or critics who look at pictures of a building or walk through and note *their* likes and dislikes. It evaluates "buildings in a systematic and rigorous manner" after construction and occupancy (p. 3).[218] The Wexner Center POE took place in the spring of 1991, two years after the completion and occupancy of the Center. The two-year period gave users time to move in and adjust to the new facility. I examined the full facility and its parts, including the gallery spaces, a performance theater, administrative offices, two libraries, a café, and a book shop. My graduate students and I interviewed 333 administrators, faculty, students, staff, and visitors for their opinions about the facility: 95 visitors responded to questions about their likes and dislikes on the exterior and interior, 217 people responded to questions about fear of crime in relation to the site, and 21 staff members (at least one for each setting in the facility) evaluated the facility and their own work space. We used structured interviews and open-ended interviews, asking individuals to describe what they like and dislike about the design. We also observed patterns of use in each place in the facility and on the site; and we examined university records pertaining to the Center. I also interviewed professionals from OSU's Office of the University Architect and Physical Facilities (which I refer to as University Architect or Physical Facilities in the followed text). Interestingly, early in the course of our interviews, two architectural faculty tongue-lashed an interviewer for daring to ask people for their opinions about the building.

The concept of an arts center and the art programs at the Wexner Center surely make a contribution to OSU, Columbus, and Ohio socially and symbolically. By putting so much money and emphasis on a building for the arts, the university may have changed its image as a football school. As the physical manifestation of the concept, the building is a flop. It does not work well for the everyday users. Two sentences in a Wexner Center annual report to the university president sum up the results:

> "The Wexner Center for the Arts . . . is expensive to operate and it was designed that way (p. 15).[200]

> "For all the publicity the building brings, its design also poses serious problem in its use" (p. 16).[200]

Staff at the University Architect's office told me of "more than the normal amount of startup problems with this building due to the building's complexity."

The following sections present key findings from the postoccupancy evaluation. Some findings had numbers and statistics associated with them. They emerged from analyses of fixed questions on questionnaires. In describing the results, I replace the numbers with their equivalent word meaning. (The ratings ranged from 4 = excellent to 1 = poor. I refer to scores of 3.5–4.0 as "excellent," scores of 2.5–3.49 as "good," scores of 1.50–2.49 as "fair," and lower scores as "poor"). Other findings simply report items, such as a roof leak or a dysfunctional loading dock, without numbers. They may reflect open-ended responses of the one or two users, familiar with the item. For example, a security officer and a café worker reported that the security officer has to lead the café worker several times a day through a maze of locked security doors to the loading dock for deliveries and trash disposal. These reports serve as adequate evidence. In each case, the problem interferes with a specific user's ability to perform necessary tasks. Others would neither know about nor experience the problem.

### Costs

One part of the POE involves costs. I looked at the construction cost and the operating cost. The latter includes costs for maintenance and for energy.

### Construction Costs

The cost of the building almost tripled from the time of the competition to the building completion, escalating from $16 million to $43 million. Though some of the increase resulted from changes in the program, University Architect staff told me that most of it came from the complexity of the design: The design specified nonstandard furnishings and furniture requiring special fabrication and assembly. It also has few, if any, square shapes. To meet the cost, the benefactor raised his contribution from $10 million to $25 million and Ohio raised its construction bonds from $6 million to $18 million.

How does the cost compare to the cost of other buildings? According to Roger Lewis, the architectural critic for the *Washington Post,* at $400 per square foot, the cost for Wexner "may be a record, or at least a near one, for a university building or an art center anywhere in the U.S." (p. 34)[136] Consider the cost for the competition-winning design for the Florida A & M Architecture school, which opened four years before Wexner – $82 per square foot. Construction costs vary across regions due to variation in costs for labor and material, and they vary across buildings types. More meaningful comparisons come from a look at costs of local buildings similar to Wexner. In telephone interviews, I obtained cost figures on university buildings from the University Architect's office. For 1996, campus buildings at OSU cost an average of between $125 and $175 per square foot. University offices stand at the low end of the range. Adjusting the Wexner cost to 1996 dollars (even at a 2 percent inflation rate) would bring its costs to $455 per square foot, approximately two to four times more per square foot than other campus buildings. Because some of the cost may relate to special security systems, air-handling controls for artwork, and wiring for sound and video, I asked about the cost of research laboratories. These facilities also require special equipment, wiring, and air-handling equipment. At OSU, they cost approximately $200 per square foot, less than half the square foot cost for Wexner.

Perhaps a signature architect's building or an arts facility might incur higher costs. The costs appear high in these comparisons as well. The University Architect reported two other recent signature architect buildings at OSU – a law library addition by Gunnar Birkerts and a Math Tower and Science Library by Phillip Johnson. Each one cost less than half the cost per square foot of Wexner. OSU did not have any other new gallery spaces, but I found two universities that had recently used signature architects to design museum space. Pennsylvania State had Charles Moore design its Palmer museum, and the University of Minnesota had Frank Gehry design its Weisman Center. The Pennsylvania State University architect Charles E. Brueggebors told me in a telephone interview that Palmer, completed in 1993, cost $174 per square foot. (For 32,277 square feet – 25,500 square feet new and 6,777 square feet renovated – the museum cost $5.6 million). Wayne Sisel from the office of the university architect at University of Minnesota told me in a telephone interview that Weisman, also completed in 1993, cost approximately $220 per square foot. (The project cost $13,475,000 for 93,833 square feet, but parking occupied 43,400 square feet. $10,866,000 of the project cost went to the 50,433-square-foot museum space). Wexner cost approximately twice as much per square foot than did these signature architect galleries.

### Maintenance Costs

Wexner's customized design also escalated maintenance costs. According to representatives of physical facilities, the design has many features that preclude the use of standard campus equipment maintenance procedures. Maintenance required more costly hand labor. Because campus maintenance vehicles cannot fit in the walkways between the raised planters, snow and leaf removal requires manual labor. Deep window wells also require specialized manual labor for leaf and snow removal. The designer used caulking to seal much of the building. Though this may have cut the construction cost, it left the university with a long-term maintenance problem. Representatives of the University Architect told me that they may have to recaulk the seals every five years.

Jill Morelli (associate vice-president, University Architect) told me that six years after the opening, the university spent $800,000 to redo the roof to fix the leaks. Although on average a roof on campus lasts thirty years (and possibly sixty years if made of copper) the Wexner roof needed a replacement in less than eight years. According to Physical Facilities, it failed to have proper detailing on flashings for the hundred or so independent sections of the roof. The $800,000 will fix most of the leaks, but Physical Facilities expects leaks in the future. The university will incur additional costs to fix the excessive lighting in the gallery areas. Correcting the problem may require total removal of the overhead glass ceiling and possibly the glass wall as well. Morelli told me that although the actual cost to correct this problem will depend on a consultant's report, she expects it to cost an additional $5 to $10 million.

In addition, the regular day-to-day maintenance costs exceed those of other buildings. In a telephone interview, Al Matthews of Physical Facilities estimated the university maintenance costs for all of its buildings. The estimate covers more than a 11 million square feet of classroom and laboratory space in more than a hundred buildings. The buildings average forty-three years old, and have a variety of designs, materials, and construction. The estimate includes a variety of items, including custodial, routine maintenance, grounds upkeep, trash removal, snow removal, water, and sewer. Matthews said that for 1994–95 the average cost for maintaining building space at OSU came to $2.96 per square foot. For the same year, the maintenance cost for Wexner was approximately $4.00 per square foot. (In phone discussions with Matthews and Gretchen Metzelaars, director of Administration at Wexner, I learned that maintenance of Wexner cost $433,583, with $249,583 university costs and $184,000 internal cost for the exhibition spaces). The maintenance for Wexner costs about 35 percent more per square foot than maintenance for other OSU buildings.

Comparing maintenance costs between buildings can be difficult. Even if standardized to a cost-per-square-foot basis, various kinds of designs and building purposes require different amounts of maintenance. However, the high day-to-day costs paired with the millions spent to correct design problems suggest higher-than-usual maintenance costs associated with the design.

*Energy Costs*

As with maintenance costs, it is difficult to compare energy costs meaningfully among different buildings. Comparisons should look at costs per cubic foot, because the cost relates to the volume of space heated and cooled. Unfortunately, I could only get figures on a square foot basis. For the 1994–95 year, the Wexner electric and steam utilities cost approximately $1.24 per square foot ($135,000). Matthews reported that the average utility cost of the 11 million square feet of academic and research buildings on campus was $0.905 per square foot. At $1.24 per square foot, Wexner's heating and cooling costs were 37 percent more than the university average. Tom Heretta (a university architect) told me over the phone that energy modeling had forecast high energy costs because of glass roofing and walls around exhibition spaces. The glass allows sunlight to heat the interior in the summer, and it allows heat to escape in the winter. Thus, the design requires more air conditioning in the summer and more heating in the winter. Although the University Architect had informed Eisenman of the potential problem during the design phase, he refused to change his design.

*Costs Summary*

In sum, Wexner has relatively high construction, maintenance, and energy costs. The higher operating costs and the amortization of the higher construction cost place a costly burden on the university, the state, and the taxpayers. This occurred at a time when OSU, like many state universities, was receiving serious cuts in state funding, requiring OSU to restructure, close programs, and raise tuition. Perhaps, other aspects of the facility make the higher costs worthwhile. Let us look at its day-to-day operations.

### Entering the Facility

*Campus Entry*

Before the new building, the Wexner Center site served as a symbol of the entrance to the campus. It connected the city to the heart of the campus, a large oval green space (The Oval) terminated by the library. As the program noted, the area (West 15th Avenue) serves as:

> The traditional entrance to the campus, provides a principal view from off-campus toward and through the Oval. . . . The West 15th Avenue axis is an area of intense pedestrian activity, a primary connection between the campus and off-campus student residential areas . . . and commercial uses (p. 3).[192]

Recall that one juror expressed concern that the "long walk" from the street through the Oval to the library continue as a straight path. The design blocks the entrance and the "long walk." Morelli reported complaints about the loss of the ceremonial entrance to the campus.

### Fear, Crime, and Security

The site arrangements evoke fear and crime. Several areas on the Wexner site appeared to have features – concealment, blocked prospect, and entrapment – that could support a potential attacker.[14] [269] By preventing a person from detecting a potential attack in time to avoid it or get help from others, the features might heighten feelings of vulnerability.

To see whether the features did evoke fear and crime, my colleague Bonnie Fisher, and I conducted several studies.[68] [179] In one, we had twenty people rate each of eight areas on the Wexner site for the feared features. The results confirmed the prediction about the presence of the features. The respondents consistently rated several areas on the Wexner Center site as high in concealment, low in prospect, and high in potential entrapment. Their open-ended descriptions of the areas included comments such as, "too many places for people to hide and surprise you," "big planters where people can jump out or drag you back there," "closed off areas," and "can't see very far."

We then measured fear for the areas around the site. We had 166 people rate their feeling of safety during the day and night for each of the eight areas shown on a map and for the full site. We had 27 females walk the site after dark and rate their direct experience of fear in relation to the areas. We tracked pedestrian behavior on the site on 87 occasions, observing more than 380 pedestrians. We interviewed staff, and we asked fourteen of the fifteen police officers who patrol Wexner to evaluate the site for ease of surveillance. We also looked at crime statistics for the site. The results of each study converged on higher levels of fear and crime for the areas with fear features (Figure 7.1). Pedestrians reported higher levels of fear, and they avoided walking in or near the areas especially after dark, when fears increase. Administrative staff complained about inadequate lighting around the buildings, the walkways, the raised planters and all entrances. They also indicated the need for more signs for security and safety. The police reported difficulties in surveillance for the same areas. The crime reports showed a higher incident of crime – in particular, vandalism – in the areas with the features evoking fear.

As a check, we asked 92 people about their feelings of fear for neighboring buildings. The results showed more fear related to physical fea-

Figure 7.1. Wexner Center spots that evoke fear and attract vandalism. Photograph by Jack L. Nasar.

Figures 7.2. The main entrances look like service entrances.
Photographs by Jack L. Nasar.

tures for the Wexner Center than for its neighbors. (One neighboring
building also evoked high fear levels, but those fear related to social factors: student parties that led to some fights.)

Many Americans and college students experience fear of crime as a
major problem.[75] [87] [188] Fear intensifies after dark and among certain
vulnerable groups, such as young females on campus.[34] [255] [294] It may
have damaging effects on health, welfare and safety, heightening stress,
limiting activities, making people feel like prisoners in their neighborhoods, disrupting community and increasing crime.[232] [234] [276] The
design of the Wexner Center heightened fears. Rather than serving as
an attractive entry onto campus, the Wexner Center site increases fear,
vandalism, and avoidance.

*Finding the Entrance*

Users, both able and disabled, reported difficulty in finding their way to
the facility from the parking ramps. Although this might not typically
represent a problem with the building design, in this case it does,
because the competition designers chose the site for the building. Once
near the entrances, visitors also report difficulty in finding their way
into the facility. The main entrances look like service entries – plain,
small, hard to find, and difficult to access (Figures 7.2). I observed visi-

Figure 7.3. Concealed library entrance (past signs and on the right). Photograph by Jack L. Nasar.

tors circling around the entrance area several times, trying to find the entrance.

Visitors also report difficulty finding the entrances to the Wexner libraries and rehearsal rooms connected to Wexner. The problems probably result from the small size and hidden location of the entries (Figures 7.3). When the facility opened, it had no signs leading to or at the entrances. University staff reported a need to add signs, but the designer did not want signs to deface his design. Eventually the university, trying to minimize the impact of signs, added some small signs and an entrance banner. The librarians say that users continue to have difficulty finding the entrance. They resorted to posting paper signs to help people find their way (Figure 7.4).

The front entrance has an additional access problem for wheelchair users. The front door, not intended for the disabled, has no sign offering directions to the wheelchair accessible entrance, hidden around a corner. At least one wheelchair user, assuming no other entrance, wheeled in the front entrance when it was open. When the door closed, the wheelchair user found himself stuck, with closed doors in front of and behind him. Neither door has an automated opener. Wexner staff at the reception desk reported having to help him into the Center.

Figure 7.4. One of several paper signs directing visitors to the libraries. Photograph by Jack L. Nasar.

### North Door and Fire Exit

A fire exit door at the north end of the gallery space looks like a natural exit from the building. Visitors regularly try to use it, setting off an alarm. After the galleries close, this fire door becomes an operating exit from the Performance Space.

### Loading Dock Conflicts

Wexner staff had to permanently close the one loading dock designed for the exhibition space, because it proved unusable. When I interviewed Stearns, the first director of Wexner, he reported that opening the loading dock door threw off the galleries' heating, ventilation, and air-conditioning system, which in turn could damage the exhibits. As a result, the Center must rely on the loading dock of a neighboring building – Mershon Auditorium. That dock connects to the Wexner Center facilities in a circuitous fashion, and it must simultaneously serve several unintended and conflicting uses: the gallery spaces, performance theater, bookstore, café deliveries and trash removal, and the auditorium.

Reliance on the Mershon loading dock creates several problems. First, it is remote from the Wexner spaces, more than a hundred yards walk from the exhibition spaces, performance theater, café, bookstore, and two libraries. Second, the route to and from it moves through secured spaces. Security staff reported that this requires them to escort staff and others through numerous locked security doors to get there and back. This can be particularly cumbersome with heavy exhibit pieces. Third, gallery staff reported that the use of the one loading dock also results in an overload of materials and persons. The café and bookstore use the loading dock for deliveries and for access to the dumpster. At the same time, the Mershon Auditorium may use it to set up for a musical performance; the Wexner Center performance space may use it to set up for a dance; and the galleries may use it to load or unload pieces. According to staff, this mixed use creates security problems. Insurance for exhibit pieces often requires a secure area for loading and unloading. For this, Wexner staff must close access to the loading dock to the other facilities while loading or unloading an exhibit. This interferes with the function of the other facilities. Scheduling the appropriate time for such closings interferes with the function of the gallery space. Fourth, to get to various destinations, materials must change levels. However, the usable loading dock does not have adequate freight elevators for the intense use, causing Wexner staff to use the passenger elevators, not designed for freight. Using these elevators also interferes with other users, such as performers.

The formal survey evaluations of the loading dock confirmed it as unsatisfactory. The loading dock workers scored it as fair to poor. It received one good rating for lighting. It scored fair for the adequacy of the space, acoustics, security, and flexibility of use. It scored fair to poor for the odor, privacy, and aesthetics; and it scored poor for temperature. In open-ended responses, some said they liked the uniqueness of the structure, the colors, and interior fittings and the large loading area. They disliked the lack of privacy, lack of temperature control, lack of direct access to and remoteness of work stations, inefficient elevators, inaccessibility of the building to handicapped, and the high maintenance required for the hardware.

### Roof Leaks

During a fundraising reception for alumni and donors, a university staff person noticed a large planter in the middle of the space obstructing movement. When she asked about it, she learned that it was there to catch water from a leak above. Tom Heretta (a university architect) informed me by telephone of approximately fifteen to twenty roof leaks. Wexner staff reported leaks throughout the facility, in the gallery spaces, in the public spaces, in the film and video theater, and in the library spaces. Recall that the replacement required a capital outlay of almost $1 million. The leaks result from the large number of joints and from exterior pedestrian paths placed above the library. The joints create detailing problems translating into roof leaks. Although staff in the University Architect's office told me that they advised the architect of this potential problem in advance, he held to his design.

### Interior Circulation

#### Entrance Stairway

Some visitors report that the stairway leading from the entry lobby to the gallery space appears disorienting (refer back to Figure 1.6). Some of them report tripping or missing the bottom steps.

#### Wayfinding

Visitors reported difficulty finding their way around the facility. When Peter Eisenman led some critics on a tour of the facility, security staff reported that he appeared on their monitors lost and circling around. A security person made his way through several locked doors to find the visitors and escort them out. Eisenman was indeed lost.

#### Gallery Ramp

A long, polished ramp runs next to the gallery spaces. It has proven difficult for women in heels, the elderly, and people using wheelchairs, causing some to slip.

#### Coatroom Access for Performance Space

Evening users of the Wexner performance space (to the north) often arrive before the galleries close. They leave their coats in the coatroom to the south of the galleries, then proceed up the ramp by the galleries, around, and then down into the performance space. After the performance, they cannot get back to their coats indoors. For security and insurance reasons, when the galleries close, a security barrier closes the gallery spaces at the top and bottom of the ramp (Figure 7.6). The barrier cuts off indoor access between the performance space and the coatroom. Visitors must go outside, walk more than 100 yards back to the front entrance, and then go downstairs to retrieve their coats. They have to do this sometimes in freezing winter temperatures with winds rushing through the outdoor alley.

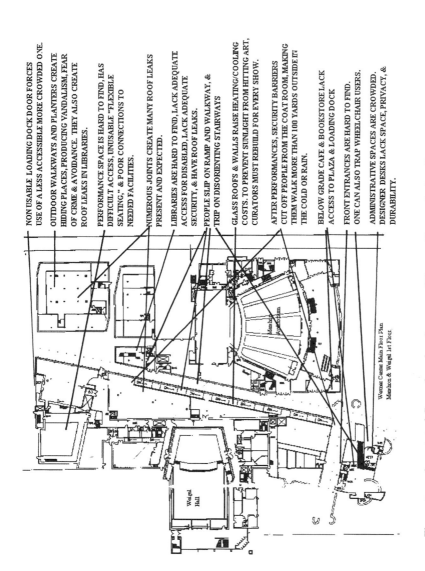

NON USABLE LOADING DOCK DOOR FORCES USE OF A LESS ACCESSIBLE MORE CROWDED ONE.

OUTDOOR WALKWAYS AND PLANTERS CREATE HIDING PLACES, PRODUCING VANDALISM, FEAR OF CRIME & AVOIDANCE. THEY ALSO CREATE ROOF LEAKS IN LIBRARIES.

PERFORMANCE SPACE IS HARD TO FIND, HAS DIFFICULT ACCESS, UNUSABLE "FLEXIBLE SEATING," & POOR CONNECTIONS TO NEEDED FACILITIES.

NUMEROUS JOINTS CREATE MANY ROOF LEAKS PRESENT AND EXPECTED.

LIBRARIES ARE HARD TO FIND, LACK ADEQUATE ACCESS FOR DISABLED, LACK ADEQUATE SECURITY, & HAVE ROOF LEAKS.

PEOPLE SLIP ON RAMP AND WALKWAY, & TRIP ON DISORIENTING STAIRWAYS

GLASS ROOFS & WALLS RAISE HEATING/COOLING COSTS. TO PREVENT SUNLIGHT FROM HITTING ART, CURATORS MUST REBUILD FOR EVERY SHOW.

AFTER PERFORMANCES, SECURITY BARRIERS CUT OFF PEOPLE FROM THE COAT ROOM, MAKING THEM WALK MORE THAN 100 YARDS OUTSIDE IN THE COLD OR RAIN.

BELOW GRADE CAFE & BOOKSTORE LACK ACCESS TO PLAZA & LOADING DOCK

FRONT ENTRANCES ARE HARD TO FIND. ONE CAN ALSO TRAP WHEELCHAIR USERS.

ADMINISTRATIVE SPACES ARE CROWDED. DESIGNER DESKS LACK SPACE, PRIVACY, & DURABILITY.

Figure 7.5. Annotated floorplan showing some Wexner Center design flaws.

125

Figure 7.6. Security barriers close the gallery spaces and coatrooms. Photograph by Jack L. Nasar.

### Café

The design placed much of the facility, including the café, below street grade. This makes the café less accessible for the public and for service. The separation from the outdoor plaza prevents interaction between café users and the outdoors space. As Lewis, the critic for the *Washington Post*, wrote:

> By stuffing the café into the armory basement, the architects and the university wasted a unique opportunity to exploit the pivotal location of the center's entrance at the gateway to the campus. The café should have been above grade, near the entrance with generous windows and dining terraces overlooking the city and campus landscapes. This would have been an act of connection. (p. 37)[136]

Instead of creating extra seating for the café and enlivening the outdoor plaza with activity, the below-grade location lowers the café's effective seating capacity and deadens the public plaza. Passersby cannot see the café from outside the facility, and no signs alert them to its presence. The café reported low sales. Although many things may have affected sales, its inaccessibility and invisibility draws away business.

Café staff also report problems getting to and from the loading dock and dumpster area. Recall that they must rely on a security guard to unlock certain secure doors. They also told me that the walk to and from the dumpster through the one working loading dock takes approximately twenty to twenty-five minutes.

### Bookstore

Nearby the café, the bookstore suffers from similar problems. It is also located below grade and lacks signs outside indicating its presence. As with the café, the bookstore staff reported low sales. The bookstore, like other Wexner facilities, has poor access to the loading dock.

Bookstore staff reported that their offices lack space for transitional storage of books. The major circulation connector between Wexner and Mershon Auditorium ran through the center of the bookstore. According to staff, this made the layout confusing. Security personnel reported it as a severe security problem. When the bookstore closed, the circulation connection closed, breaking the interior connector between Wexner and Mershon Auditorium. The university had the bookstore redesigned two years after completion of the building.

In the formal evaluation of the bookstore space, the staff generally reported fair to poor scores. They evaluated the odor and aesthetics as good. They judged the temperature and security as fair to good, the acoustics and flexibility of use as fair, and the adequacy of the space, the lighting, privacy, and storage as poor.

### Gallery Spaces

#### Difficulty Displaying Insured Artworks

Two of the four galleries face glass walls and roofs. This lets in sunlight, interfering with the central purpose of the exhibition space – displaying works of art. Gallery staff report that many museums and lenders have insurance policies requiring protection from ultraviolet light and sunlight. They will not lend their works unless the Wexner Center guaranties that no direct sunlight will touch the art. Direct sunlight can also produce glare on the surfaces, hindering viewing the works.

Wexner staff report that for each exhibition they must design and build temporary walls and ceilings to provide extra display space and to block sunlight (Figure 7.7). After the exhibition, the staff tears down the barriers and starts anew for the new exhibition. According to Wexner staff: "Every time they install an exhibition . . . they construct the equivalent of a two bedroom apartment" (p. 5).[118] In at least one case (an historic costume exhibit), they reported having to postpone the opening to deal with the light problem. Because of standards for

Figure 7.7. Glass roof and walls require temporary gallery enclosures for each exhibit. Photograph by Jack L. Nasar.

temperature and humidity controls for exhibitions, the temporary remodeling efforts create another problem. The temporary ceilings disrupt the flow of air, by blocking the ventilation air returns above it. Patrick Maughham, The Director of Security at the Wexner Center, told me that the temporary barriers also block the security cameras.

According to the annual report from the Wexner Center: "Among the most serious (problems) are . . . uncontrollable light transmission which limits exhibition design possibilities and causes great concern for conservation standards required by lenders to various exhibition. *This last issue will seriously compromise the Center's ability to attract loans from other institutions* (p. 16).[200] Recall that correcting this problem may cost approximately $5 to $10 million.

### Space

Beyond the lighting problems, the gallery spaces have much unusable space because they lose one wall to the long ramp along side, and one wall to the lower entries. The annual report on the center described the "inefficient placement of galleries" as one of several "serious problems in its (the building's) use." (p. 16).[200] In addition, the report cites the "location and size of air return vents" as a "serious problem" (p. 16) interfering with the creation of installations. The combination of problems forces the curators to place exhibits more rigidly than they would like.

The fire exit from one gallery leads to a lower-level corridor in the Center. The fire exit from another gallery leads to an adjacent building. In each case, once through the doors, users would not find adequate signs directing them to an exit. During a fire, wheelchair users would have to find an elevator to get out, but no signs direct them to the elevator.

### Maintenance

Floor surfaces in the ramps and elsewhere get "slippery when wet," a problem for a public space. They also have high maintenance costs associated with them. Because of the design, painters must repaint the interior walls for every exhibit.

Lighting in the galleries and throughout the facility is supplied by specially fabricated fixtures that have an industrial look. These fixtures require maintenance workers to spend extra time when changing a light bulb. According to maintenance staff, the covers wear poorly, get shopworn, and, as nonstandard pieces, make replacement difficult. Over time, maintenance workers have used standard fixtures, creating an inconsistent appearance.

### Security

The stationary, immovable security cameras in the gallery spaces conflict with the mounting of exhibits. The barriers built for the exhibit must not block the security camera. In several exhibits, however, the cameras end up facing a blank wall, making them useless. Security personnel had to develop other ways to handle potential security problems. Because insurance often requires surveillance in each gallery, this means hiring additional security staff to cover each gallery. In addition, because of the layout, the gallery areas turn into a passageway. This requires extra security personnel to secure the exhibits and stop

Figure 7.8. Crowded designer-desks in administrative area showing signs of wear. Photograph by Jack L. Nasar.

unwanted trespassing. After hours, they must also close both ends of the ramp, cutting the space in half.

### Administrative Spaces

Users of the administrative offices complained about the fixed furniture, crowding, and the inadequacy of the work and storage space. Twelve of them must squeeze into one specially fabricated designer desk, difficult to subdivide for the needed privacy or space for them to do their work. The desk lacks file or storage space. Staff added privacy barriers and split the desk, but it still remains crowded. The designer desks suffer from deterioration (Figure 7.8). Many bookshelves cannot hold books, because the designer, maintaining his desired geometry, specified the shelves too narrow to hold books.

Staff also complained about the overhead lighting, the glass doors, and see-through partitions, which lessen privacy. Some offices have windows at knee level. This limits the workers' view out, and gives the female staff the feeling that outsiders have a view up their dresses. The staff have placed cardboard over the low windows to block the view. The Director complained about electrical outlets in the middle of his office floor, which prevented him from placing his desk where he

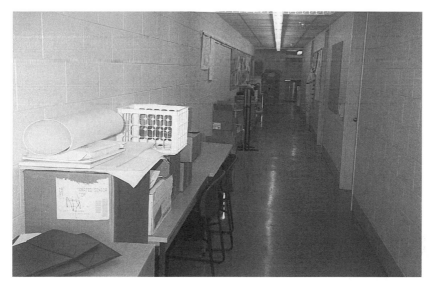

Figure 7.9. Hallways used for storage. Photograph by Jack L. Nasar.

wanted it. He also said that he could not put books on his book-shelves, because the shelves, following the 12-$\frac{1}{4}$ degree grid shift, were too narrow.

The director noted that the administrative space is separated from curatorial spaces by long and inconvenient distances. At the building opening, the 4,948 square foot administrative space did not offer enough space to house the administrative staff. Spaces are crowded and lack adequate storage, forcing some people to store materials in a hall-way (Figure 7.9). The Director had to distribute staff throughout the facility and had to lease additional space off campus to house a depart-ment. This segregation created a coordination problem between departments and further separated staff from spaces where they had to conduct their daily work.

Staff rated the space as good to excellent for adequacy of space (though this is belied by the renting of additional space across the street for Wexner functions). They also rate the temperature, odor, and acoustics favorably. They rated aesthetics and security as fair to good; and they rated privacy and flexibility of use as poor. The in-house man-agement rated their office space as excellent, the lighting, furniture and equipment as good, but they gave fair ratings to storage and shelves, privacy and aesthetics.

*Security Space*

Security personnel (like others) said they have difficulty moving from one end of the building to the other when the exhibition area closes. The design offers no direct route. For security reasons, the security staff can only issue a limited number of keys. They describe their control room as chaotic, and say that the limited space forces an arrangement of monitors that makes observation difficult. They say they need a larger briefing room, more office, lockers, storage space, and prefer better lighting and security cameras on the public walkways around the facility. They reported difficulty securing the bookstore, because of the path through it.

*Space for Visiting Artists*

When the building opened, the administrative staff and security personnel took over the space for visiting artists. The Center lacks the space intended for visiting artists, who get assigned space elsewhere on and off campus.

### Libraries

The Wexner facility houses a Fine Arts Library (FIN) and a Cartoon Research Library (CGA) that share one building entrance and stairway. FIN is a circulating library and CGA is a rare books, manuscripts, and special collections library. My evaluation of the libraries used a published evaluation of FIN by its head librarian Susan Wyngaard[313] in addition to interviews and observations of use. Although several things worked well in the libraries, the evaluations identified significant problems.

On the positive side, FIN users said they liked the movable bookshelves and the soothing color scheme; and Wyngaard said that she liked the spaciousness of her office and the glass wall allowing her to observe the public. CGA users also liked the soothing color scheme and the canvas wall texture, making it easier to hang things, though the room has a more complex function. Users of the two libraries had mixed evaluations. Respondents complained about the lack of daylight and information about conditions outside, due to the basement location. They complained about the tables being too narrow for work and too low, causing them to bump their knees. They gave fair to good scores to security, flexibility of use, and adequacy of space, good scores for temperature, aesthetics, and acoustics,and high scores for odor, and lighting. Staff at the two libraries gave poor scores to health, safety, and signs, fair scores to location and privacy, and good scores to the ambiance and control.

The POE identified four broad categories of problems with these facilities:

1. Difficult to find
2. Poor access for disabled and elderly
3. Inability of staff at circulation desk to observe and secure the libraries properly
4. Miscellaneous technical problems

### Difficult to Find

Users said they had difficulty finding the entrance to the libraries. The libraries have an unceremonial entrance resulting from their location, the size of the door, and inadequate signs or cues to lead people to them. Although the university added small signs later, the signs are too small to resolve the problem. Both librarians report that users, once inside, still lack adequate cues, signs, or lighting to lead them to the appropriate library. They have difficulty finding either FIN or CGA. However, a letter from the CGA librarian Lucy Caswell reported an unexpected effect of the poor legibility:

> We have not had the problems with street people that we expected. There was, for awhile, a homeless man who moved back and forth from Main Library to the libraries in Sullivant. We were sure that our building would be included in this circuit. Unfortunately, he died, but there are other folks I see sleeping on High Street who haven't come in here.

### Poor Access

Visitors have to move through a long outdoor aisle, unsheltered in stormy weather. Caswell also told me that the marble strips in the walk become extremely slick in rain. The aisle works as a wind catcher, accelerating the wind, sometimes making walking difficult. Librarians report that when the entrance floor becomes wet it becomes slippery and especially dangerous for elderly and the disabled. Glare from windows irritates users, especially the elderly. Users descend a steep stairway from the glare into a dark basement area to enter the libraries. This leads some visitors to feel uncomfortable or to trip.

Both Caswell and Wyngaard report that the facility has a large, wasted, unused space in lobby areas and in the mezzanine area. Intrusive posts get in the way of movement. At each library, wheelchair users cannot get through the entrance doors alone. They must wait

Figure 7.10. A sign added to direct wheelchair users to library elevator. Photograph by Jack L. Nasar.

for a staff member to notice them and help them through the entrance. The librarians reported approximately five wheelchair users per week in one library, and approximately two per month in the other.

The FIN librarian reported that at planning meetings she discussed the need for access to the second floor book stacks by disabled library patrons. Though Eisenman resisted an elevator, he eventually complied because of codes. He placed the elevator out of sight. Staff have posted signs directing wheelchair users to the elevator (Figure 7.10).

CGA has problems with the freight elevator and loading dock. Caswell wrote me that:

> We lend for exhibition; receive large gifts in kind delivered in moving vans, etc. A related problem is the design of the entry door to CGA. Large boxes or the cherry picker (for replacing light bulbs in the double-height ceiling area or repairing roof leaks) cannot get through without having the center post removed. A second related problem occurs for the temporary storage/staging area. CGA was supposed to have space in the basement just outside the freight elevator. This space has been taken over by Wexner, and is not available to CGA. A space such as this was in CGA's program of requirements (because of concerns about collections contaminated by insects, fungus, etc.) and is another example of something not provided.

Figure 7.11. Library alcove at left could conceal an attacker.
Photograph by Jack L. Nasar.

### Surveillance and Safety

During planning and design, Wyngaard told the designers of the need
for visual access to the stacks to prevent vandalism or theft. They disregarded her concern. She told me that the design blocks library employ-
ees from doing the needed surveillance. It also has several nooks and
crannies out of view. The circulation desk supervisor's work area is separated and quite distant from the circulation desk, making hands-on
management of the circulation desk nearly impossible. The circulation
desk supervisor had to install a mirror in order to observe the circulation desk from her work space. Even so, the enclosed office blocked
visual access to the stacks and study tables. After occupancy, the university installed "wall-and ceiling-mounted video cameras throughout
the library with a series of monitors placed inside the circulation desk"
(p. 39)[313] The design also poses surveillance problems for CGA.
"Spacing of posts is a major problem . . . in the public reading room
where one blocks sight lines" (p.39)[313]

At night, one staff member closes the library. This can be dangerous,
because she cannot see whether someone has lingered, hiding in the
stacks. An alcove (Figure 7.11) along the hallway to the emergency
door can hide a potential attacker. According to Wyngaard, "The librarians attempted to discuss potential security problems with Eisenman,

Figure 7.12. Repair work on roof leaks on underground library. Photograph by Jack L. Nasar.

but he disregarded and downplayed" their concerns (p. 39).[313] Female staff, who must pass this alcove nightly to lock up, fear the walk.

### Miscellaneous Technical Problems: Fine Arts Library (FIN)

The POE found a variety of problems relating to the building systems, columns, bookshelves, reading room, and designer furnishings and furniture.

*Building Systems.* The librarians report that the roof leaks over library books, study areas, and computer equipment. The University Architect had warned that the raised planters and paths would lead to leaks (Figure 7.12). Problems with heating ventilation and air conditioning (HVAC) create climate zones and excess humidity, potentially damaging books.

*Columns and Bookshelves.* To maintain the various grids in the design, the designers placed columns that resulted in a loss of "over 800 linear feet of shelves" (p. 38)[313] The bookshelves sagged under the weight of the books. Although Wyngaard indicated the need for a three-foot span to support the books, Eisenman specified a four-foot span to fit his geometry. After construction, the university had to add metal braces under shelves to eliminate the sagging. The braces "reduced the vertical dimensions between the shelves" requiring the librarians to "rewrite the library's definition of an oversize book" (p. 38).[313] Nearly six years later, the librarians were still altering the cataloging data and shifting books "from the regular size to the oversize shelving area, a labor-intensive task, necessitated by the design" (p. 38).[313]

*Designer Furnishings and Furniture.* The librarians and users complained about nonstandard and custom-built furniture that does not serve their purposes. Beyond problems with the bookshelves, users report that other custom furnishings (such as the card catalog, library tables, book and exhibit cases, and lighting) do not work. Caswell reported that the custom-built circulation desk and shelves deteriorated quickly and did not work well from the start. For example, she said that the designer did not include a bookdrop in the circulation desk. Soon after construction, staff had to cut a book drop into the desk to allow users to return materials to the library. In 1996, the library tore out the deteriorating circulation desk and shelves and replaced them. In public areas, the replacement shelves and desks look almost identical to the ones they replace. In areas out of public view, the staff opted for more traditional shelving and furniture, inconsistent with the original design concept. Staff report that these designs better meet their needs.

The reading room has an irregular shape, as does its furniture, designed to fit the shape. This reduced the seating capacity of the room. Designer lighting also is a problem. The underground space lacks natural daylight. The design called for alternating warm and cool fluorescent lights to mimic daylight. Physical Facilities had told the designers that when these tubes failed staff would replace them with traditional (lower cost) tubes. Now when lights fail, maintenance staff "replace them with stock available from the university's storehouse," leaving the lighting with an irregular pattern.

An unused card catalog stands, according to the designer, as an icon and shrine. Because the library had closed the card catalog for years, offering on-line public access, Wyngaard reported that she neither wanted nor needed a new catalog. She had wanted to move the old oak catalog to the new library temporarily, but the designers said they wanted to design every item in the "interior, right down to the ashtray on the receptionist's desk" (p. 38).[313] The librarian said that the symbolic but unused catalog cost extra money to fabricate and install and occupied space needed for seating or stacks.

Students bump their knees on the custom-built desks, and wheelchairs do not fit under the desks. This forces wheelchair users to park in the aisle and put books in their laps. Narrow space between tables also makes the space impassable for wheelchair users. After construction, the libraries requested new money to get appropriate furniture and equipment.

*Miscellaneous Problems: Cartoon Research Library (CGA)*

CGA users reported problems that parallel those found in FIN.

*Building Systems.* Caswell reported that the HVAC "does a very poor job of dust filtration." It also created a flood. In a note to me, she wrote:

> The HVAC machines are located above the reading room. In the blue-print stage, I remember asking about the possibility of flooding from this arrangement, and was assured that a flood couldn't happen because of the way the machine room was designed. A maintenance worker left a valve open and there was a flood. Nothing on exhibition was damaged, but the wall covering had to be replaced.

*Columns and Bookshelves.* Caswell also described problems with the bookshelves: "The spacing of posts is a major problem . . . in the stacks where aisles and shelves are blocked by their arbitrary placement to fit the grid." In addition, Caswell reported that the bookshelves in the storage room do not fit the specific need for storing books and boxes. Nor do the shelves work in the stack area. She wrote: "The non-standard stacks (both in their 4-foot length and in distance between shelves) are very inefficient. CGA is now out of space and urgently needs to replace the stacks on the ground floor with compact shelving." In 1996, CGA had a laminate repair/replacement program. For it, Caswell told me in a telephone interview: "The custom-built shelving was removed everywhere except the book stack area. It was replaced with the type of shelving specified in the original program of require-ments for the building but not supplied by the architect."

Staff reported that the designer desk for CGA does not provide ade-quate space. It lacks the necessary space to lay out papers to do the work; the computer does not fit; and the desk needs more privacy (secu-rity) from the public. When I interviewed the curator, she said that her office did not have enough space, that she could not arrange the furni-ture in a way that worked for her, that many of the bookshelves were unusable, and that the office lacked adequate sound insulation from the seminar room into the office. She described the office as "claustro-phobic" and "noisy." She characterized the shelf space as "useless and wasteful." She has "abandoned the office" for an "office space within the stacks," that "offers more flexible space, but is unsatisfactory in its lack of privacy for telephone calls and meetings."

*Reading Room.* Staff reported that the reading room in CGA is too narrow and uncontrolled, crowding users and failing to provide the necessary silence for reading. Caswell wrote me that "the first design I saw had a double height ceiling . . . a desirable feature to 'open' the space. . . . I was not told that the design had been rotated to place the high ceiling in the stacks and learned this only when I visited the construction site. The aesthetics of the reading room were compromised and valuable stack/storage space was lost."

*Designer Furnishing and Furniture.* Staff note that the designer display boxes have several sections, making it difficult for users to see the displays. They also note that the wall display surfaces have sections interfering with the mounting of exhibitions. As with FIN, CGA had problems with a catalog/altar and custom-built tables. CGA also received an unneeded card catalog/altar, but Caswell wrote to me that in CGA, "it has been taken apart in an effort to use the space more efficiently." As for the custom-built tables, Caswell wrote that they "are extraordinarily heavy and very difficult to move. We need to be able to shift them to accommodate sorting needs of various types of materials that are processed, and this cannot be done. We end up sometimes with Rube Goldberg type arrangements of book trucks, typing stands, etc. to get the job done."

### Performance Space (Black-Box Theater)

Administrative personnel evaluated the performance theater as good for security but poor functionally (too small), for maintenance, and design.

#### Wayfinding and Access

To get to the performance space, users must enter the facility, go down a flight of stairs, walk up the long ramp along the galleries, turn into what looks like a dead-end space, go down a small flight of steps, and turn to enter. According to staff and users, the space is difficult to find.

Wheelchair-disabled users cannot get to the upper-level seating. They can only sit on the ground floor. The fire exit from the performance space leads to stairs, which would prevent a wheelchair user from escaping a fire and which might lead to a blocked fire exit.

#### Unusable Adaptable Seating

The architectural plans specified "a 225-seat flexible performance space." The flexible seating proved both unusable and smaller than specified. As stated in the annual report: "To date it has been impossible to put the full riser system in the room because it is too big and too heavy for the room. The real capacity of the performance space is 110 seats." This reduces the potential revenue for the space for a three-night performance (assuming $12 tickets) from $8,100 to $3,960.

### Connections

Managers complain that the performance space is too far away from other performing arts activities, with which they share extra services. It is on the opposite end of the building from the film and video space, and administrative offices. The separation hinders needed communication. Because of the failed loading dock door, users of the performance space have a long walk to the loading dock. We have seen that the location (and closing of the galleries) causes audience members to have a long walk outside to get their coats. The poor connections also create problems for performers. According to managers, the closed galleries block the performers' access to the café, making it more difficult to get ice, water, and other amenities.

### Film and Video Theater

Managers evaluated this space as good for function and security but poor for maintenance and design. Users reported several problems with the functioning of this theater. They reported that the theater has a small screen, set back in the stage. This reduces the appeal and impact of viewing a film or video because of the smaller image seen by the audience. They reported inadequate space for desks and storage and a need for more flexible lighting. They also mention the need for more exterior doors and more flexible doors. The doors only open in one direction. When crowds move in and out, this can block circulation. The design also generates noise. As a renter of the space for conferences, Caswell wrote me: "I find it problematic because of the noise people make when they enter. Many continue to chat, not realizing that the program has started." Users report that the theater is too far from a working loading dock, making the movement of equipment difficult. Disabled users can sit only in the back of the facility.

### Weigel Hall

The Wexner design added connections to and spaces for the Weigel Hall music area. Users complained about wayfinding, accessibility, the institutional appearance, and the dizzying design of music rehearsal rooms. The new entrances to Weigel are hidden. Once in Weigel, users report difficulty finding their way to the rehearsal rooms. In addition, the stage door lacks clear signs, and the raised wooden floor jamb causes equipment to become snagged, causing damage to the wood. Because of poor signs, users cannot determine which restroom is for males and which is for females. Performers note that the location of the music rehearsal room at the top of a narrow staircase makes accessibility for large instruments a problem. Disabled users have difficulty getting to the performance space. They must negotiate a long maze of corridors and doors (without power door openers) to get from their first floor entrance to the second floor performance space. Users complained about the institutional look of the high ceilings, tunnel hallways, lighting, and equipment stored in hallways.

The white fluorescent lighting and white walls in the music rehearsal space create glare. The acoustic panels have a dense dot pattern that interferes with reading music and gives some users, particularly conductors, headaches. As one faculty member said, the space has "no blackboards, no windows, and walls with dots . . . in short, nothing to break up the space, and the surface appears to swim." When asked about the rehearsal rooms, most students interviewed said that the interior design is very important. All of them said they saw movement in it, and most saw vibration (89%). Most of them also said they disliked the pattern (86%), found it distracting or somewhat distracting (79%), and as busy or somewhat busy (87%). Most respondents also rated it as disrupting, as wearying, and as creating after-images (58%).

### Comparison to Other Buildings

Do the problems in Wexner differ in number or severity from those in other buildings or other campus buildings? Yes. They appear to be more numerous and severe. Though variation in methods and reports of POEs hinders precise comparisons across buildings, examination of several sources suggest that Wexner stands out for its problems. My examination of published POEs found few buildings described as performing so poorly. This does not mean that all buildings work well. Texts describe many flawed designs, such as Frank Lloyd Wright's Johnson Tower, which the client had to close as unusable, or I. M. Pei's Boston's Hancock Tower, which had windows pop out onto the plaza below and created winds blowing pedestrian off their feet.[29][81] The texts do not, however, present systematic POEs.

In one extreme negative case, the client eventually tore the project down as unusable. Constructed in 1955, Pruitt Igoe housed 12,000 low-income residents in thirty-three eleven-story buildings.[20][148][189] The overburdened and underfinanced public housing authority made several critical changes in the design to cut costs, but they kept the basic scheme intact. The design won an award for multifamily housing and received critical praise. For example, *Architectural Forum* praised it for its construction efficiencies, refreshing site plan and landscaping (a river of open space), skip stop elevators, bringing row-house convenience to high-rise dwellers, changing the pattern of public housing, a new prototype for mass housing, providing decent safe homes, and saving people. *Forum* gave particular praise to the galleries, conceived as "vertical neighborhoods," safe playgrounds," "open air hallways," "a porch," "a laundry," and "storage." The idea of galleries on alternating floors had appeared in a 1952 design competition project.[257] When sociologist Lee Rainwater studied Pruitt Igoe, he found a different picture.[86 226] Due to the lack of public toilets on the lower floors, children playing outside, urinated and defecated in the elevators, elevator shafts, hallways and elsewhere. The stairwells, elevators, and galleries came under the control of criminals who robbed, assaulted and raped people. Fearful of the galleries, residents referred to them as "gauntlets." The laundries and storage lockers stood unsafe and unused. Pruitt Igoe developed a vacancy rate of 70 percent. The housing authority tried to save the project through new investments, closing building, and then dynamiting three buildings. When that failed, they tore it down. It had proven unlivable, dysfunctional, and too costly to manage. Constructed for $36 million, Pruitt Igoe ended up costing the authority $57 million.

More typically, published POEs indicate a mix of strengths and weaknesses. For example, consider a POE of four senior centers in Albuquerque. The POE found "problems with unprotected, confusing or dark entries, irregularly shaped, wasteful spaces, windowless spaces, inadequate kitchen facilities, some lobby and office spaces with circulation problems, and outdoor activity areas . . . unused." The POE also found strengths, including "the lobby areas, and pool rooms' excellent potential for socializing, security of gift shops; dance floors in multipurpose rooms, and a very flexible arrangement for food service lines (pp. 101–102).[218] A POE of a building at the University of Kentucky found generally favorable reactions." After ten years of occupancy, the client organization considered the building functionally appropriate, especially in the laboratory areas . . . (and) occupant surveys indicating 'good quality ratings for virtually all aspects of the building" (p. 133).[218]

POEs of two buildings at Ohio State University also showed neither the number nor severity of problems encountered in Wexner. In a POE of a new math tower and classroom space, students and I interviewed 191 people.[176] For a POE of a chemistry addition, we interviewed 78 people.[175] For each POE, we also observed patterns of use and talked with the University Architect staff who oversaw the projects. What did the POE's find? The chemistry addition had some problems with circulation, crowding near a classroom and difficulties finding one's way around, but otherwise people gave it favorable ratings. Occupants scored the building, and most of its spaces and features at a "good" level. Passersby and occupants scored its visual appeal at the good to excellent level. In contrast, Wexner had fair to poor ratings. Although the math tower scored better than Wexner, it did not do as well as the chemistry addition. It had problems with acoustics. A noisy mechanical system interrupts a main goal of the facility – quiet, to allow the professors to think. It also had problems with flexibility, disabled access, its anti-pedestrian exterior, basement flooding, building wear, cheap appearance of the interior, uneven heating and cooling, difficulties in finding one's way around. Yet, most occupants scored the building as adequate (53%) or more than adequate (34%). They rated all of the spaces as either fair or good, giving particularly favorable scores to a lounge, the main office, and their personal office spaces. Passersby and occupants gave favorable ratings of the exterior, though they felt it needed more vegetation. (The architect had rejected vegetation, because it would block the view of his building.)

Finally, anecdotal evidence from the University Architect's office confirms the comparative negative performance of Wexner. Morelli, the University architect, told me that her office works on approximately a half billion dollars of projects every year. Staff in her office informed me that compared to the other projects, the Wexner Center is "unrivaled for its problems."

### Conclusion

The results of the Wexner POE raise some ethical questions about the competition and the conflict between elite art and popular use. It demonstrates the arrogance and out-of-touch quality of some members of the architectural profession. The POE uncovered few favorable qualities and a host of serious problems with the design. It identified design problems disrupting secondary or support functions, such as the bookstore or café, as well as design problems disrupting the main function of the facility – the display of visual or performance arts. The surveys of users showed that the design obstructs the intended function of every space in the facility. The building fails to satisfy any of the three major tasks of architecture set out by Vitruvius. It lacks convenience, durability, and, to most observers, beauty.

Such problems are probably not unique to this competition or to signature design. Design, which stress the elite artistic statement, will tend to have such problems. One sees this in the many dysfunctions in Frank Lloyd Wright's work: His buildings often cost five times more than the original budget. His roofs leak, his cantilevers sag, and his fireplaces seldom work.[81] He designed one house without bedrooms, closets, or screens (pp. 341–42).[81] His famous Johnson Laboratory Tower used helio lighting, "overheating the building and threatening to parboil and blind its occupants" (p. 373)[81] The company shut it down as unusable. Still, it received enough praise from critics to appeared on the list of the most cited buildings of the twentieth century (Chapter 3). In response to a client's complaint about a fireplace that did not work, he explained, "she had mistaken its nature. It is designed to burn pole wood and not ordinary cordwood. One sets the pole wood vertically in the fireplace and permits the pole to blaze all the way up to the top . . . and very little smoke will come down the flue. . . . Of course treated as an ordinary fireplace, it is bound to smoke" (p. 422).[81]

Evidence of potential problems with signature architecture emerged in my POEs of the math tower and the chemistry addition. We found that the chemistry addition performed relatively well compared to the math tower. A local commercial architect designed the chemistry addition, but Philip Johnson, one of the most acclaimed signature architects of the twentieth century, designed the less functional math tower. As Christopher Degenhardt, a Fellow in the American Society of Landscape Architects, noted, "If design becomes so selfish and so arrogant that it does not and will not respond to a client's needs, then we're not serving the client properly" (p. 177).[8] Signature architects often do this, and competitions can aggravate the problem because of the absence of adequate contact and consultation between the client, users, and the architect after the selection of the winner. A more responsive designer and better management by the client might ease the problems.

Competition juries, designers, and clients have a moral and ethical obligation to at least respect the dignity and welfare of the visitors and end users who will regularly experience the completed project. The Wexner POE points to an abandonment of this responsibility. As Les Wexner noted, the university was not an active client. In a telephone interview with me, he said, "in hindsight, I should have been the client. Without me, they (the architects) had none." Publicity and public artistic statements may represent legitimate public purposes or goals for some facilities, but the design must still minimize risks to the dignity and welfare of others. For a public entity like the Wexner Center, a higher standard applies. In a democratic society, the process should lead to solutions that benefit the public – durable solutions that work for and delight the client, users, and the public. The next chapter describes such a process. It involves monitoring the design from programming through postoccupancy evaluation.

# 8

# MODEL FOR RUNNING
# DESIGN COMPETITIONS

> A competition succeeds or fails to a substantial degree depending on
> the process of conducting it. Casual programs, confused information
> and careless juries . . . are a disaster for the ultimate architectural
> product (p. 21).[153] – Richard Miller, Wexner Center Competition
> Advisor

I have presented a variety of studies, opinions and examples of design
competitions. The evidence points to competition architecture as out-
of-touch with the client, occupants, and public it should serve. My studies of design competitions through history suggest that they do not tend
to deliver lasting masterpieces. The studies of Wexner Center point to a
jury and architect seriously cut off from the client, users, and public.
Other research confirms a disconnection between popular and
designer values. In a democratic society, public buildings should be
accountable to the public. I believe that several actions can help make
competition solutions satisfy and work for the client, users, and public.

### Decide on the Appropriateness of a Competition

First, clients should consider the appropriateness of a competition. As
the architect Mark Feinknopf said, clients first need to ask: "Are you
spending money for the right thing?" For a simple project with a domi-
nating artistic or symbolic goal, such as the Vietnam Veterans Memorial,
competitions may be appropriate.[8] For more complex projects and
goals, the problems associated with competitions may override the initial publicity.[215] "To be successful," the architect Michael McKinnell
told me, a competition "has to be for a building for which the brief can
be stated very exactly." Chuck Nitschke, another Wexner competitior,
noted that competitions take "the selection process out of the client's
hand, which is extremely dangerous. . . . The client normally has to
build what the jury picks, and the jury, even though they are competition professionals who are trying hard, they don't know anything about
the client's needs" (Appendix B). Competitions also tend to lose "the
rich dialog among designer, client and user" (p. 148).[8] Architects agree

that the lack of contact with the client in competitions has adverse effects on solutions.[31] As Ann Strong, a supporter of competitions, wrote:

> *Competitions can come between the architect and client.* The traditional design competition system aims to provide a set of rules which ensures that everybody who takes part does so on an equal basis. Anonymity is retained throughout. No contact is permitted between the competitors and the promoter, assessors and advisors other than in specified written form until the final selection has been made. The brief is issued, designs submitted and a decision reached. The result? Scrupulous fairness, *but no dialogue. The promoter cannot discuss hopes and expectation, no hints can be given as to what would be acceptable and what would be off-putting, competitors cannot probe, alternatives cannot be explored,* questions tend to be factual if not banal, as no competitor wants to reveal his or her line of thinking" (p. 6, italics added)[271]

Yet, as Nitschke said, "the most valuable phase of the architectural process is the period of time the architect works with the client to determine what the client needs. The client and architect become intimate team members working together, which is a synergy that always works" (Appendix B).

For a complex project, clients might spend their time more productively in picking the best architect for the project. Clients can study the works of designers, check out their references, interview a few, and pick the one most likely to satisfy the needs of the project. Because the process returns control to clients, it should yield a better building for them. Handled well, this approach may generate as much publicity as a competition. Perhaps the "better" building could serve as a basis for publicity.

If a client opts for a competition, the chance of success improves with a well-prepared and managed one. According to competition advisors in Germany, a well-prepared competition costs the sponsor "about 1.5 to 2 percent of the estimated building costs," but the sponsor can recoup this expense in cost savings associated with the winning design (p. 40).[116] Government bodies might consider legislating guidelines for competitions that use public money or land or that occupy prominent sites. To achieve more democratic solutions, I suggest the actions outlined in Table 8.1. A successful solution requires a solid program, a well-managed jury and design review process, and a postoccupancy evaluation. Several of the actions shown in Table 8.1 also make the competition fairer to entrants. The application of these actions may vary, depending on the objective of the competition. A competition for ideas might use a different approach than one seeking a developed design.

Table 8.1. *Model for more successful and democratic competitions.*

*PROGRAMMING*
* Prepare a detailed program

*MANAGING THE JURY PROCESS (DESIGN REVIEW)*
* Set up a structure that allows in-depth evaluation of entries
* Select a professional advisor open to a diverse jury and comprehensive solutions, and select a jury of individuals representing diverse interests related to the facility
* Prepare a prejury evaluation (PJE)
* Set up an unbiased evaluation process
* Use open proceedings with a formal record
* Monitor design development through design review

*POSTOCCUPANCY EVALUATION (PREDESIGN RESEARCH)*
* Monitor the results after the competition, after construction and occupancy

### Phase I: The Program

First, a competition needs a detailed program (spec or brief) evaluating the feasibility of the site, the space planning needs, and the fit between the two.[116] The AIA agrees, stating, "the success of an architectural competition depends largely on the care with which its program is formulated and written" (p. 9).[6] Architects and clients also agree. When asked about factors influencing their decision to enter a design competition, most architects in a *PA* poll cited the importance of "a complete and clear program" (p. 16).[31] Interviews with seventy-three architects found that they thought programming produced "successful projects and happy clients" (p. 37). The architects also thought that programs facilitated "the design process, marketing, project management, . . . client confidence in the project and firm, and (it saved) client and firm time and money" (p. 52).[299] As Chuck Nitschke said in his interview: "The most important element in any architectural project is the program. . . . A sophisticated program process should be developed before the competition is started . . . and published in a form that is easily read and understood." Charles Gwathemey agreed: "There needs to be a clear objective and moral obligation to writing a program, fulfilling the program, and judging it all on the same terms" (p. 191)[8] A mail survey also found that most sponsors, jurors, and entrants agree on the importance of a well-planned program, and most of them report competition programs as often poorly defined.[248] Inadequate programs are a prominent cause of abandoned projects.[271]

Table 8.2. *Composite programming model: A listing of the procedural steps used by seven programmers.* (p. 253)[243]

| Composite Listing of Programming Models |
| --- |

*Plan the Program*
    Identify participants and organize programming team
    Identify programming objectives
    Identify program context
    Identify information needed
    Define with client – process, sequence, task, schedules, rules, responsibilities
    Identify primary information sources
*Understand Client's Organization and Philosophy*
    Nature of organization, image and philosophy
    Organization function and communication process
    Satisfaction and dissatisfaction with current facility
    Identify user objectives
*Establish Project Goals*
    Functional goals
    Form-related goals
    Time-related goals
*Organize Information Search*
    Collect and organize project related facts
    Questionnaires and interviews
    Literature search
    Observation of existing operations and facilities
    Background information from client
    Review similar building types and operations
    Collect facts related to building function
    Collect facts related to building form
    Collect facts related to building economy
    Collect facts related to time (historical, present, future)
*Analyze Information*
    Analyze collected facts
    Functional space standards
    Tabulation of space requirements
    Spatial diagrams
    Interaction patterns among activities
    Written description of functional units
*Develop the Concept*
    Uncover, test, and develop conceptual alternatives
    Develop functional concepts
    Develop form, economy, and time-related concepts
*Identify Budget-Related Problems and Needs*
    Functional needs
    Form needs
    Economic needs
*Consider Project Impact*
    Impact on client's organization and operation
    Community and ecological impact
*Program Review and Revision*

A good program involves more than general statements about the number of rooms and sizes. The client should hire a programming architect or develop the expertise to create the program. There are many useful guides to programming one can use (see sidebar).

---

PROGRAMMING RESOURCES

Ed White's *Introduction to Architectural Programming* is an early guide to programming.[298] William Pena's *Problem Seeking* describes the five-step process used by Caudill Rowlett and Scott Architects and Planners.[211] Wolfgang Preiser has edited several collections – including *Facility Programming*,[216] and *Professional Practice in Architectural Programming*[217] – that give overviews of programming, description of programming activities, and case studies. Henry Sanoff's *Methods of Architectural Programming*,[242] and *Facility Programming*,[243] offer comprehensive reviews of programming models and step-by-step descriptions of how to do one. Donna Duerk's *Architectural Programming: Information Management for Design*,[61] and Mark Palmer's *The Architects' Guide to Facility Programming*[207] cover similar ground.

---

Programmers face two questions about how to proceed: What programming steps should they follow; and what concerns should the program address? Regarding the steps, the architect–researcher Henry Sanoff summarizes the steps of various programming models into a composite model (Table 8.2). Each action, such as "plan the program," may have several steps associated with it. The programmer may not find every step appropriate to each programming exercise. Different ones apply to different projects. Although the actions and steps look linear, Sanoff describes them as iterative. Information from later steps can feed forward to later steps and back to earlier steps. For example, "information on budget-related problems and needs" may affect the later step "program review and revision" or change the earlier step "project goals."

The program should offer criteria for concerns relevant to the particular project. The concerns fit into the broad categories of appearance, convenience, and durability.[292] Table 8.3 shows a list of potential concerns under each category. For each one, the programmer would specify guidelines or performance criteria for the design to satisfy. Different building purposes would have different concerns, priorities, and sets of criteria. Some projects may have unique criteria not listed. To get accurate information on the broad range of concerns, the programmer

Table 8.3. *Performance criteria for an architectural program.*

*Appearance*
    Identity (denotative meaning)
    Emotional quality
    Connotative meanings (status, symbolism)
*Convenience*
    Activities of user to be supported
    Circulation
    Comfort
    Convenience
    Environmental characteristics to support needed activities
    Flexibility
    Goals of the facility
    Legibility
    Personalization
    Privacy
    Safety (from accidents and hazards)
    Security from crime (and surveillance)
    Social interaction
    Territoriality
    Visibility
*Durability*
    Energy systems
        Acoustics
        Heating, ventilation, air conditioning
        Lighting
        Olfactory
        Radioactivity
    Environmental impact
    Siting and foundation
    Technique
        Assembly
        Economy
            Construction cost
            Maintenance costs
            Operating costs
        Phasing
        Quality of materials and finishes

should consult a variety of individuals related to the delivery and occupation of the facility. In addition to formulating the criteria for the jury, the client should also make clear how to interpret and weigh them. The program should indicate which criteria are most essential to satisfy, which are less essential, and which are relatively unimportant.

All designers entering a competition should receive the program in advance. The jury should also receive the program, with adequate time to read and digest it before evaluating the entries. This should help the designers and the jury use the criteria in the intended way. As the architect Charles Gwathmy said in his comments on competitions, "There needs to be a clear objective and moral obligation to writing a program, fulfilling the program, and judging all entries on the same terms" (p. 191).[8] However, Cesar Pelli told me, "I have served on some twelve juries . . . and I have concluded that today, most architects choose according to their stylistic allegiances, with little or no regard to how well the building will respond to other critical requirements." By laying out the expectations and sticking to those expectation, the client may reduce this potential problem.

Although programming may cost some money up front, it should save money by improving the efficiency of the solution for the client and occupants. It helps coalesce the thought of diverse users and resolve conflicts before the architect is hired; and it makes the competition fairer and more attractive to competitors. Research confirms that programming reduces costs by eliminating unnecessary features.[9] For example, a POE and program for low-cost self-built housing in Brazil identified unused features for elimination in future versions of the house.[177] Also the POE/Programming process for public housing, New York City Plazas, the Marriott Hotel, the Federal Bureau of Prisons, and hospitals (described in Chapter 6) saved money for clients.

### Phase II: Managing the Jury Process (Design Review)

#### Structure the Competition to Allow In-Depth Evaluations

The different competition formats – open, limited, invited, and two stage – have different implications for the review of entries.[36] An *open one-stage* competition, which allows many designers to enter anonymously, may attract hundreds of entries and may generate "the widest exploration of potential solutions" (p. 3).[6] A *limited competition*, which restricts entries to certain requirements by region or skill, may do the same, while giving clients some extra control. By keeping anonymity, these approaches can reduce costs for entrants, and they can lessen potential jury biases relating to the reputation of the entrants. On the downside, the large numbers of entries in open competitions make it difficult for the jury to evaluate much more than appearance. The anonymity also removes information about previous experience with the designer. Thus, an open or limited competition format may work best for a simple project with an overriding goal, such as the Vietnam Memorial in Washington D.C. Even with a simple project, the client may have to pair the winner with a reputable practice-oriented firm, and spend time refining the schematic design into a workable solution.

For a more detailed evaluation of the entries, clients can use an *invited competition*, in which they invite and pay a small number of architects to compete. To decide on who to invite, some clients use a *two-stage competition*. They use an open or limited competition to choose a short list of designers, who they invite to submit more detailed plans. A two-stage competition might attract entries, ideas, and allow for client and jury feedback, but it costs more, and it still suffers from many of the problems of the open competition.

Though I do not recommend competitions for complex projects, if a client wants one, I recommend a *one-stage invited* competition. The client does research and talks with various firms to select participants. If inviting national firms, the client should set up a procedure, such as the one used in the Wexner Center competition, for pairing them with local firms (familiar with local codes and construction practices). Clients should not skimp on the program, assuming the invited designers will handle it. One needs a comprehensive and specific program in advance. Such a program can improve the fit of the designer to the building purpose. Because invited competitions have a small enough number of entrants to allow in-depth evaluations, the jury can evaluate the entries relative to the program. Though knowledge of the reputation of the entrants may bias the jury evaluations, instructions from the client to the jury about adhering to the program may lessen such biases. To increase dialog during the process, the client should also provide review sessions for the designers at several points during the design process. In my interview with the architect Michael McKinnell, he described the review sessions in one competition as "extremely helpful" to both the architects and the client. To avoid favorable treatment to one designer over the others, the client could assemble questions from all of the designers up to a specified date, and then send a written response to all questions to all entrants.

### Selecting the Professional Advisor and Jury

In selecting the professional advisor and jury, the client is probably selecting the winner. According to the architect Steven Izenour, "clients who use design competitions don't understand that by picking the jury you're in effect picking the architect. You've given away the most crucial choice you have to make" (p. 198).[8] Similarly, The British Secretary of the Royal Fine Arts asserted:

> The crucial decision is to appoint the jury. If you want a Classical building set up a jury that is likely to award it to a Classicist and those people will apply. Of course, the opposite is much easier, because most architects are modernists (p. 46).[27]

For a building that works and satisfies popular values (as well as designer values), the advisor should be open to broader input on the design. The advisor must also "discipline the jurors: see to it that they do their homework and that they have a decent foundation for their decisions" (p. 184).[8] The client might explore the track record of the advisor or talk with potential advisors to find one suitable to the public purpose. Rather than having a jury dominated by architects, artists, art historians, and designers, the client should seek a jury that represents the diversity of interests and issues in the creation and use of the building. In my interview with the architect Cesar Pelli, he agreed, saying that architects no longer look at the "whole picture," the "totality" of the building. To get at the whole picture, the jury might have a "design" architect, a programmer, specialists in mechanical systems and structures, specialists in construction costs and processes, representatives of various user groups, and representatives of the client. The makeup of the jury would vary with the building purpose and competition objectives. The AIA suggests that such a jury would not attract leading designers, because they would see "design" playing a lesser role. Yes, "design" as creating an artistic statement might play a lesser role, because the jury would attend to other things as well. Whether this would restrain architects from entering remains uncertain. A *PA* poll suggests otherwise. It found that less than a third of the respondents said they considered the stature of the jurors as an important factor influencing their decision to enter a competition (p. 18).[31] An interesting problem and good program should attract entrants. To synthesize the diversity of needs into a three-dimensional building still represents a complex and interesting design problem. If competition clients took the position that solutions will be accountable to the public, this would leave little choice for the "competition-oriented" architect. Given a limited supply of available competitions, they would need to enter. If government bodies required or legislated accountability or if the federal government put together a standard set of recommendations in the same way they do for other local ordinances, accountability could become standard practice.

The selection process should avoid conflict of interest or even the appearance of any conflict of interest. For example, in The Wexner Center competition, Richard Miller, the professional advisor to the jury, was a faculty member in the School of Architecture at OSU. The Director of the School, Gerald Voss, had been the former college roommate of Eisenman, the eventual winner. Richard Cobb, chair of the jury was dean at Harvard, which had Eisenman among its faculty. Though these factors may have had no effect on the outcome, they certainly raise questions about impropriety in the expenditure of public money.

### *Prepare a Prejury Evaluation (PJE)*

Once the designers have submitted their designs, prejury evaluation (PJE) can help pick the design that will convey the desired meanings to the public. Recall that the PJE of popular reactions to the Wexner entries (Chapter 6) did better than the jury in predicting popular responses to the completed building. I describe and demonstrate many aspects of conducting a PJE in Chapter 5. Ideally, it would identify in advance the kind of meanings that the winning design should convey. One could do this by using a tested list of adjective descriptors of building meaning,[54] [123] [170] and asking people to select the adjectives that best reflect the kinds of meanings the building should convey. The PJE should also use realistic views of the designs, relevant respondents, and measures of meaning. It should use color photographs depicting comparable eye-level views of each entry. The views should have standardized sizes and graphic quality. The PJE should have respondents representative of the people who will experience the eventual building. It should have the respondents rank-order the entries on the meaning scales with the order of scales and entries varied across respondents. The scales might include judgments of preference, excitement, relaxingness, perceived status, but they might also include other scales deemed relevant to the project goals (as seen in the visual quality program). Additional questions might ask people why they responded in the way they did, what they like and dislike about each entry. This can provide specific information about the evaluation and rationale.

### *Set Up an Unbiased Jury Evaluation of the Entries*

To familiarize the jury with the project, the client should ensure that they have the program, PJE results, and in-depth site visits. Beyond that, the adviser should plan the process with care. Various aspects of the presentation and evaluation process may bias a jury decision. Just as scientists attempt to understand and systematically rule out biases in their research, competition planners should try to understand and rule out biases in the selection process. Eliminating such biases helps make the jury choice more closely reflect the quality of the entries rather than other unrelated factors. Setting up such a process should also make the competition fairer to competitors, making it more attractive to them.

The *PA* poll found that most architects (67%) noted "the assurance of fairness in rules" as an important factor influencing their decision to enter a competition (p. 18).[31]

The type of presentation and the way it is exhibited can become one possible source of bias. Jurors might choose one design over another because of the way it looks rather than quality of the design. In an interview with Anthony, the architect Rodney F. Friedman described a case where a friend said he knew he was going to win a competition due to its placement "because the secretary at the jury liked my scheme best. The staff . . . put it in the middle of the room under the brightest lights. Everybody else's proposal was somewhat in the dark" (p. 185).[8] To minimize this kind of bias, the advisor should develop standards for the size, medium and placement of presentation and hold to the standards, so that everyone submits under the same rules. This can also save time and money for the entrants. Lacking such standards, they might feel driven to spend time and resources trying to outdo the presentations of the others. In the Wexner Center competition, the university requested each entrant to submit a scale model at quarter-inch scale. The winning team built their model at half-inch scale, twice the size of the others. Though this may have given them an unfair advantage, the competition advisor did not disqualify the model. To prevent entrants from disregarding the rules, the client must not accept materials that do not fit the standards.

Another potential source of bias can arise from the order in which the entrants present their work to the jury. As James Scott, a designer with Eisenman's local partner, said in his interview, "we were . . . looking to go first so we could set the playing field. And we also wanted to go first because we could get a greater amount of set-up time." The first presenter might bias the way jurors look at subsequent entries, and the last presenter might leave them with some memorable words or images. To lessen such order effects, social science research regularly counterbalances the order of experimental conditions. For competitions, the designs are the equivalent of experimental conditions. Competitions could use a similar process in which different jurors see the entries in different orders. Instead of having entrants present their work sequentially, the advisor could set a time for competitors to stand by their entries, perhaps in different rooms. Each juror could rotate through the competitors in different orders discussing each entry. Although this would require competitors to present their work several times, it should strengthen the one-on-one dialogue about the designs. Taping such discussion would allow sharing it with other jurors or the public.

As an alternative, jury members might view videotapes of the presentation in different orders of presentation. Savvy competitors might put special efforts into putting together an impressive tape. To avoid this, the client could set up the time for presentation taping for each entry. The client would then make arrangements for a standardized taping of each presentation. After viewing the tapes, the jury could meet with each competitor to ask questions and discuss the entry. The advisor should also structure these meetings (perhaps in the poster format mentioned earlier) to minimize order effects.

To get better information about the competitors, the client and the jury could visit the offices of the invited designers, identify and interview the individuals who will work on the project, as one might do in selecting a designer in a traditional noncompetition process. As the architect Rodney Friedman said, "juries need to visit the firms to see whether they indeed have the capacity to do the work, and to make sure that they aren't smuggling in six or seven students and having them build models feverishly late at night."

Another potential source of bias relates to the evaluation criteria. The client and each juror might have different things in mind when they think of "best design." To ensure that the jury evaluates the entries on relevant criteria, the client or advisor can create a checklist of items to consider in the evaluation. The checklist should reflect major areas of the design program.

Another source of bias comes from the group process. The typical jury procedure has the jurors meet to discuss and evaluate the entries. Research suggests that the group process may skew the choice. One study examined jury decisions on funding for artists, comparing group deliberations to individual votes.[99] When the investigator polled jurors after the decisions, he found that collective deliberations did not reflect the individual opinions of the jurors as well as the individual assessment and vote did. In the group decision-making process, one or more jurors may sway the group vote away from the individuals' actual preference. As Erickson said, "The ardent campaigning of the "star" jury member for their "favorite" . . . (can win) the day" (Appendix B). To lessen this bias, the jury should make the decision via confidential individual voting that takes place several hours after the discussion.

### Use an Open Proceedings with a Formal Record

To make the results accountable to the public, the client should make all jury discussion open and available to the public. Law courts and public hearings have public records of the proceedings. Competitions could also use open proceedings with a written or taped record. The AIA recommends otherwise. In the *Handbook of Architectural Design Competitions,* the AIA states:

No one other than the jury, the professional adviser, and the adviser's official assistants should be admitted to the room. . . . Most observers of the competition process would argue . . . that *design juries must hold their deliberations in private* (p. 16).[6]

Why should competition deliberations occur behind closed doors? The AIA argues that "to expose a jury's process to public view may make sound collective judgment more difficult, if not impossible to achieve" (p. 16).[6] For a public building, the public should have the right to observe the process. This means open proceedings. One can structure the observation such that it leaves the jury undisturbed during its deliberations. As in courtrooms, the observers can follow rules that maintain order and prevent biasing influences on the jury. As a compromise, clients could use a combination of a public forum to solicit opinions and discuss various entries, and private voting for the decision making.

The taped or written records (as in court proceedings) would allow people to refer to the record. The record should go beyond the deliberations. It should also include the presentations by the designers, the jury questions and the designer answers, and decision. The jurors and client could refer to the record for clarification. The presence of the record alone could also make the experts (jurors and entrants) accountable for their statements. Lacking such a record, the public and client may hear that the jury arrived at an unanimous decision but not know how. Did the jury find none of the solutions as adequate, select the best one, and vote for it unanimously? Did one entry nudge out another in a close vote, after which the jury voted unanimously for the winner? Or did the winner emerge as the unanimous favorite on the first vote? Such information could help the client in making the final decision about how to proceed. With a record and an open proceeding, the client and others would have the needed information.

### Monitoring Design Development through Design Review

The selection of a winner is not the end of the process. It starts a new phase. The client does not have to build the winning entry as it is. Perhaps, the jury saw none of the entries as adequate, but had to choose one as the best. Even with an adequate entry, additional dialog between the client, users and designer should improve it. The Finnish model encourages dialog after the competition (p. 152).[8] In Finland, the competition winner receives the award for the project, but the design is developed further in cooperation with the competition promoter. In town planning competitions, certain elements of the winner and other entries (possibly second-and third-place entries) serve as the basis for further work on the project, with the winning team doing the work. In some large-scale urban design projects, the winning team does the master plan in cooperation with the client, and other entries do some buildings with the winner as a consultant. The winner receives the recognition, but the client retains more control of the final building. Although the AIA may want clients to build the winning entry, the client may get a better design by considering other entries, using aspects of other entries, and working closely with the designer to refine the solutions. This needs to be done with care and honesty to prevent abuse of the architects.

With the prejury evaluation, the public record of the proceedings, and the jury recommendation, the client can make an informed decision about which architect to select to design the facility. The prize money goes to the winning architect, but the client need not take the exact design. Through design review, the client can shape the design to better fit the program requirements and the needs of the client and occupants. After selecting the architect, the client must work closely with the architect to shape the design so that it works as desired. This means holding the design to the program, to the desired appearance characteristics, to the budget, and time unless a change in needs creates a change in the requirements. Consider Stanford University is process for enforcing the program through design review. Stanford requires the program to specify measurable goals and expects compliance on those goals. As part of design review, Stanford hires a cost estimator to do a mid-process cost-estimate comparison to the dollars available. The university eliminates projects and architects if they do not comply with the programmed goal expectations.

### Phase III: Monitoring After the Competition

#### Postoccupancy Evaluation (POE)

After completion and occupancy, the client should evaluate the building to see how it performs relative to the program, the jury criteria, and other (unexpected) dimensions. The client might also formally evaluate the competition process to learn what worked and what did not. Doing this can suggest ways to improve competition processes. Recall that POEs systematically evaluate projects after construction and occupancy to identify what works and what does not work for the users.[74][88][218] Taking place in the real life setting, they attempt to identify strengths and weaknesses of the facility from the perspective of the user.[88] They provide systematic and objective information about the functioning of completed and occupied facilities.[218] For design competitions, POE can also make the architect and jury accountable for building performance. POEs also identify and solve correctable problems, improve occupant attitudes, and create a knowledge base to improve the performance of future projects.[218] In doing this, they can save money. Only 2.8 percent of a building's life-cycle cost comes from construction; 3.6 percent comes from operations and maintenance; and 94 percent come from personnel.[289] Excluding wages, operating costs consume 50 to 60 percent of a building's cost over its life cycle.[210] [289] By making workers more efficient and cutting maintenance and operating costs, POE's can reduce operating costs and personnel costs. Not surprisingly, a study examining costs over many POEs found that every dollar spent on POE saved $75.[52]

According to one estimate, researchers and practitioners have done more than 50,000 POE's (Robert Bechtel telephone conversation), and many have had favorable impacts.[88] Consider some examples. In 1969, the architect–planner Oscar Newman evaluated crime in New York City public housing to develop guidelines for crime prevention through environmental design.[189] He examined crime statistics for 100 projects, finding higher crime in high-rise projects and in areas that lack natural surveillance. He compared two neighboring projects with similar tenant characteristics and physical arrangements, but different heights, and found higher rates of crime and more maintenance problems in the high-rise project. He used the analysis to develop a program for *defensible space* design that enables residents to maintain safety. Following the program, he redesigned a low-rise and a high-rise project, and tested the results. The low-rise showed a 50% reduction in crime, and increased sense of safety and control. The high-rise had less success, in part because of problems with equipment and management and security responsiveness. Newman expanded his concept to neighborhoods, introducing defensible space features into Five Oaks in Dayton, Ohio.[190] Within a year, internal traffic dropped by 67 percent, accidents by 40 percent, nonviolent crime by 24 percent, and violent crime by 50 percent. Prices for single-family homes increased by 15 percent. The decrease in crime occurred against a relatively stable rate of crime elsewhere in Dayton. Many neighborhoods have adopted his principles to create safer and higher-quality living environments.

In 1969, the landscape architect Donald Appleyard began an inquiry into the effects of traffic on neighborhoods.[11] He initially used a battery of measures to assess three San Francisco streets differing in traffic level. The measures included observations of noise level and buildings, extensive interviews to find out about street images, annoyances, activities, interference of traffic inside and outside the home, and adaptations to traffic. He discovered a host of negative qualities associated with high traffic – including less social interaction, fewer acquaintances with neighbors, heightened concern about traffic as a hazard, and more complaints about noise, dirt, and fumes. In an expanded study, he surveyed residents of twenty-one streets, and confirmed the widespread harmful effects associated with increased traffic.[11] His findings have led some cities to divert or slow down traffic in neighborhoods.

In 1971, William Whyte observed patterns of use of the plazas to see how well they worked.[301] Ten years earlier, a New York City zoning law had given developers bonuses for adding public plazas to their project. Using stop-action cameras, Whyte developed a running record of eighteen plazas. He identified several factors contributing to the rate of use, including seating, connection to the street, food, and trees. Prime among the factors was seating, or what he called *sittable space*. The more ledges, benches, steps, and places for people to sit, the higher the levels of use. Whyte followed this analysis with a POE of one extremely successful park. Supplementing the film records with interviews and on-site observation, he discovered some features of that park that contributed to its success. New York City used his findings to program the quality of future plazas. The city amended the zoning law to require plazas to have Whyte's features to quality for the bonus. Whyte also used the findings to program the redesign of one plaza, which he then evaluated after completion. His research succeeded in transforming dead and unsafe public spaces into spaces contributing to the vitality of the city.

Several government agencies have adopted POEs as a routine procedure, in part for cost savings.[40] The Federal Bureau of Prisons used POE to evaluate and refine the design of its jails. In the early 1970s, the Bureau constructed and evaluated two correctional centers, one in New York and one in Chicago. The POE team, led by psychologist Rich Wener, interviewed designers, inmates and staff members, observed the behavior of inmates and staff, and examined institutional records.[296] The Bureau used the POE information to guide the program and design of the new Contra Costa County detention center (California) that opened in 1981. POEs of this jail three years and eight years after it opened revealed a functional success.[317] Although the inmate population had doubled the intended capacity, the jail still earned high scores for safety and satisfaction from management, deputies, and inmates. It had relatively low levels of vandalism and repair costs; and it scored better than other recently build jails, even though all but one of them had not exceeded their intended capacity.

In the private sector, the Marriott Corporation used POEs to program the design for its courtyard hotels. POEs identified one important cost saving. Hotel guests disliked narrower rooms, but did not notice decreases in room length. "A reduction of 18 inches in each room of a 150-room hotel" saves Marriott "$80,000 . . . (in 1985 dollars)" (p. 15)[225] A five-year POE of more than seventy offices with responses from more than 5,000 workers identified ways to improve productivity, job satisfaction and performance through design.[33] A POE on hospitals also pointed to efficiencies. The research team evaluated three layouts – radial, single corridor, and double corridor.[279] They found that the radial design had fewer absences and accidents, and saved the nurses time moving between the nursing station and patients. In that design, each nurse spent 97 hours per year more time with the patients. The findings led many hospitals and intensive care units to adopt the radial plan. Another study in hospitals also produced widely used findings.[294] Hospitals have experienced pressure to shorten patient stays, because various programs pay them a fixed amount regardless of how long a patient stays. The study found that hospitals could shorten patient recovery time (and thus cut costs) by giving patients rooms with views to nature.[284]

POEs also have unique value for competition architecture. They can make the jury and architect more accountable for the project's performance and they can improve our understanding of the actual performance of these public projects. Because competition buildings tend to involve complex or new building tasks for many users,[215] the chances for problems increase. Finding and correcting those problems can have greater consequences.

Investigators have published few if any POE's of competition architecture. With a record of POEs on competition architecture, we can start to build up a better knowledge base about the performance of competitions. One can supplement this information with evaluations of the process by jurors, entrants and others involved in the competition. Such information can help improve future design competitions.

In sum, if clients want a good building from a competition, they should develop a comprehensive program, manage the jury to follow the program in an unbiased way, and evaluate the building after occupancy. In managing the jury process, they should select the appropriate kind of competition and the appropriate kind of advisor and jury, prepare a PJE, set up an unbiased evaluation of the entries, use an open procedure with a formal record, and monitor the design development.

Even for a competition that does not follow all of the steps, the PJE could improve the competition product. Assessing consumer reactions should also improve future designs and competitions, as it does in industry with the widespread use of consumer evaluations of products. Public information about performance, from consumer surveys such as those in *Consumer Reports*, has had some success in leading producers to improve their products for consumers. Perhaps, similar results will apply to architecture.

# 9

# TOWARD A NEW
# DEMOCRATIC
# ARCHITECTURE

We can follow one of two roads. The one we have followed so far, of having artists choose what is best for people, has left many communities with costly oddities that neither work nor have appeal for most people. The other road offers a chance to reach a more desirable place, one in which the public and users derive enjoyment from design. If, after looking at the signature architecture and public art in our communities, we conclude that we deserve something better, then we should no longer accept the counsel of those who insist on the primacy of elitist artistic statements. We should follow a more democratic course that values public meanings and needs in all phases of the project. This requires consideration of public meanings in programming, design review, and POE. We should also broaden our perspective from competition architecture to architecture and public art.

Noncompetition design may follow a course similar to competitions. When a client hires a designer, or when a community empowers a panel of artists to pick a public sculpture or artist for one, the client or community may hesitate to meddle with the expertise of the artist. As with competition architecture, this can result in flawed solutions. Although the artists may sense the state of "high" art, they do not know – or, in many cases, care – about popular meanings. In opting for elite artistic statements, they may neglect human and technical concerns and misjudge or overlook the likely public meanings. The result may satisfy the aesthetic standards of some artists, but convey unfavourable meanings to others.

Most U.S. cities have design review boards, which regularly make judgments about designs to improve the appearance of the designs and the community.[137] (In design review, plans for a new structure or changes to an existing structure must receive approval from the design review board, before they can proceed). Although communities empower design review boards to act for a public interest, research shows that their decisions fail to have the intended effects on perceived appearance. Five studies of the performance of design review found low correlations between the decisions of blue-ribbon juries, or design review boards and public preferences.[263] [264] [265] The judgments of the boards differ from those of the public they serve. In contrast, research shows high correlations between initial public preferences and subsequent public responses to completed buildings.[264] [265]

The broad framework I propose for competitions also bears on noncompetition design, design review, and solicitation of proposals. The three phases – programming, design review, and postoccupancy evaluation – represent an integrated set or holistic model for planned changes. The model is a master guide for the future of all kinds of planned changes in the physical environment. Although some of the actions do not apply to noncompetition architecture, the three-phase framework does. Underlying the framework is a different attitude toward design – a democratic one.

### Democratic Architecture

Much architectural design rests on formalistic approach – an authoritarian, top-down, and exclusive orientation that values monumental and costly artistic statements. To get more pleasing design products, we must move toward an approach driven by democratic values. Table 9.1 shows some of the changes such a move entails. A democratic approach replaces authoritarian, top-down, and exclusive decisions with democratic, bottom-up, inclusive decisions. It replaces monumental and costly artistic statements with human-oriented, lower-cost solutions concerned with context and popular meanings.

The three phases of the broad framework conform with a democratic approach. *Programming* involves the users and produces design guidelines that respond to their requirements; *design review* monitors and shapes the design to embody the qualities desired by the people who will live with it; and *postoccupancy evaluation* assesses the results to improve current and future designs for people. Each of the actions described in the previous chapter also advance a democratic approach. Beyond programming and postoccupancy evaluation, the actions for managing the jury rest on democratic values. Establishing a structure for an *in-depth evaluation* helps ensure that the jury can look beyond artistic statements to do a comprehensive evaluation of the entries. *Selecting a diverse jury and an advisor* attempts to democratize the jury and open the process to value popular meanings and concerns. *Prejury evaluation* brings information on popular meaning to the jury. The use of an *unbiased evaluation process* should lessen potential biases and give

Table 9.1. *Differences between the formalistic and democratic design approaches* (adapted from Francis[71] and Sommer[258]).

| Formalistic Design | Democratic Design |
|---|---|
| Authoritarian | Democratic |
| Top-down design | Bottom-up design |
| Exclusive | Inclusive |
| Decisions come from the designer | User and client involvement |
| Monumental | Human-oriented |
| High cost | Low cost |
| Concerned with Artistic Statement | Concerned with meaning and context |

the jury a democratic vote. *Open proceedings with a formal record* is a central component of a democratic process.

The broad framework also applies to noncompetition projects and public art. Rather than relying on hunches of artists, clients, communities and design review boards can use scientific procedures (like those described in Chapter 4) to *program* guidelines for the desired appearance. They can *manage the process* by maintaining an active roll in picking a designer with the skills and inclination to listen, to involve them in a participatory process and to heed their needs. To help guide *design review*, they can use procedures similar to the PJE to gauge likely meanings conveyed by a design or design alternatives; and through monitoring the plans, they can push the designer to satisfy the program requirements. For an example of the importance of championing the program requirements, consider the chemistry laboratory addition discussed in Chapter 6. It had the best score for visual quality of the seven OSU buildings I evaluated for visual quality. Paul Young, a member of the office of the University Architect, told me that the desirable appearance resulted from the University Architect's office pushing the commissioned architectural firm to comply with the program and the campus master plan. The firm's first design differed substantially from the one eventually approved by the University Architect. Perhaps learning from the Wexner experience, the University Architect pushed the firm through repeated versions of design. The firm eventually replaced its lead designer with one willing to heed the university's requests for a design more compatible with the surroundings, a design that the public now enjoys.

As with competitions, after completion and occupancy of the building, clients, and communities can monitor the result through *postoccu-*

*pancy evaluation.* This can identify ways to improve appearance, and often, it can develop low-cost improvements. The POE of the math tower (Chapter 6) pointed to vegetation and a more pedestrian friendly plaza as ways to improve the image of the building. The university has implemented both recommendations. Institutional and corporate clients who build many buildings can also use the POE results as pre-design research for programming new facilities. POE's of design review identify shortcomings and specific directions to improve future results.[263] [264] [265]

### Awards for Democratic Designs

My suggestions for improvement go beyond the specific design process to community actions and design education. At a community scale, POE can take the form of an alternative kind of design award. Design awards, critics and professional design magazines typically follow a formalistic approach praising the artistic statement seen in photos, prior to the opening and occupancy of the facility, and often before construction. Though such assessments may reflect and shape designer values,[161] they miss the actual day-to-day performance of places. Because design magazines sell advertising to industry selling building products, they encounter a conflict of interest. When they show an artistic picture of the building, usually with no person in sight,[161] they highlight the items their advertisers sell. Criticism of the performance of these products would cut their advertising revenue.

Communities can balance the formalistic awards and criticism with more democratic awards that recognize the actual performance of places for the users and public. The psychologist Robert Sommers suggested that no one could nominate a building for an award until twelve months after it has opened and until someone has systematically obtained opinions of building occupants (p. 136).[258] These kinds of awards would consider the meanings of the place, how well it fit its context, how well it worked, how much the inhabitants like it, and how well it fulfills their day-to-day needs.

Some local and national awards have begun to do this. Started in 1985, The Rudy Bruner Award for Excellence in the Urban Environment emphasizes the actual performance of places. It invites nominations for a variety of urban places in North America. The jury consists of experts on design research and on human behavior and environment. The jurors visit the sites, interview people, observe use, and bring their expertise to bear on selecting the innovative applications of design research to produce successful places for people.

Massachusetts set up a Governor's Design Awards Program. This program sought projects "comprehensively beneficial to their users, viewers, and the surrounding built and natural environment" (p. 114).[19] It took nominations from citizens, designers, and developers for their favorite projects. Regional juries, consisting of an architect, a landscape architect, a city planner, a historic preservation expert, and a member of the Regional Advisory Panel, visited the projects and spoke to the users. The regional juries passed on regional winners and rationale for the selections to the state-level jury. The state gave awards at five regional ceremonies and one statewide ceremony, and they publicized the awards with an exhibition of the winners that traveled around the state. Winners included such popular places as Heritage State Parks, the Boston Public Library, and Faneuil Hall Marketplace.

San Diego has the Orchid and Onion awards that take nominations from the public in a variety of design categories.[8] A jury of the public and professionals decide on the best (orchid) and worst (onion) places that get cited at a formal banquet. The Recchie Awards, in Columbus, Ohio, also takes nominations from the public and design firms. The Recchie Awards broadens the emphasis from architecture to all kinds and sizes of popular places. In addition to buildings, they have considered such places as parks, playgrounds, and highway entrances. Jury members visit the sites, talk with users, and report back to one another before making the choice. In 1997, the *Environmental Design Research Association* and *Places* magazine received funding from the Graham Foundation to start a national Design Research Awards program. As with the Recchie Awards, this program considers all kinds of places, but it does so at a national scale. Nominations can come from the public, civic groups, and designers. The nominations must document the extent to which the design enriches the users. A diverse jury of design researchers, public officials, and design professionals evaluate the entries. As with competition juries, the results of any such jury deliberations depends on the criteria and quality of the jury. With a well-managed process, these kinds of awards can bring attention to the real consumer successes, which can serve as models for successful development elsewhere.

### Balance in Architectural Education

Architectural education needs some adjustment to help produce future architects supportive of democratic values in design. Architectural education is out of balance. A Carnegie Foundation report found architecture faculty and students "too often disconnected from other disciplines, . . . remote from the concerns of clients, communities or the larger challenges of the human condition" (p. xvi). The report goes on to state: "The gulf dividing architecture schools and practice has grown perilously wide" (p. xvi).[35] Written by Ernest Boyer (president of the foundation until he died) and Lee Mitgang (a senior fellow at the foundation), the report resulted from a 30-month study of architectural education. The Boyer-Mitgang team read accreditation reports of approximately fifty architecture schools and participated in an accreditation visit. They visited twenty-four architectural firms and fifteen accredited architectural programs for several days each. They interviewed 300 students, 50 faculty, and 25 deans and department chairs at those programs and received mail surveys back from approximately 500 students, faculty and alumni of those programs. They also received 80 replies to surveys mailed to deans and chairs of all 103 accredited architecture programs in the United States. The Carnegie report called for a more balanced curriculum and a more applied as opposed to theoretical orientation of the design studios.

The typical curriculum emphasizes design over the technical aspects of architecture and stresses the building as an art object. The emphasis on "design" as art in architecture was born with the Ecole des Beaux Arts in Paris and strengthened with the Bauhaus school of design in Germany. The artistic emphasis came to the United States almost 100 years ago. Prior to that, architectural curricula did not treat design as sacrosanct. At the turn of the century, design was treated as the least important aspect of the architectural curriculum. By 1930, it had risen to the top, where it remains today.[8] Walk into most architectural schools in the United States or look at the brochures they send to perspective students and you will see abstract designs with little connection to everyday reality. Studio instructors socialize the student's values toward a professional ethos rejecting popular culture and the nondesign or technical aspects of architecture.[58] Research has shown how the values of students can shift in response to such an emphasis,[161] and it reveals a shift in values as architecture students advance through their architectural education. As they advance, they tend to respond more negatively to popular and vernacular designs.[223] Today, the formalistic concepts and practices imported from less democratic societies do not apply. The Carnegie report notes that students complain about studios as being "more about personalities than principles, a place where the ideology of the instructor became the true curriculum" (p. 87), and most faculty and alumni agree that studios failed to "integrate key aspects of practice." (p. 87).[35] Research on the design studio found that "many practicing architects felt that their schools had shortchanged them in nondesign topics" such as how buildings get built (p. 23).[35] None "felt

Table 9.2. *Steps toward a more democratic architecture.*

1. Balance design education
2. Programming
   - Program desired popular meanings and visual quality
3. Design review
   - Conduct popular evaluations of a design or design proposals
   - Monitor design development relative to the program
4. Postoccupancy evaluation (predesign research)
   - Evaluate meaning and visual quality of completed project and revise where possible
   - Have community and national recognition of democratic design

that the schools had provided too little training in design" (p. 23).[35] A *PA* poll also looked into the question of design education. *PA* summarized the results with a quote from an architect who described architectural education as "too removed from reality," and the design emphasis as "totally inappropriate for a field full of technical, management and construction-related challenges" (p 92).[221] Boyer and Mitgang agree, concluding that the "method and climate at most schools might be contributing to a disdain for technical and practice oriented topics" (p. 23).[35] They call for a greater emphasis on the public needs of health, safety, and welfare that remain part of licensing laws in most states (p. 33), on "how environments affect human well being, productivity and happiness (p. 38), on "preservation and restoration" in cities (p. 41), and "sustainable design" (p. 44) to help preserve the planet. They stress a redefinition of the design studio away from "design" as "aesthetic and theoretical" to design as the "integration of knowledge" (p. 73). In sum, the Carnegie report on architectural education calls for a more democratic approach to design.

Although following the democratic framework may not guarantee more humane designs, it make such designs more likely. Table 9.2 summarizes my recommendations for achieving this end. A process that attends to more than the artistic statement should yield solutions that go beyond such statements. Balancing design education can help produce architects open to a broader approach. Involving the public in the process, assessing public preferences, developing a program and a visual quality program, and monitoring design development should produce more satisfactory solutions. Monitoring the performance of projects after construction and publicizing projects that work for the public has an educational value that can lead to improvements in the future. Greater emphasis by communities on democratic design and by architectural education on a balanced education can make such designs more likely. For clients, these actions can produce efficient products that convey desired meanings. For designers, these actions may renew public interest and attention to design. For the public, these actions can make places and communities more livable. All groups can win.

# APPENDIX A

## THE USE OF THE PREJURY EVALUATION

For the PJE and to get at the public image of the Wexner competition entries, I interviewed a small sample of people about their reactions to the entries. Before advocating the use of the method, we needs to look at its value. This has three components. (1) How *reliable* is the method? This refers to the consistency of judgments. Just as a yardstick should consistently measure distances in similar conditions, measures of public response should produce consistent results. If they did not, we could not rely on the measures as useful. (2) What is the *validity* or truthfulness of the conclusions? This refers to the degree to which the differences in response to the entries result from their design and the degree to which the differences apply to real-world conditions. (3) How *useful* is the method? This refers to the value of the effort and resources relative to the results obtained. In sum, we want to know if the results of a PJE have value in guiding competition decisions, and if they are worth the effort.

### Reliability

Did people respond consistently? Contrary to the popular view of preferences and meaning as highly variable across people, the respondents showed strong agreement. I compared the responses of alumni, faculty, students, and residents, and I compared the responses of males and females. The rankings by the various groups showed strong similarities, particularly for the most liked entries. Tests for differences between the groups found little difference in response (see sidebar; see also Appendix C, Table C.7). The tests found minor differences between males and females on two items. Otherwise, both males and females ranked Erickson first, Kallmann second, and Graves third. Alumni, faculty, students, and residents concurred in selecting Erickson as the best. Three of the four groups ranked Kallmann as second and Eisenman as fourth. Overall, each group agreed on the meanings conveyed by the entries.

## SOME MINOR GROUP DIFFERENCES

For the item "acknowledges the importance of the landscape," females ranked Eisenman significantly less favorably than did males ($Z = 2.00$, 1 df, $p < .05$). For the item "adventurous and challenging," females ranked Graves significantly more favorably than did males ($Z = 2.05$, 1 df, $p < .05$). Students ranked Kallmann as tied with Erickson for best; alumni and faculty ranked Kallmann as second, and residents ranked it fourth. All groups ranked the winning Eisenman design as fourth best, except for the residents who ranked it second. Females ranked Pelli fourth and Eisenman fifth, and males did the reverse, but this difference only achieved marginal significance ($Z = -1.85$, 1 df, $p = .065$).

Tests of similarities across groups and individuals also revealed strong consensus in response (sidebar). I looked at Pearson correlations between group ranks for each scale. The correlations between the resulting sets of seventy-five rank scores for each group confirmed similarities in response across the groups. The results showed high correlations between responses of the males and females and among the four respondent groups: alumni, residents, students, and faculty. I also tested the degree to which each individual agreed with the others in their judgments. Again, the results showed evidence of agreement in response across the respondents.

## AGREEMENT AMONG GROUPS AND INDIVIDUALS

The analyses revealed highly significant Pearson correlations on the scores of each group compared: Males and females ($r = 0.71$, $p < .01$), alumni and faculty ($r < 0.78$, $p < .01$), alumni and students ($r = 0.51$, $p < .01$), alumni and residents ($r = 0.35$, $p < .01$), students and faculty ($r = .56$, $p < .01$), students and residents ($r = 0.41$, $p < .01$).

Across the full sample, respondents showed fairly high agreement in their responses. One can see this in the Cronbach alpha interobserver reliability coefficients[56] of 0.81 for Eisenman, 0.80 for Kallmann, 0.80 for Pelli, 0.77 for Erickson, and 0.75 for Graves.

The findings agree with a large body of research finding consistencies in people's evaluations of places.[38] [129] [174] People agreed in their evaluations of the five entries. This not only indicates the reliability of the measures, but it also indicates that the PJE can safely use the composite data from the full sample.

### Validity

Two questions have bearing on the validity of the findings: (1) To what extent do differences in the competition entries (the independent variable) cause changes in response (the dependent variable)? (2) To what extent do the findings apply to the real situation, population, and responses of interest (i.e., people's natural responses to the completed building)? The first question refers to the PJE's *internal validity*, and the second refers to its *external (or ecological) validity*.

### Internal Validity: Did the Designs Make the Difference?

Did the five designs or some other factor account for the difference in scores across the entries? To answer this, I looked at the sampling, presentation of entries, and measurement of meaning. The evidence suggests that the differences in scores resulted from differences in the meanings of the designs.

*Sampling.* I used an experimental design (called repeated measure design), in which each person evaluated all five entries. As all respondents rated all of the designs, the results do not have biases from different groups in the different conditions. The sample of 65 persons also exceeds the minimum number of persons needed for statistical comparisons between the entries. A sample of 30 would have met the statistical assumptions for the parametric test of differences across the conditions; and research shows it as a large enough sample to obtain an effect.[261] The comparisons of responses across subgroups (such as males and females) may have benefited from a larger sample in each group, but for the desired comparisons among the entries, the PJE had an adequate sample. Sample size also has relevance to the generality of the findings, discussed later.

*Presentation of Entries.* For control, the raters should see similar material for each entry. To find out about differences in responses to the designs, one needs to minimize differences in depiction or viewing angle. For Wexner, the designers used different presentation media and styles, which could bias responses. Presumably, a competition should pick a design for its content, not the quality of the presentation. Although the submission guidelines did not standardize the presentation and views, the PJE did assemble comparable images and views.

Rather than bringing the original drawings and models to participants, I used photographs of the materials. Each respondent saw seven
photographs (four in color and three in black and white) of each entry.
The photographs of each entry showed comparable views from the
west, east, south, north, northeast, southwest, and overhead. For each
entry, the seven photographs, mounted in the same order on a board,
captured much of the presentation materials in a standardized way.
Still, differences in presentation graphics rather than the design could
bias the rankings. (For juries a similar bias may occur). Though I did
not test for this potential bias, other research did. It has found that the
design itself accounts for more of the variation in response than does
mode of presentation.[262] Though graphics may have influenced the
respondents, it probably had a minor influence compared to the
design; and if clients standardize entry requirements, they can heighten
the influence of the design.

*Measuring Building Meaning.* The interview had respondents
rank each entry relative to fifteen statements about building meaning.
Respondents saw each statement on a separate index card. The interviewer varied the order of cards by mixing them and drawing one at
random. The interviewer also varied the order of the five boards depicting the entries. Presenting one card and one board, the interviewer
asked respondents to give their honest opinion of the entries by placing
them in order relative to the statement on the card. The interviewer
repeated the procedure for all fifteen scales. Varying the order of
boards and questions across respondents lessened potential biases from
question order and recency effects.

The PJE could have used other kinds of scaling procedures. For example, it could have had respondents rate each entry on a set of semantic
differential items (such as pleasant–unpleasant, novel–commonplace, or
exiting–dull). It could have presented respondents with a list of adjectives
(such as pleasant, unpleasant, novel, commonplace, exciting, dull) and
have them check the adjectives that apply to each entry. Instead, it had
people rank the entries on various items. Research shows that rank-order
procedures yield results similar to and consistent with those obtained
through the other scaling procedures.[38] [85] With twenty or more respondents, the information approximates metric measures allowing estimates
of intervals between points. It has the added benefit of getting responses
more efficiently and getting greater agreement among observers.[55] Rank-
order scales are an efficient way to get rich data.

*Summing It Up.* The PJE controlled for potential biases, such as
order of presentation, scales, selectivity, mortality, and experimenter

cues. In spite of possible differences in graphics, research suggests that the designs account for most of the variance in response. The results should reflect the raters' impressions of the designs. It yields reliable information about ranking of the entries.

### External Validity: To What Extent Do the Results Apply?

The findings reported in earlier chapters suggest that the PJE results did generalize. Chapter 2 showed longitudinal data indicating that decisions of competitions juries and experts do not lead public taste, but that scientific study of popular preferences did hold over time. Chapter 6 showed that the PJE accurately forecast subsequent popular reactions. Still, we should look at the method to evaluate its generality. To establish the degree to which the methods support the generalization of the findings, I consider the respondents, presentation of the entries, and measures.

*Respondents.* Several aspects of the sample have bearing on its generality: the sampling procedure, sample size, replacement of nonresponses, and the proportion of nonresponse. For purposes of application, the respondents should come from groups and individuals likely to experience the design. The groups in the sample represented potential users of and visitors to the Wexner Center. The PJE sampled respondents from four groups: OSU students, faculty, alumni, and local residents in Columbus, Ohio. Students, faculty and residents would pass by the Center regularly. Alumni might see it during a visit, and the university might ask them, along with the other groups, to donate money to it. A more diverse sample might have also included other groups, such as tourists, who might experience the facility. Still, the sample captured representatives of most user groups.

The sample size also has relevance for generality. In evaluating the size of the sample, one should think about the purpose of the research. The PJE did not need the kind of precision of political polls, where the pollster can report the percentage in favor of each candidate, the margin of error, and the probability of getting that error. This kind of precision would require a much larger sample. As the precise percentages have less importance than the relative scores for the entries, the PJE can use a smaller sample. It had enough respondents to make the statistical comparisons. Nevertheless, I would have preferred a larger sample to allow for more precise estimates of the responses of the population.

We should also look at the process of selecting respondents to see how well they represent the populations to which we want to generalize. For representativeness, some form of *probability sample* is recommended.

It allows one to estimate the probability that any individual or group of individuals had of getting into the sample. The PJE used two kinds of probability samples – a *stratified random sample* and a *cluster sample*. Faculty and alumni were selected at random from directories, phoned to request participation, and visited for the interview. This represents a *stratified random sample* in that the population was split into relatively homogenous groups or strata where responses across groups may vary. Then a *random sample* was drawn from each stratum. For residents (another stratum), districts or clusters in the city were selected on the basis of location – north, east, south, west, and central city. Within each district, four houses were chosen at random for interviews. This represents a *cluster sampling* approach. In each case, the PJE obtained a probability sample.

The process for replacing nonresponses can also affect generality. For the random sample, replacements were selected at random. For the cluster sample, if no one came to the door, the interviewer visited two more times at different times of day. If no one appeared after three visits, the interviewer picked a neighboring house for the interview. Research indicates that this approach to replacement may produce better results than those obtained by selecting the replacement at random.[272] As a form of a *probability sample*, these kinds of samples have strong external validity.

I could not get a probability sample for one stratum – students – because no directory listed all students on and off campus. Instead, the PJE sampled students at four campus sites. I picked a variety of sites on different parts of campus to get a more representative sample. I eliminated further bias, by using a random selection procedure to select participants at each site. Still, because this is a *nonprobability sample*, I do not know how well it represents the full population of students. Yet, there is little reason to suspect that the diverse student sample would differ from the full population of students.

Nonresponse could potentially make the responses of a sample differ from those of the population. The PJE obtained high rates of participation from each group. More than 90 percent of those contacted agreed to participate. Unfortunately, of the eighty people interviewed, I had to drop 19 percent for problems in their completion of the survey. The percentage of nonusable forms varied from 15 percent for faculty to 20 percent for alumni, residents, and students. Thus, the analysis relied on data from approximately 77 percent of those contacted. If the remaining 23 percent differed from the others, the results may not apply to the population.

In sum, the sample is representative on most counts, though it may have some possible biases from nonresponse and nonrepresentative sampling of students. It does more closely reflect the public than did the jury of experts and outsiders.

*Presentation of Entries.* Respondents judged the entries seen in photographs. Though this simulation lacks the movement and sound present in the real place,[12 79 230] jurors see the same kind of material. In choosing views to show, I used realistic eye-level views that represent the views users would have approaching and walking around the building. Research consistently shows that responses to such views depicted in color slides or photographs accurately reflect on-site experience.[64 102 120 203 247 249 318] A review of more than 152 environments evaluated by more than 2,400 observers found that preferences for places shown in photographs correlated highly with preferences on-site to the same places.[263] If the completed building remains true to the design, the responses to the photographs of the entries should accurately reflect responses to it.

*Measuring Building Meaning.* For external validity, the PJE should measure responses relevant to what people would experience when encountering the completed buildings. Because four items (pleasant, active, exciting, and relaxing) come from research on dimensions of emotional meaning,[238] the PJE did capture relevant dimensions of evaluative response. The remaining eleven items come from the jury report describing their rationale for choosing the winning entry. The items measure various connotative meanings representing the jury's interpretation of inferences the public would make about the design. I could have measured response to these items in several ways. I used the rank-order procedure, in part, because it closely reflects the comparative decisions used by a jury.

The self-report verbal measures alone may identify responses lacking in emotional involvement. One could supplement verbal measures with physiological measures, unobtrusive measures of behavior, or questions about how much people care about the building meaning. Still, the verbal measures do reveal the direction of the popular opinions about the entries.

### Usefulness of the Method

The method proved efficient. Each survey took about five minutes to complete. People readily completed the rankings and they seemed to enjoy doing it. For a relatively small investment of time, the method succeeded in obtaining popular meanings for the entries. The rank-order method could work well with larger sets of entries, as well. Several studies have had respondents rank-order or categorize up to sixty scenes.[85] [164] [167] With more entries, the PJE might reduce the number of scales to prevent the interview from taking too long. It can still obtain popular meanings for the entries in an efficient manner.

### Future Research

From the studies of one competition, I cannot say with certainty how well the method and pattern of findings will generalize to other competitions. However, the validity of the methods and other empirical evidence of differences between designers and nondesigners suggest that the pattern of results does apply. I would like to see additional tests of PJE for other competitions. Research also could look into whether the size or purpose of the project or the makeup of the jury makes a difference. It could evaluate the use of PJE for other kinds of building purposes and for other kinds of design competitions, such as those in interior design, landscape architecture, or urban design. It could evaluate the applicability of PJE to other countries, such as Germany, which have different approaches to design competitions.

Research could also look at several methodological questions to help refine the use of PJE. For example, it could look at the relative merits of obtaining scores through ranking, semantic differential scales, or checklists. It could consider what mode of presentation and viewing angle would best generalize to the eventual responses to the completed building. It could look at physiological and behavioral responses. It could also evaluate various approaches to sampling. Is an opportunity sample of likely passerby adequate? Are samples large enough to make precise estimates of population opinions worth the extra time and expense? One might also want to compare the results of PJEs based on reviews of the research versus popular surveys. How can one best prepare jurors to make judgments that more closely reflect popular appraisals? Do the various processes that I recommend for running a competition bring about better results? How does open versus closed deliberation influence the jury choice? Sponsors might also want to know if and under what conditions the presentation of PJE results to a jury would affect their choice. Though researchers have examined some of these questions in other domains, knowledge for competitions would rest on more solid ground with the direct study of competitions.

The most pressing topics include examining PJEs in other contexts, looking at the character of entrants in competitions with juries not dominated by designers, examining the effectiveness of the proposed variations in the jury process, and evaluating the design merits in PJE buildings over the long term.

# APPENDIX B

## COMMENTS ON DESIGN COMPETITIONS BY PARTICIPANTS IN THE WEXNER CENTER COMPETITION

This appendix presents excerpts from interviews with the Wexner Center competitors and with Leslie Wexner, the benefactor. The interviews come from several sources. I interviewed Leslie Wexner and four of the five national architects competing in the Wexner competition by phone. (My attempts to interview Michael Graves did not succeed). Unfortunately, portions of my interview with Wexner were lost through problems in taping over the phone. Following each interview, I sent each person a transcript for their approval or final editing. Eisenman, Erickson, and Pelli did some minor editing on the transcript. My doctoral student Peg Grannis interviewed three of the Ohio architects in person. She also showed them the text of the interviews for their approval. We asked the participants what they liked about design competitions and what they disliked about them, and what they liked and disliked about the Wexner Center competition. The interviews also had an open-ended format to probe for more information. Additional information comes from two sources: an interview by David Goldblatt and Kay Bea Jones with Peter Eisenman about the Wexner Center competition,[83] and interviews by Kathryn Anthony with architects about design juries in education and practice.[8] I reprint those portions of her interviews with the Wexner competitors Eisenman, Graves, and Cesar Pelli that had to do with design competitions. She asked what they felt about competitions, what advice they had to improve juries in professional practice, and what words of wisdom they had for competitors to catch the eye of the jury.

From these sources, this appendix includes comments by Leslie Wexner, each of the five national finalists – Eisenman, Erickson, Graves, McKinnell, and Pelli – and three of their local partners – James Scott (a designer with Trott, the local partner of Eisenman), Mark Feinknopf (the local partner of Erickson), and Chuck Nitschke (the local partner of Kallmann, McKinnell and Wood).

### *Les Wexner, President, The Limited*

The structure of that competition – the jury selection, the jury, I had no concern in that . . . The most important buildings in the university to me, buildings that have a meeting place, might be the Arts Center or the Faculty club, and they still do. That's where you can have an inter-disciplinary dialogue.

I did not see the spec. So I don't know what the university requested. When I came to be aware of the project, the building had been designed. And in my judgment (my avocation is an architect and I had certainly known Dick Trott,) so I was happy that he was involved, and subsequently Peter Eisenman. Both of them wanted me to kind of act as the client, because I was the benefactor . . . I didn't really understand that they didn't have a client. The university as a client is deadly. I thought that as the benefactor, the creative work of the architect should be respected. So I didn't want to be the client. I thought that would be unfair. In hindsight, I should have been the client. Without me, they had none, and I think the flow and systemic problems were driven by aesthetic, creative ideas rather than practical things that a more practi-cal kind of person would notice.

I've only been in the building a couple of times. Dick probably more than Peter really wanted pushback and client involvement. It seems like every two weeks, I would get a plan or Dick would call me and say you know, you really should get involved.

The process is only as good as the jury's understanding of what's dri-ving the project. And I think this project was driven by an aesthetic intellectual idea, and no one ever said it. It's funny, I would never have hired him on my own. If I were looking to hire an architect or designer for the university and I made a list of architects, Peter Eisenman would be the last one on the list. Theoretical architecture for institutions is not something that would last over the years.

I never even read the charge to the jury. It's too late, and I didn't think about it. The notion that a building has to work practically. . . . It has to be attractive to park. It has to have low maintenance. . .

Peter Eisenman is a great salesman. He's Richard Meier's cousin and I think he suffers from that . . . He's one of the few people I've met who talks about his *psychiatrists*. . .

Its hard for an architect to do good work without a client, and institu-tions as clients are no good. Is there a person or persons who understand architecture, design, space, reverse space? They didn't have that. None of them understand anything about architecture. . . .

When you sit down to write the spec, it should have a user, a builder, people involved.

### Peter Eisenman, Principal, Eisenman Architects, New York City

Rather than accepting site and boundaries of objects and sites it [the Wexner Center] "breaks between." In other words, it takes two buildings which were joined and breaks them apart and opens up the site and makes it by traditional standards, a nonbuilding. The idea of the Wexner Center was not to make yet another object-shelter-enclosure as dominant values. And the Wexner Center is a fracturing of a dominant enclosing building, both in terms of the armory, which is fractured into pieces in terms of the two existing buildings, which then are fractured apart and itself becomes a remnant. And the site is full of remnants and that was an attitude that one had been working with for a number of years, this breaking down of the traditional envelope (p.282).[83]

I can't tell you the reason but I have a sense that people are going to react to the Wexner Center. They can't help but react. It is something very physical, no matter what the theory. They don't have to know any theory to go in there. I've heard that many students hate the building. They don't know the theory and they hate it. They don't hate the theory of the building. The hate something about that building that is very disquieting to them. To their idea of what buildings are. So obviously it is affecting them in a very real way. I mean, if they were neutral to the building this would be different, right? Or if they said, "Oh, that's nice." But they don't like it. Now, they have not been taught to like it and if they don't like it for very good reasons it is because in that building is an aesthetic of "not like" in a certain way. But it also releases, if you are willing to go with it, another aesthetic of an enormous pleasure at the same time (interview by Goldblatt and Jones, pp. 289–290).[83]

I believe open competitions are great for young architects. But I think professional design competitions are also abusive. I think I would never enter an open competition again because it's too costly, I think that closed competitions abuse architects, since they are not paid a realistic fee. However, I think they often produce very exciting buildings because you don't have the client limiting you. So I think competitions are good as long as you have a good jury and you have a proper fee. But they're not very good otherwise (interview by Anthony, p. 183).[8]

In my telephone interview, Eisenman said:

Competitions have their good and bad points, both from the architects' and the clients' point of view. In a competition, architects are pressed to do their best work. They have to think about what they can do to win. It is very different working to win than when an architect already has a commission. Architects very often produce their best work in a competition. On the other hand, the client is often stuck with something that he or she does not want, because the client has no input in the process. When there is a sophisticated client, even without a competition that client can bring out what a competition brings out. If there is no sophisticated client, even a good winning project may get slowly eroded by all of the bureaucratic middle managers who do not have ownership of the design. Competitions are for owners willing to take risks; they represent long-term investment. Unless a competition is limited, most signature architects will not go into them because losing to a student or a young architect has no reward. Often it depends on the kind of jury. One gets quite knowledgeable about which competitions to enter and which to avoid.

Competitions therefore work best at both ends of the scale: At one end, they push well-known signature architects to do more than mediocre work, and at the other end of the scale, they discover new talent that may not get a commission without winning one. I recommend competitions to young architects who could not get such a commission in any other way. For myself, I am very careful about going into competitions because they take an enormous amount of energy and time. For a $25,000 invited competition, we figure on spending at least $50,000 more. For example, the one that Richard Meier and I did for the Church of the Year 2000, his model alone cost $25,000. If you go into a high-stakes poker game with Richard Meier, Cesar Pelli, and Frank Gehry, you had better be prepared to throw a lot of money at it. The client is like the dealer; he cannot lose. He gets a design, models, drawings, and publicity. For clients looking for fundraising, clearly one issue is the amount of publicity competitions generate. They receive the media attention that such a competition generates.

What made the Wexner Center competition important were the quality of the jury, the particular architects involved, the nature of the project, its site, its program, and its visibility. What made the competition work was Ed Jennings, president of The Ohio State University, who refused to allow the bureaucracy to change the project. He kept its integrity. If it had not been for Ed, the competition would have devolved into a mundane, ordinary building. In fact, if you do not have the CEO on your side, whether one is in a competition or not, one is not going to get anywhere, because middle management is only interested in short-term benefits. That is always problematic, because signature architecture is a long-term proposition.

What you realize about juries is that no matter how diverse the group seems at the start, they always pretty much agree on a level of quality. I have never run into partisan bickering. Jurors recognize the need to transcend their own interest. I have never been on a jury in which we did not end up in a unanimous decision, even though we radically disagreed. That is a positive sign, especially with juries where you have four hundred entries. It is very easy to pick out twenty.

It is amazing how people do not realize how to do competitions. Arthur Erickson, for example, who is a good architect, never knew how to deal with competitions.

Improving competitions: I think the best competitions are those where there is a level of equality among participants, a certain peer respect. One does not want to go up against a young architect, if one is a gorilla. Equally, there is a need for peer understanding and respect on the jury. Oftentimes juries are not up to people they are judging. Equally, competitions need enough compensation, but not so much that people take the thing seriously. They also need a serious commitment by the owner to build the results. Obviously, this is difficult to achieve, and very few reach such an ideal. Most competitions do not get built, either because the sponsors do not like the results or they do not have financing in place. Sixty percent of the competitions that I know about or participate in are not serious. They do not get built. So *caveat emptor*, but we never think about whether a competition will be built. That is not the issue. The issue is to do an exciting project, and maybe not even to win.

### Arthur Erickson, Arthur Erickson Architectural Corporation

I am encouraged by the public that it (Erickson's entry) was in your collective opinion the best. On two other competitions which I felt we lost unjustly, ours was also voted by an overwhelming majority, the best. One was the Portland building, which launched Graves's career, with the unequivocal judgment of Phillip Johnson. The other was the Chicago Library, which we had five times the vote of anyone else, but judged by Vincent Scully. In both cases, the ardent campaigning of the "star" jury member for their "favorite" won the day to my regret and the ultimate demise of my respective offices. There is a book or at least a lengthy essay being written on the Portland case – the building put Portland on the architectural map, but has always in my view, evoked the image of Babylonian heterea. (Author note: *Heterea* refers to an image of a woman employed in entertainment, such as flute playing or dancing). In all cases when I saw the work of the competitors, I was certain we would win. For the Wexner Center, the key jury member was Henry Cobb, which surprised me, since I thought his work more experiential than intellectual and therefore more favorable to ours. Maybe he didn't want to admit he couldn't understand it. The winning scheme was a far-fetched intellectual exercise, and to me his presentation made no sense – a step toward the Disneyfication of America in its token historicism. In Chicago, I couldn't believe the results, for everyone, including several of our competitors assured me that we were the obvious winner. But, Austro-Hungarian romanticism won out!

However, my firm has also thrived on competitions. We were launched by the Simon Fraser University Competition in the '60s, won and triumphed with our entry for the Canadian Pavilion at Expo '70 in Osaka, and were able to launch an American office in L.A. with our California Plaza. Therefore, I believe in the value of competitions, especially for offices starting out. I have also been on the jury for countless competitions internationally and so have sympathy for the jurors' view.

The nature of open competitions is to flush out new talent and new ideas. As a juror that is what you look for. Since that kind of competition is based on the early tentative program, there is lots of room for modification and adjustment for the architect and the client. The results – such as the Tokyo Forum competition – are usually excellent.

However, the above three competitions were limited competitions with full program and client input and a substantial fee (which is never commensurate with the costs) to a chosen half-dozen architects. In each case, submissions are thoroughly worked out and costed – to the extent of substantial design development. In this kind of competition, the danger to the client is from a jury who is judging it as an "ideas" competition. They believe their reputations stand on a memorable new direction in architecture resulting in – not the best solution to the problem given. So in all these cases, the building has been a disappointment to the owners and the public – and the jury escaped unscathed.

### *Mark Feinknopf, Feinknopf, Macioce, Schappa Architects, Local Partner of Arthur Erickson (In-person interview by Peg Grannis)*

I've done a lot of research work with the Department of Development. I am a professional that works very closely with our clients to develop programs and to understand their needs and to try to develop out of that role a responsive environment that allows that client to be the most creative in that environment.

I think there are some real flaws in the competition process. You don't get that out of a competition. You get that out of really understanding what's going on. It's not the great monumental image, but the environment inside for people, that's where I am focused. I want to see cities designed for people. That's why we do projects that begin to strengthen the fabric of the community. A one-shot deal just becomes that, a one-shot deal, and if it's out of context it can be just as much a detriment as it can be positive.

So the first thing is: Can you through the competition process really meet the needs of a client? And I have some real questions about that. Secondly, you put the architect, due to the image that they created, in a position of controlling the whole process. I don't think anybody on a team should be put in the point of a total dictatorial position, and that's what you do. In other words, you're creating a piece of something and everyone else has to live in it. From that point of view, I think the client is at a disadvantage. The people who work everyday at the Wexner Center are at a disadvantage. The spaces don't work very well.

Also, because this is on the cutting edge, do you really get the quality of space and the amount of space for the dollars that you spend that you would have if you had really gone through a different process? Why should you do it on a public project? You lose something in that. You lose something in creating the monumentality and the other things. The arts facility has several objectives and it being a piece of art can be one of those objective.

From the client's view there is the question: are you spending money for the right thing? And do you get the program met thoroughly? Or do you get it met partially and give that?

As an architect, I've learned a lot from seeing buildings built in competitions and I think, on a technical basis and on some other bases, competitions can tend to push the art beyond where it might go otherwise. It makes people conscious of architecture. It makes people talk about it. You don't take those buildings for granted and you don't today. They really become important pieces of the environment, but I personally believe that we as a society have spent too much time aggrandizing individual architects, individual buildings, and have not spent as much time really saying, how do you really create the best environment for people? The total environment. We want to raise people's total consciousness of what is community, and out of community, what are the symbols that represent that community.

I'm less interested in how to make a monument than how do we build community. How do we build an integrated place where people want to go? So I get very interested in those kinds of things which bring people together and the experiential aspect of that, as opposed to here's a building that made the front of *Architectural Record*.

The architectural competition had a far less exciting potential than some of the other things that we do. How do we rebuild rivers? How do we rebuild community? How do we rebuild the social structure? How do we really create spaces and environments that help people feel good about themselves, which can enhance healing as opposed to harming it?

### Michael Graves, Michael Graves Architects, Princeton, N.J.

Those who administer professional design juries often try to construct a jury that's like a "Chinese menu," with one of each: a designer, a technocrat, a business person, a woman, a man, somebody tall, somebody short. The awards that are given by a group of people like this, all well meaning, generally become a compromise. Or else, a couple of strong individuals on the jury who are skillful and clever enough dominate the event. It's human nature. There's nothing wrong with this system except that you can get a very mixed, mediocre result.

I think that the award of buildings through competition juries is much, much more political than people ever realize. And this is true for a variety of reasons. For instance, if an architect is young and has good ideas but hasn't built very much, and is up against an architect with lots of built work and also with good ideas, and both schemes are equally good, the jury will probably award the prize to the younger architect because he or she hasn't yet had a chance. Depending upon the nature of the competition, the jury might pair that young architect with someone who has greater experience in the technical field. And this is done with all good intentions. Nevertheless, there is definitely a political dimension to it.

I'm not sure that competitions are the best way to select an architect. I really am not. The interview process involves the client selecting an architect – the person as well as the work. And the interview process works both ways. The client interviews the architect and the architect interview the client. In the end this process is really superior to juries, simply because there is a chance for dialog.

I certainly have had my successes in entering competitions and winning a few, and they helped enormously in my early practice. But at the same time the way juries for professional design competitions are conducted today is usury, to a great extent. The amount of money lost by well-intentioned architects is frightening and immoral. It takes so much money to win because it seems the ante is increased with each successive competition. (Interview by Anthony, p. 189)[8]

### Michael McKinnell, Principal, Kallmann, McKinnell and Wood, Boston

As far as competitions are concerned, we owe our existence to the competition system, because we started as a firm by winning the Boston City Hall competition. It was the first competition for a major civic building since the San Francisco town hall after the fire. We do not have a history for civic buildings in America. It was a very bold gesture, initiated by marvelous man James Lawrence, an architect determined to break the stronghold of patronage in the city and to open the possibility for a design commission to the competition system. We were fortunate enough to win, without the firm or credentials, for what was an extremely large and complex building. The city had the good sense, for them the daring position, to allow us to proceed in joint venture with Boston firm.

Obviously, I'm very much in favor of the competition system. We have entered a number since then, and been successful in some, not in others. We just won a competition for a building in the Hague, Netherlands, for the headquarters for the Organization for Prevention of Chemical Warfare. It was an invited competition. We've won others and been unsuccessful in quite a few.

I'm very much in favor. I think that quite apart from obvious benefits of opening career possibilities to young or even not so young architects who would not be apparently eligible for a commission to prove themselves and to set their careers in place as a consequence, quite apart from that, one of the reasons we persist in entering is that it allows one to do what one thinks is right on the basis of a brief, and to be judged by one's peers. It is a vehicle for the exploration of ideas.

The competition system is splendid in principle. To be successful, it has to be for a building for which the brief can be stated very exactly. The drawback of the competition system is clearly one that eliminates the interchange between the client, in their broadest sense, and the architect in the generation of the ideas. So, for instances in which an architecture might develop which the architect can't conceive of merely by his own interpretation of the brief, it is not a good idea.

We recently engaged in limited competition for a Berlin embassy, for which five or six firms were invited to compete. An embassy is an extremely complicated program of requirements, particularly in operational and security sense. The Federal Building Authority (F.O.B.), the organizer of the competition, had two review sessions in which architects were able to separately present work, one third and two thirds of the way through. This was extremely helpful in allowing the F.O.B. to ensure that their practical requirements were being met by many of the competitors. It afforded the client protection against a willful and absurd solution, which seems reasonable, as they were paying. On the other hand, it is all but impossible for anybody to view six schemes without implicitly drawing on the knowledge of the other schemes. There might be a tendency towards entropy. I am sure we were not alone among the competitors in wondering to what degree what had been said about our scheme had been generated by reaction to other schemes. It is difficult to straddle the two conflicting requirements: on the one hand to use the competition system to engender ideas free of any influence, and on the other hand to ensure that competitors will produce schemes which are not absurd from the client's point of view.

On the Wexner Center, in many ways, I'm very glad that Peter won, quite apart from the fact that he's my oldest personal friend in America. We roomed together as students at Columbia. It first allowed his trajectory as a practicing architect to take off, which he had been struggling with before that. We are all the beneficiaries from that. Second, it validated the notion that a competition can produce a building that would have been very unlikely to be produced had the commission been a normal one, if he had to endure and benefit from the weekly interaction with a client. So, in both respects the Wexner competition was admirable.

The results of competitions are twofold. One of the downsides is the very serious abuse of architects. The abuse paradoxically mounts when the competition is an invited one among prestigious architects, because the client at that moment knows very well that the architects, because of their competition, are known, and are competing against their peers, would engage in greater efforts than if it were an open and anonymous competition. This is a very serious abuse of architects in this regard. We calculate very carefully, we will spend far, far more than any amount of money that the client is willing to offer us. This includes even the F.O.B. competition for the Berlin Embassy, where each of us were given $100,000. I guarantee that all of us lost substantial amounts of money. Even the winner is losing money.

We have been fortunate that the competitions that we have won have been built. In one that we entered but did not win, the final for extension of the Parliament buildings in England, they did not proceed with it.

*Chuck Nitschke, Nitschke Sampson, Dietz, Inc., Local*
*Partner of Kallmann, Mckinnell and Wood (In-person*
*interview by Peg Grannis)*

I wondered about the enthusiasm that architects traditionally have for architectural competitions. It's a wonderful way to get work. It's a wonderful way to get fame. And it's an exciting sort of thing, that traditionally true architects have put a lot of time into.

I have suspected that this is an internal phenomenon that our profession has discovered and nurtured within itself without ever realizing what we are doing or what it is costing the profession. So I have had a general worry about the profession eating itself up by giving its true talent to competitions for very little results.

The general public doesn't really care because they don't understand why architects do all this work for nothing and they say, "Well if architects are willing to contribute all this work for nothing that their work must not be worth anything. If they're willing to give it away for nothing, then why should I pay for it?" So the general public is confused over this competition thing. I've seen people, businessmen, shake their heads and say, "Why would architects do that?" There is no other business or profession in the world that gives away so much professional time and talent. Why would architects do that?" So they shake their heads and say, "Architects are odd balls. They are not part of the mainstream, and certainly they can't be trusted to do a good job if they have this attitude toward each other that they want to give their time for something that is very risky."

When I was asked by the university to compete on the Wexner Center, I was honored by the invitation, and so we discussed this in the office. I said, "This is going to be a huge contribution of our time and effort to the good of the university, so let's do it and we might win. In fact, we will try very hard to win, but let's not be surprised if we don't." Our team had put a quarter of a million dollars cash in our submittal. We had a very pretty picture. We got published in a book. Nobody thanked us. They did give us $25,000. It just barely paid for the airline expenses between Boston and Columbus. And the university didn't thank us. The architects didn't care. So it was strictly for us. We felt pretty good because we felt we had the best solution, but we realized that our solution wasn't what the university was looking for.

In a competition intended to create a special moment for the general public and publicity for the university, they don't want a practical solution. They want something that's kind of flamboyant. And oh boy! That's what they got! Very huge and successful in attracting attention and it will continue for a few years, and then it will start to rust and then it won't work. So let's remodel it and see if we can make it more usable. But that will happen several years after its true value has paid the university handsomely.

The most valuable phase of the architectural process is the period of time the architect works with the client to determine what the client needs. The client and architect become intimate team members working together which is a synergy that always works. This competition did not have a client.

When you're working without a client . . . we had this architect, who was the facilitator, a nice guy, Rich Miller, but he didn't know what the program was, and I kept asking and he said, "You'll have to do that yourself. The university had not determined what they need. They just want something that's out of your mind." And that's exactly what it was. All of the solutions were kind of out of people's minds. It was kind of mindless many times, meant to create an image or a situation that would attract the attention of the jurors. Sometimes they were kind of crazy, but always kind of fun, and that was the solution.

So, what was really hard on me was that we were one side of the essential team that results in a successful project. We did it ourselves without the help of a client. We kept inquiring is that the normal way that competitions are handled. Rich Miller said, "Yes we followed the rules of the AIA precisely." In kind of a traditional way, the client gives the third rail to the architect. The architect designs the building, you bid it, find out how much it's going to cost, you go back and redesign it. That's the normal process.

But I was disappointed in our solution, because I had a lot of intelligent reasons for doing what we did, but no one ever asked those questions, probably didn't care. The jury came in on a weekend. Without real preparation, they were asked to pick something out of this pile of very exciting, interesting, expensive solutions, which they did. They did their job, but in response to tremendous investments that all of these architects put into it, it was kind of a weak result. Nobody got out of it, including Eisenman and Trott, what they put into it. They lost their shirt also, dollar for dollar. But they lost more than we did probably, and we didn't even get the award. We did get the fame. That's the nice thing. At least, the winner gets the publicity, and, for architects that have egos, maybe that's most important.

So, I am not an advocate of competitions because I don't see any rationale for having them other than to gain publicity for the client at a very low cost. So the Ohio State competition was extremely successful, extremely, one of the most successful competition every held, I think, because that building that came out of it was flamboyant and for an arts center you couldn't ask for anything more flamboyant or more exciting. It put Ohio State on the map at the time when they were trying to become internationally recognized as a top-quality, forward-thinking university. So I will say, if anyone ever asks me, the Wexner Center competition was one of the most successful competitions ever held.

Now the solution will have to be tested by time. And when you look at the continuing displays of programs they have up there, it's really a challenge to use. The directors kind of tear their hair out. What are we going to do next? We have to hire artists or convince artists to create art that will fit in this building. But that was the goal of the building to challenge artists, to challenge creative thinking and risky projects. It's very successful.

We were told that the whole program was that the results of this competition must be a building that is avant-garde, that is future challenging, something that we have no idea what the future is going to be. This building ought to stretch creative people's minds and talents beyond any dimension they have now. This building has to stretch creative people. And great. It's successful, really successful.

It had no program. It had to come out of the architects' heads. And I don't think the university could have gotten such a successful solution through a normal architectural process by hiring an architect. Even though you hire the world's best architect, the solution would not have been that creative, or crazy, or illogical, or demanding, or whatever words you want to use that relate to the building. This is one situation where the competition really worked.

Now that doesn't mean I felt it was a good idea at the time. It was a foolish decision on my part to accept the challenge, because it was so expensive. I've decided no matter how famous you might get by winning a competition, it is something like winning the lottery. The chances of winning are terribly low. Unless you are financially independent, you don't have to make money from your profession, you'd better not get into it, because if you don't win, it is a very expensive lesson. So, when we get invitations to do other competitions, we always very quietly say, "We're sorry, we respect your program but we can't contribute at this time." I guess we don't do it, because our egos are not as strong as our desire to be financially responsible architects. We work awfully hard to produce jobs that satisfy client's budgets as well as their programs. And we like to do the same thing for our own projects. We like to work hard so that the work we produce keeps us in business also. We're not highly paid architects. We're average paid, but we work awfully hard to do a good job. Entering a competition is just draining. We just can't afford to do that. So I would never enter another one. Anybody that would ask me, I'd recommend that they don't unless they were financially independent and could do this just for a lark, or for potential fame they might get.

Jury members are just busy people. They come from around the country for one day. They haven't done their homework. They don't know anything about the thing. So what they learn is what's presented to them that first day. So, it's an uneducated jury, where if the client were the jury and if the client had worked with the architect, he knows what will satisfy his needs. So what you have done by selecting an outside jury, you've taken the selection process out of the client's hand, which is extremely dangerous. I mean, the client normally has to build what the jury picks, and the jury, even though they are competent professionals who are trying hard, they don't know anything about the client's needs. So, you are really lucky if the jury picks something that satisfies you. It is a terribly risky process. Any client is crazy – unless he's only looking for publicity.

The most important element in any architectural project is the program. If the client has spent a lot of time figuring out what he needs, so that in the program it is clearly illustrated and demonstrated and shown in graphic form as well as words, so that when the architect, who is the competitor can say, yes, I know what the client needs. Because he's never going to be able to talk to the client, everything the architect learns, he has to learn from the written program. Architects traditionally have not done a good job demanding good programs. The traditional architecture process is the owner gives the program of needs to the architect. The architect evaluates those, asks questions, and agrees with them. Then, once the program is agreed upon between the owner and the architects, then the design begins. A sophisticated program process should be developed before the competition is started, which means that the owner should hire a sophisticated programming architect to do a good, good, good program, and you're talking about tens and thousands of dollars, even hundreds of thousands to do a good program. That is absolutely essential. You can't have a volume of words that is difficult to read. It has to be put together so that it is precise, understandable, have everything analyzed So, if I were going to develop a new competition process, I would say that the program must be developed by a skilled architect-owner interrelationship and published in a form that is easily read and understood, because when competing architects get to the design they don't know who wrote the program and they don't have to ask questions. They kind of wing it. They fly by the seat of their pants. Let's try this. If the program has a bunch of check things, here are things you must know – click, click, click, click, click. If the design architect would read these things in detail and it won't be so iffy for the architect, and he won't make mistakes.

Going back to the Wexner Center, and setting up the agenda for the jury, Trott and partners were first up. They spent time developing their strategy of how they were going to present their work and the part of their work they were going to emphasize. And from what you told me, there was no program. This was really wide open and something that you would really want to happen. I'm sure that if you spoke to the university, they'd say we have a program, that Rich Miller put one together. But compared to a real program it was very inadequate. He had never seen a real program. Therefore, I am saying that the program had to be more sophisticated for the clients to use.

If you have a viable idea, I'd say to win a competition, you have to have an askew idea. It has to be diagonal. It can't be upside down, but it has to cut through several lines of conventional thought. That's what Trott did. If someone else came in with something equally creative, and anything creative is the result of diagonal thinking, somebody else would have been in good competition with Trott. But since they had such a creative approach, nobody else could approach it. We had a good solution, but maybe somebody else did to. Ours was practical. Ours really was a good result. It had nothing to do with the interesting ideas like recreating the towers and slicing through these buildings, and theirs was just totally creative, not off the wall, but an unexpected solution, so they would have won no matter what order they had presented in the program.

The minute I went into that whole program [I was] saying that we have to win because our solution is good for the campus. It's going to strengthen the entrance. It's going to cover up that ugly Mershon Auditorium. It's going to strengthen the approach to the Oval, which is sacred. We had a lot of good ideas. We had the best solution. Except the antisolution was better than ours, because that's what the university wanted. We were not that creative. If we had been, we might not have had the guts to even present it, it was so wild. Eisenman had that talent and the guts to do it. I went in saying we have to win until I saw that solution on the board, and I said, "No way." That is just what the university wanted. I would have selected it, too. Somebody poured a quarter of million dollars into a bunch of pretty pictures, and that was quite a mission. I saw it immediately. There was the winner.

Parking at the Wexner Center was never even considered, never solved, never part of the challenge, never part of the program. . . . I imagine that roof leaks will be the major problem with the Wexner Center. Looking at the building, there are probably twelve major water leaks right now, that are going to keep getting worse, and are very difficult to identify. I don't know whether that's true or not. If I were the architect, I would wake up on rainy nights wondering where the next leak is going to come from. That doesn't mean it is bad design. It is just difficult to detail a design so complex.

If their criteria is vague, I think that through a competition, they can get more than their money's worth. If their criteria is a working solution and practical maintenance, they are getting stung nine times out of ten. . . . I think the average owner who has a competition won by name-brand architects many times does not get a solution that he had hoped for and more maintenance expenses than he had hoped for. If he can trade off name and the recognition for these kind of practical things, fine.

You pay a premium for making an impractical design practical to build. It costs more, more in steel detailing, more in wall detailing, more in waterproofing, more in drainage, more in whatever. Owners will spend a lot more money once they get down to it. Eisenman just took a chance. Let's build something. We don't know what it's going to cost. We'll win the competition and work out the costs later. That's what they did, and it worked. That's called teasing the owner to pay for whatever it's going to cost. In the real world of architecture, architects are fired if they design a building that can't be built within budget, a great way to lose a client, but in a competition maybe it's a great way to win a client.

### Cesar Pelli, Principal, Cesar Pelli & Associates, New Haven, Connecticut

Design competitions have great potential because they open up opportunities to talented architects that may be young and unrecognized to become recognized. But they are always risky. There's no assurance that the best design is going to be chosen. The final pick is always subjective. It's what's in the mind of the jurors, and is affected by personal preferences and momentary fashions. Design competitions offer that great opportunity to unknown or lesser-known architects to come to the fore. However, they have the problem that one is designing in a vacuum. Good, solid designs usually develop through the architect working closely with clients and users. There is a great deal of give and take, where ideas are explored, rejected, or modified to make them properly suit all of the needs of the clients and users. That, to me, makes for a richer, more real project than what one can conceive all alone in competition (p. 207).[8]

In my telephone interview, Pelli, said:

I have strong feelings about competitions, both in favor and against them. I like them and support them because they open opportunities to younger or unrecognized talent. This is particularly true of open, international competitions.

Competitions have been very good to me and my career. Early on I won first prize on a major competition, in 1969, for the "U.N. City" in Vienna. Although the Austrian government did not honor its promise to build the scheme of the first-prize winner and built instead that of the fourth-place entry (by a Viennese with strong political connections), still, the competition was important to me. I did not get the commission, but it made other people pay attention to my work. The American Embassy in Tokyo project came directly from it. The selection group, having seen my design for U.N. City, recommended to the U.S. State Department that I and my firm (Gruen Associates) be interviewed and we were selected. The American Embassy in Tokyo was a good and critical project for me. However, the experience with the Austrian government was not pleasant and I have not entered other public (or open, or unpaid) competitions since then. But, with my present firm of Cesar Pelli and Associates, we have entered many invited (and paid) competitions. Winning the competition to design the World Financial Center and carrying the project successfully through construction transformed the nature of our firm. It was a very public demonstration that our firm could be entrusted to design large and complex projects. We also obtained the commission to design the Petronas Towers by winning a competition and, more recently, we won a competition to design a major hotel in Japan, now built, and also a very important competition to design a Performing Arts Center in Miami, now well advanced in design. Last December, we won a competition to design a large complex, including a very tall building, in Hong Kong. We have accepted to participate in a competition for a large, multi-building project in Korea and in one for a new airport in Madrid. There is no doubt the competitions have been critical and beneficial to my firm and to me personally. They have also been very important in shaping the careers of other architects such as Piano and Rogers.

Competitions also have drawbacks. The first is that competitions distort the design process. A design for a good building is the result of a special type of collaboration of architect with clients and users. This is not possible in a competition.

The second drawback is the natural bias of those that judge. I have served on some twelve juries, know of the particulars of many others, and I have concluded that today, most architects choose according to their stylistic allegiances, with little or no regard to how well the building will respond to other critical requirements. Now I have come to believe that a competition will be more thoroughly and fairly judged by clients than by architects. Clients tend to look at the whole picture, not only the style of the building, but also how well it will function, how will users like it, what problems the scheme may present. It would be the reverse, but in general, today most clients look at the totality of the design, while architect look primarily at the image of the buildings. Certainly not all architects do this. Some take the time to study the plans and judge the entries on their merits, but that is not common today.

The third drawback is the enormous waste of time and energies of very many architects: Those who do not win. Even in invited competitions, where architects are paid to participate, the amount is never enough to cover costs. We are vulnerable because architects do not enter competitions for the money, but for the opportunity to design a wonderful building. We don't think about the money when we design; but, in the end, we feel it anyway. We still have to pay the bills. Because competitions tend to be unfair, it is important to have clear rules that define a simple, well understood and fair playing field. The request for presentation materials should be modest and appropriate.

Invited competitions are particularly hard to control. Many architects end up very bruised. It is essential that presentation requirements be well defined. Otherwise, the sky is the limit because architects are very competitive. Not specifying the presentation has a form of abuse built in.

On the O.S.U. Wexner competition: It was well run and done with the clear intention of being a very special competition. It was well prepared and had a good jury headed by Henry Cobb. Afterward, a book on it was printed. Overall, it was a high-class effort and a pleasure to participate in it. It was already a distinction to be invited because other competitors were architects one respected.

Our entry suffered from a political problem. The site presented to the competitors as available for the new building included the southern tip of the Oval. The president, during an informal gathering, suggested that this site be seriously considered because it has many advantages. In our studies, we concluded that a building there could give better form to the Oval and would allow for the least restricted plan for the museum and we placed our design there. A week or so before the presentations were due, we heard that some O.S.U. students had requested and obtained a promise from the president that he would not allow anything built on the Oval. We also heard, from our Ohio associates, that this promise probably took us out of the race. During the presentation, it was obvious that some members of the jury were very uncomfortable as I explained why I believed the southern tip of the Oval was the best site. They kept fidgeting in their chairs. It may have made no difference in the end but, for us, the rules were changed too late, which we thought was unfair. The president had encouraged us to study this site and he should have stuck to his guns. However, in every other respect it was a serious competition that ended on a positive note. Peter Eisenman won with an ingenious and good scheme. This competition was very important to his career because it certified him as a practicing architect, not only a theoretician. I like Peter's design and building and I am glad this competition was so helpful to him.

*James Scott, Designer with Trott & Partners, Partner*
*with Eisenman (In-person interview with Peg Grannis)*

I think the one thing about competitions that is good is that they bring fresh ideas to the table. They in some ways push the profession to explore its own values and how it solves problems. And it's kind of like in an effort to *quote* "win the competition" you look for something that will make yours stand out as being more unique.

We spent a lot of time analyzing our competition. . . . Just like any football coach, you scout your teams. So, we were scouting our competition to understand what their response might be. You compete on all these different levels, just in terms of when we presented. When we presented, first, second or third, was real important to us. In fact, we were pushing to go first to set the stage for every everyone else. By going first we could put the bug in the jury's ear for what they look for in everyone else's design. We could set the playing field. We also wanted to go first because we could get a greater amount of setup time. By going first we were able to get into Mershon. We rented Mershon out the day before so that we could set up the room and the environment to best enhance our presentation. The people who came after us only had a couple of hours to set up theirs. We had much greater time to set up our stuff and manipulate the environment so that our design came off in a bit better light.

On the drawbacks of competition, the plus is you get world-class unique design that pushes architecture forward and makes statements for the city and for whoever. On the down side, they're very expensive. To play to win costs big money. That's why a lot of architects are hesitant to get into them. It's a big financial risk. Another drawback, this feeling that when they grouped local architects with *quote* "international national signature architects" there may be some resentment from local architects, feeling that they're not good enough to compete.

People would probably say you don't get the best building for the money that you would if you did it with a more traditional architectural commission. And I think that that criticism is like it costs more to do a Wexner Center. There's this feeling that those type of buildings cost more. And in some cases that's probably true.

Then you have the postrationalization about engaging the university and the city. I don't know where that came in. I think it was more of a strategy game to win the competition. I don't know what that competition cost – $100,000 – but I'm sure it didn't cover the costs of producing that stuff. And I think what was good about that competition was that it was the first one in Ohio and maybe even in the Midwest that really brought architecture to the forefront of people's minds. So, it was a great incentive for us – a great incentive to try to do more that just a standard solution, to actually explore other alternatives, and in that sense competitions are good for everybody. Maybe not so good for the people who compete because you lose money, especially if you don't win. I think the winner in the broader sense and the long range sense in everyone – the city or environment or whoever is sponsoring the competition gets a better building. The profession as a whole wins in the long-range sense because it brings their work and their profession to the forefront of people's minds so that people start thinking about it more and actually asking more of the architecture, to strive for something unique.

It the criticism of the jury is that they didn't pay much attention to the program, it is probably because the people who were presenting presented things other than that. They steered the jury away from that.

# APPENDIX C

## SELECTED TABLES
## OF RESULTS

Table C.1. *The 25 pairs of winning and losing entries.*

*1892–1916*
1882 Reichstag in Berlin
1903 Helinsky Station
1903 Stockholm Town Hall
1903 Austrian Savings Bank
1916 White Pine House

*1920–1929*
1922 Chicago Tribune
1925 Harding Memorial
1926 House Competition
1928 Diplomat's Club
1929 Museum

*1930–1946*
1930 Chapel
1931 Auditorium
1946 House Competition
1946 House Competition
1947 Termini Station

*1956–1967*
1956 Library
1956 House competition
1956 Embassy
1965 Museum and Auditorium
1967 Civic Center

*1980–1991*
1981 Library
1982 Louisville Tower
1983 Codex Building
1986 Museum
1991 House Competition

Table C.2. *Characteristics of the architects and nonarchitects interviewed.*

| Group | Architects ($n = 50$) | Nonarchitects ($n = 50$) |
|---|---|---|
| Gender | | |
| Male | 92% | 38% |
| Female | 8 | 62 |
| Age | | |
| 20–30 | 20 | 16 |
| 31–40 | 30 | 34 |
| 41–50 | 24 | 16 |
| 51–60 | 16 | 24 |
| 61 and older | 10 | 10 |
| Years in Practice | | |
| 0–5 | 10 | 18 |
| 6–10 | 36 | 30 |
| 11–20 | 22 | 24 |
| 21–30 | 24 | 18 |
| 31–40 | 8 | 6 |
| 40 years + | 0 | 4 |

Table C.3. *Frequency chosen as more liked or as better design.*

| Scale | Winning Entries | Losing Entries | Choice $\chi^2$ | Group × Choice $\chi^2$ |
|---|---|---|---|---|
| More Liked | | | | 16.24 $(1, n = 2496)$*** |
| Architects | 610 | 639 | | |
| Nonarchitects | 508 | 739 | | |
| Combined | 1118 | 1378 | 27.08 $(1, n = 2496)$** | |
| Better Design | | | | 8.93 $(1, n = 2495)$** |
| Architects | 609 | 637 | | |
| Nonarchitects | 535 | 714 | | |
| Combined | 1144 | 1351 | 17.18 $(1, n = 2495)$** | |

$**p < .01.$ $***p < .001.$

Table C.4. *Frequency chosen as more liked or better design over five time periods.*

| | Liked | | | Better Design | | |
|---|---|---|---|---|---|---|
| Time Period | Winning Entries | Losing Entries | $\chi^2$ (1 $df$) | Winning Entries | Losing Entries | $\chi^2$ (1 $df$) |
| 1882–1916 | 190 | <u>310</u> | 28.80** | 187 | <u>312</u> | 31.26** |
| 1921–1929 | 245 | 254 | 0.16 | 251 | 249 | 0.008 |
| 1930–1947 | 220 | <u>278</u> | 6.80* | 244 | 255 | 0.144 |
| 1950–1967 | 263 | 236 | 1.46 | 249 | 250 | 0.002 |
| 1981–1987 | 200 | <u>300</u> | 20.00** | 213 | <u>285</u> | 10.40** |

*$p < .05.$ **$p < .01.$

Table C.5. *Frequency chosen as more liked or better design by each group over time.*

| | Most Liked | | | | | |
|---|---|---|---|---|---|---|
| | Architect Choices | | | Nonarchitect Choices | | |
| Time Period | Winning Entries | Losing Entries | $\chi^2$ (1 $df$) | Winning Entries | Losing Entries | $\chi^2$ (1$df$) |
| 1882–1916 | 96 | <u>154</u> | 13.46** | 94 | <u>156</u> | 15.38** |
| 1921–1929 | 134 | 116 | | 111 | 138 | |
| 1930–1947 | 131 | 118 | | 89 | <u>160</u> | 20.74** |
| 1950–1967 | 118 | 132 | | <u>145</u> | 104 | 7.06* |
| 1981–1987 | 131 | 119 | | 69 | <u>181</u> | 50.18** |

| | Better Design | | | | | |
|---|---|---|---|---|---|---|
| | Architect Choices | | | Nonarchitect Choices | | |
| Time Period | Winning Entries | Losing Entries | $\chi^2$ (1$df$) | Winning Entries | Losing Entries | $\chi^2$ (1$df$) |
| 1882–1916 | 99 | <u>150</u> | 10.45** | 88 | <u>162</u> | 21.90** |
| 1921–1929 | 136 | 114 | | 115 | 135 | |
| 1930–1947 | 132 | 117 | | 112 | 138 | |
| 1950–1967 | 119 | 131 | | 130 | 119 | |
| 1981–1987 | 123 | 125 | | 90 | <u>160</u> | 19.60** |

*$p < 0.05.$ **$p < 0.01.$

Table C.6. *Houses chosen as more liked and better designed over five time periods.*

| | Liked | | | Better Design | | |
|---|---|---|---|---|---|---|
| Time Period | Winning Entries | Losing Entries | $\chi^2$ (1 *df*) | Winning Entries | Losing Entries | $\chi^2$ (1 *df*) |
| 1882–1916 | 33 | <u>67</u> | 11.56** | 32 | <u>68</u> | 12.96** |
| 1921–1929 | 52 | 48 | 0.16 | 42 | 58 | 2.56 |
| 1930–1947 | | | | | | |
|   House 1 | <u>73</u> | 27 | 21.16** | <u>70</u> | 30 | 16.00** |
|   House 2 | 40 | 59 | 3.66 | 49 | 51 | 0.04 |
| 1950–1967 | 47 | 53 | 0.36 | 51 | 49 | 0.04 |
| 1981–1987 | 35 | <u>65</u> | 9.00* | 34 | <u>65</u> | 9.71* |
| TOTAL | 280 | 319 | 2.54 | 278 | 321 | 3.09 m.s. |

*$p < .05.$ **$p < .01.$

Table C.7. *Ranks by groups on composite score (from all fifteen items).*

| | Ranks of entries | | | | | |
|---|---|---|---|---|---|---|
| | 5 = Best | | 1 = Worst | | | |
| | Design | | | | | |
| Group | Erickson | Kallman | Graves | Eisenman | Pelli | F (4 *df*) |
| Male | 5 | 4 | 3 | 2 | 1 | 35.08* |
| Female | 5 | 4 | 3 | 1 | 2 | 22.75* |
| Alumni | 5 | 4 | 3 | 2 | 2 | 14.60* |
| Students | 5 | 5 | 3 | 2 | 1 | 15.30* |
| Faculty | 5 | 4 | 1 | 2 | 3 | 23.10* |
| Residents | 5 | 2 | 3 | 4 | 1 | 12.41** |

*Note:* Composite scores on the 11-item scales produced the same ranks as those for the 15-item scale.

*$p < .01.$ **$p < .05.$

Table C.8. *Public evaluations of the entries on each item.*

*Mean Rank Scores of Entries (from 5=Best to 1 = Worst)*

| | Best | | | | Worst | Kruskal Wallis Worst $\chi^2$ (4, $N = 65$) |
|---|---|---|---|---|---|---|
| *Embodies participation and accessibility*[a] | Erickson 3.02 | Kallman 2.83 | Graves 2.50 | Eisenman 2.07 | Pelli 1.92 | 29.97* |
| Is good use of site | Erickson 2.92 | Kallman 2.48 | Pelli 2.28 | Graves 2.18 | Eisenman 2.11 | 14.39* |
| Enhances pedestrian approach to university | Erickson 3.25 | Kallman 2.83 | Eisenman 2.23 | Graves 2.12 | Pelli 1.91 | 49.39* |
| Is accessible | Erickson 2.83 | Graves 2.62 | Kallman 2.54 | Pelli 2.17 | Eisenman 2.00 | 15.36* |
| Acknowledges the importance of landscape | Erickson 2.86 | Kallman 2.78 | Eisenman 2.48 | Graves 2.45 | Pelli 1.97 | 16.09* |
| Pleasant | Erickson 2.83 | Kallman 2.77 | Graves 2.65 | Pelli 2.18 | Eisenman 2.11 | 14.79* |
| Relaxing | Erickson 2.98 | Kallman 2.74 | Pelli 2.40 | Eisenman 2.22 | Graves 2.20 | 15.31* |
| *Responds to campus setting*[a] | Erickson 3.15 | Kallman 2.66 | Eisenman 2,33 | Graves 2,24 | Pelli 2.16 | 21.15* |

(continues)

Table C.8. (continued)

*Mean Rank Scores of entries (from 5=Best to 1 = Worst)*

| Best | | | | Worst | Kruskal Wallis Worst $\chi^2$ (4, $N=65$) |
|---|---|---|---|---|---|
| Serve as magnet and focal point | | | | | |
| Erickson 3.29 | Pellli 2.42 | Kallman 2.36 | Eisenman 2.36 | Graves 2.06 | 27.96* |
| Extends the parklike environment | | | | | |
| Erickson 2.75 | Kallman 2.53 | Graves 2.50 | Eisenman 2.28 | Pelli 1.90 | 13.92* |
| Active | | | | | |
| Erickson 3.61 | Kallman 2.72 | Graves 2.30 | Eisenman 1.96 | Pelli 1.92 | 63.02* |
| *Is adventurous and challenging*[a] | | | | | |
| Erickson 3.55 | Kallman 2.76 | Graves 2.36 | Eisenman 2.19 | Pelli 1.67 | 63.87* |
| Is dynamic | | | | | |
| Erickson 3.69 | Eisenman 2.34 | Kallman 2.32 | Graves 2.28 | Pelli 1.91 | 60.89* |
| Exciting | | | | | |
| Erickson 3.49 | Kallman 2.57 | Eisenman 2.39 | Graves 2.19 | Pelli 1.88 | 48.60* |
| Provokes speculation and uncertainty | | | | | |
| Kallman 2.68 | Eisenman 2.63 | Graves 2.45 | Pelli 2.28 | Erickson 2.12 | 7.33 |

*$p < .01$.

[a] Index item for a factor from the PJE factor analysis (Chapter 5).

Table C.9. *Characteristics of mail survey respondents (N = 92).*

| Group | Percent | Group | Percent |
|---|---|---|---|
| *Gender* | | *Discipline* | |
| Male | 60% | Design | 80% |
| Female | 37 | Non-Design | 11 |
| *Age* | | *Frequency Walked By Wexner Center* | |
| 0–24 years | 4% | Never | 4 |
| 25–34 | 26 | 1–5 times | 14 |
| 35–44 | 31 | 6–10 times | 18 |
| 45–54 | 25 | Once/week | 12 |
| 55+ | 8 | More/week | 32 |
| | | Daily | 14 |
| *Position* | | *Frequency Walked Inside Wexner Center* | |
| Faculty | 48% | Never | 40% |
| Staff | 41 | 1–5 times | 48 |
| Graduate Student | 9 | 6–10 times | 8 |
| Undergraduate | 2 | Once/week | 2 |
| *Years on Campus* | | More/week | — |
| 0–5 years | 29% | Daily | 2 |
| 6–10 | 24 | | |
| 11–20 | 26 | | |
| 20+ | 16 | | |

*Note:* Percentages do not tally to 100% because of nonresponses.

Table C.10. *Comparison between PJE and mail survey scores.*

| Item | PJE (N = 65) Standardized Mean (Rank) | Mail survey (N = 92) Standardized Mean |
|---|---|---|
| Serves as magnet and focal point | .340 (3.5) | .582 |
| *Embodies participation and accessibility*[a] | .265 (4) | .423 |
| *Responds to the campus setting*[ab] | .298 (4) | .409 |
| Is dynamic | .335 (2) | .673 |
| Makes good use of site | .278 (5) | .516 |
| *Is adventurous and challenging*[a] | .333 (3) | .685 |
| Is pleasant[b] | .278 (5) | .521 |
| Is exciting | .348 (2) | .645 |
| Is active[b] | .240 (4) | .671 |
| Is calming | .305 (4) | .346 |
| Is atypical | No score | .892 |

*Note:* I standardized both scales from 0 to 1. For the 5-point PJE, 1 (Worst) became 0; and 5 (Best) became 1.0.
For the 7-point mail survey scale, 1 (Strongly disagree) became 0; and 7 (Strongly agree) became 1.0

[a] Index item for a factor from the PJE factor analysis (Chapter 5).

[b] Poles reversed from the survey (neglects campus setting, unpleasant, inactive) to make higher numbers positive.


Table C.11. *Mean designer and nondesigner responses to mail survey (from 1 = strongly disagree to 7 = strongly agree).*

| Item | Designers (n = 10) | Nondesigners (n = 92) | F (1 df) |
|---|---|---|---|
| Magnet/Focal Point | 5.70 | 4.42 | 4.13* |
| Embodies participation | 4.10 | 3.50 | n.s.[b] |
| Responds to campus setting[a] | 4.90 | 3.38 | 4.45* |
| Dynamic | 6.20 | 4.96 | 3.98 (p = .05) |
| Good use of site | 5.70 | 4.00 | 5.27* |
| Adventurous/challenging | 6.22 | 5.07 | n.s.[b] |
| Pleasant[a] | 5.70 | 4.02 | 5.47* |
| Exciting | 5.40 | 4.80 | n.s.[b] |
| Active[a] | 6.30 | 5.00 | 4.72* |
| Calming | 3.90 | 2.99 | n.s.[b] |
| Is atypical | 6.34 | 6.30 | n.s.[b] |

[a] Poles reversed from the survey (neglects campus setting, is unpleasant, is inactive) to make higher numbers positive.

[b] Not statistically significant

*$p < .05$.

Table C.12. *Comparisons of mail survey scores by different groups (from 1 = strongly disagree to 7 = strongly agree).*

| By Group | Faculty ($n = 51$) | Students ($n = 11$) | Staff ($n = 40$) | $F$ (2 $df$) |
|---|---|---|---|---|
| Livability | 4.21 | 3.64 | 2.83 | 13.55*** |
| Responds to campus setting | 4.58 | 2.73 | 2.55 | 7.31*** |
| Adventurousness/Challenge | 6.04 | 3.82 | 4.20 | 10.69*** |

| By Sex | Male ($n = 55$) | Female ($n = 34$) | $F$ (1 $df$) |
|---|---|---|---|
| Responsive to campus setting | 3.95 | 3.05 | 4.19* |
| Adventurous/challenging | 5.57 | 4.60 | 5.36* |

| By Age | Under 30 ($n = 23$) | 30–39 ($n = 26$) | 40–49 ($n = 35$) | 49+ years ($n = 20$) | $F$ (3 $df$) |
|---|---|---|---|---|---|
| Responsiveness to campus setting | 3.50 | 3.84 | 3.47 | 4.56 | 3.54* |

*$p < .05.$ ** $p < .01.$ *** $p < .001.$

Table C.13. *Comparison between mail and on-site surveys (from 1 = strongly disagree to 7 = strongly agree).*

| Item | Mail Survey ($n = 92$) | On-site Survey ($n = 90$) |
|---|---|---|
| *Embodies participation and accessibility* | 3.53 | 4.43 |
| Makes good use of site | 4.09 | 4.57 |
| Is pleasant [a] | 4.12 | 4.94 |
| Is calming | 3.07 | 3.51 |
| *Responds to the campus setting* [a] | 3.45 | 3.72 |
| Serves as magnet and focal point | 4.49 | 4.83 |
| Is active [a] | 5.02 | 5.38 |
| *Is adventurous and challenging* | 5.10 | 5.56 |
| Is dynamic | 5.03 | 5.75 |
| Is exciting | 4.86 | 5.42 |
| Is atypical | 6.34 | 6.20 |

*Note:* None of the differences – Embodies participation [$F$ (1 $df$) = 12.63, $p < .01$], Pleasant [$F$ (1 $df$) = 7.76, $p < .01$], Calming [$F$ (1 $df$) = 4.19, $p < .05$], Dynamic [$F$ (1 $df$) = 6.96, $p < .01$] – remained statistically significant after Bonferoni adjustments for multiple-comparisons.

[a] Poles reversed from the survey (neglects campus setting, is unpleasant, is inactive) to make higher numbers positive.

Table C.14. *Characteristics of on-site samples.*

| | At Wexner (N = 90) | At Other Buildings (N = 59) | |
|---|---|---|---|
| Sex | | | n.s.[a] |
| Male | 50% | 44.1% | |
| Female | 48.9 | 54.2 | |
| Age | | | n.s.[a] |
| 18 or less | 7.8% | 10.2% | |
| 19 | 26.7 | 10.2 | |
| 20 | 14.4 | 15.3 | |
| 21 | 12.2 | 16.9 | |
| 22–28 | 28.9 | 30.5 | |
| Older | 7.8 | 15.3 | |
| Mean | 22.5 years | 24.1 years | |
| Years at OSU | | | $F = 4.995$, 1 $df$, $p < .05$. |
| 1 or less | 40.0% | 25.4% | |
| 2 | 23.3 | 20.3 | |
| 3 | 16.7 | 20.3 | |
| More | 17.8 | 32.2 | |
| Mean | 2.27 years | 4.22 years | |
| Position | | | n.s.[a] |
| Undergraduate | 67.8% | 74.6% | |
| Graduate student | 15.6 | 11.9 | |
| Staff | 3.3 | 3.4 | |
| Faculty | 0.0 | 3.4 | |
| Frequency Walking by Building | | | n.s.[a] |
| 1. Never | 1.1% | 3.4% | |
| 2. 1–5 times | 10.0 | 8.5 | |
| 3. 6–10 times | 5.6 | 10.2 | |
| 4. 1/week | 16.7 | 10.2 | |
| 5. few times/week | 41.1 | 14.1 | |
| 6. Daily | 25.6 | 25.4 | |
| 7. Mean | 4.63 | 4.73 | |
| Frequency Walking Into Building | | | $F = 35.29$, 1 $df$, $p < .01$. |
| 1. Never | 56.7% | 28.8% | |
| 2. 1–5 times | 31.1% | 15.3 | |
| 3. 6–10 times | 8.9 | 18.6 | |
| 4. 1/week | 0.0 | 10.2 | |
| 5. Few times/week | 0.0 | 18.6 | |
| 6. Daily | 3.3 | 8.5 | |
| 7. Mean | 1.66 | 3.00 | |
| Major | | | two-way $\chi^2 = 4.46$, 1 $df$, $p < .05$. |
| Design-related | 15.6% | 1.7% | |
| Other | 82.2 | 62.7 | |

[a] Not statistically significant

Table C.15. *On-site responses to Wexner and other buildings (from 1 = strongly disagree to 7 = strongly agree).*

| | Wexner (N = 90) | Other Buildings [a] (N = 60) | F (1 df) |
|---|---|---|---|
| *Embodies participation and accessibility*[b] | 4.43 | 4.75 | |
| Makes good use of site | 4.57 | 5.55 | 14.72*** |
| Is pleasant[c] | 4.94 | 5.55 | 7.08** |
| Is calming | 3.51 | 4.88 | 47.17*** |
| *Responds to the campus setting*[b][c] | 3.72 | 5.41 | 31.30*** |
| Serves as magnet and focal point | 4.83 | 5.23 | |
| Is active[b] | 5.38 | 5.16 | |
| *Is adventurous and challenging*[b] | 5.56 | 4.69 | 12.04*** |
| Is dynamic | 5.75 | 4.98 | 13.69*** |
| Is exciting | 5.42 | 4.72 | 9.02** |
| Is atypical | 6.20 | 4.50 | 68.31*** |

[a] Others = Composite for James, Enarson, Library, and Chemistry
[b] Index item for factor.
[c] Poles reversed from survey (neglects campus setting, is unpleasant, is inactive). Higher numbers are positive.
**$p < .01$, with Bonferoni adjustments, this becomes statistically insignificant.*** $p < .001$.

Table C.16. *Analysis of variance results for on-site responses to Wexner and four other buildings separately (from 1 = strongly disagree to 7 = strongly agree).*

| | Wexner (n = 90) | James (n = 15) | Enarson (n = 15) | Library (n = 15) | Chem (n = 15) | F (4 df) |
|---|---|---|---|---|---|---|
| *Embodies participation and accessibility* [a] | 4.43 | 5.13 | 5.40 m.s. | 4.40 | 4.07 | 2.56* |
| Makes good use of site | 4.57 | 6.27*** | 5.93*** | 5.27 | 4.71 | 6.16*** |
| Is pleasant [b] | 4.94 | 6.20** | 5.53 | 5.33 | 5.13 | 3.11* |
| Is calming | 3.51 | 4.87*** | 5.60*** | 4.93*** | 4.13 | 15.49*** |
| *Responds to the campus setting* [ab] | 3.72 | 5.63** | 6.00** | 5.60** | 4.40 | 10.04*** |
| Serves as magnet and focal point | 4.83 | 5.60 | 5.27 | 5.60 | 4.47 | 2.41 m.s. |
| Is active [b] | 5.38 | 5.80 | 5.57 | 4.73 | 4.53 | 2.69* |
| *Is adventurous and challenging* [a] | 5.56 | 5.50 | 4.47 | 4.40* | 4.40* | 4.45** |
| Is dynamic | 5.75 | 5.87 | 4.80* | 4.87*** | 4.40*** | 6.72*** |
| Is exciting | 5.42 | 4.80 | 5.07 | 4.67 | 4.33* | 2.76* |
| Is atypical | 6.20 | 5.67 | 3.93** | 3.60** | 4.80 | 27.73*** |

[a] Index item from a factor.

[b] Poles reversed from survey (neglects campus setting, is unpleasant, is inactive) to positives.

$*p < .05$ Bonferoni adjusted. $**p < .01$ Bonferoni adjusted. $***p < .001$ Bonferoni adjusted. m.s. = marginally significant, $p < .10$.

Table C.17. *Ratings of Wexner compared to ratings of Math Tower and Chemistry Addition.*

| Scale | Wexner Center | Chemistry Addition (*n* = 86) | Math Tower (*n* = 30) |
|---|---|---|---|
| *Pleasant* | 4.94 | 5.57* | 5.36* |
| *Responds to Campus Setting* | 3.72 | 5.81* | 5.13* |
| *Calming* | 3.51 | 4.72* | |
| *Atypicality* | (6.20) | 2.12* | 3.06* |
| *Exciting* | (5.42) | 4.51* | |

*Note:* When compared for comparable scales (pleasant, responsive to campus setting, calming, exciting, and atypicality), Wexner emerged as significantly less pleasant, less responsive to the campus setting, less calming, more exciting, and more atypical. For the Chemistry Addition, the measure for Responds to Campus setting was Fits with Surroundings. For the Math Tower the measure for pleasant was Overall Appearance, and the measure for Atypicality was Poor Fit with OSU image.

*$p < .01$ (in comparison to Wexner).

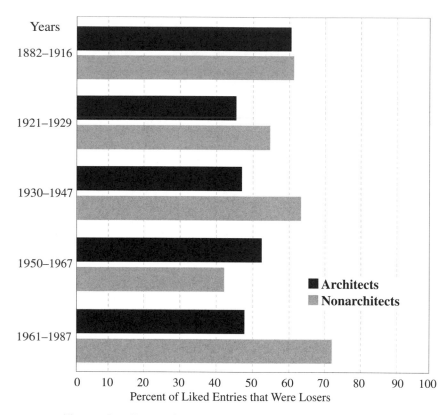

Figure C.1. For each group and time, the proportion of entries selected as *liked* that were competition losers. *Note.* Architect and nonarchitect choices of winners and losers differed significantly in 1930–1947 ($\chi^2$ [1, $n = 498$] = 13.68, $p < .001$), 1950–67 ($\chi^2$ [1, $n = 499$] = 5.66, $p < .02$), and 1981–87: $\chi^2$ [1, $n = 500$] = 31.08, $p < .001$). They also had a marginally significant difference for 1921–29: $\chi^2$ [1, $n = 499$] = 3.71, $p < .10$).

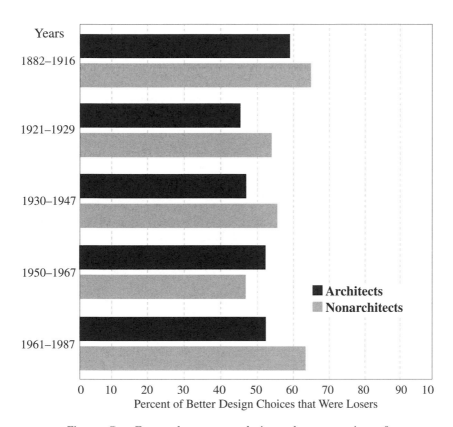

Figure C.2. For each group and time, the proportion of entries judged as *better designs* that were competition losers. *Note.* Architect and nonarchitect choices of winning and losing entries differed significantly in 1882–1916 ($\chi^2$[1, $n = 500$] = 3.87, $p < .05$) and 1981–87 ($\chi^2$ [1, $n = 498$] = 9.97, $p < .01$). They also had a marginally significant difference for 1950–1967 ($\chi^2$ [1, $n = 499$] = 3.70, $p < .10$).

# REFERENCES

1. Alberti, L. B. (1956). *On painting* (J. R. Spencer, Trans.). New Haven: Yale University Press (Original work published in 1435–36)
2. Alexander, E. R., Casper, D. J., & Witzling, L. P. (1990). Competitions for planning and urban design. Lessons from experience. *Journal of Architectural and Planning Research, 7,* 142–159.
3. Alexander, E. R., & Witzling, L. P. (1990). Planning and urban design competitions: Introduction and overview. *Journal of Architectural and Planning Research, 7,* 91–104.
4. Alexander, E. R., Witzling, L. P., & Casper, D. J. (1987). Planning and urban design competitions: Organization, implementation and impacts. *Journal of Architectural and Planning Research, 4,* 31–46.
5. American Institute of Architects. (1988a). *Encyclopedia of architecture, design, engineering and construction.* New York: Wiley.
6. American Institute of Architects. (1988b). *Handbook of architectural design competitions.* Washington, DC: American Institute of Architects.
7. Anderson, K. (1989, November 20). A crazy building in Columbus. *Time, 133,* pp. 21, 84, 89.
8. Anthony, K. H. (1991). *Design juries on trial: The renaissance of the design studio.* New York: Van Nostrand Reinhold.
9. Anthony, K. H. (1992, March 1). *ACSA Task Force on 'Schools of Thought in Architectural Education.* Paper prepared for the Associate Schools of Architecture.
10. Appleton, J. (1975). *The experience of place.* London: Wiley.
11. Appleyard, D. (1981). *Livable streets.* Berkeley JCA: University of California Press.
12. Appleyard, D., Lynch, K., & Myer, J. R. (1964). *The view from the road.* Cambridge, MA: MIT Press.
13. Aquinas, T. (1945). *Basic writings of St. Thomas Aquinas, Vol. 1* (A. C. Pegis Trans.). New York: Random House (Original work published in 1225–1274).
14. Archea, J. C. (1985). The use of architectural props in the conduct of criminal acts. *Journal of Architectural and Planning Research, 2,* 245–259.
15. Arnell, P., & Bickford, T. (Eds.) (1982). *A tower for Louisville: The human competition.* New York: Rizzoli.
16. Arnell, P., & Bickford, T. (Eds.) (1983). *Southwest Center: The Houston competition.* New York: Rizzoli.

17. Arnell, P., & Bickford, T. (Eds.) (1984a). *A Center for the Visual Arts: The Ohio State University competition.* New York: Rizzoli.

18. Arnell, P., & Bickford, T. (Eds.) (1984b). *Mississauga City Hall: A Canadian competition.* New York: Rizzoli.

19. Bacow, A. F. (1995). Designing the City. A Guide for Advocates and Public Officials. Washington, D. C.: Island Press.

20. Bailes, J. (1965). The case history of a failure. *Architectural Forum, 123,* 22–25.

21. Banerjee, T., & Loukaitou-Sideris, A. (1990). Competition as a design method: An inquiry. *Journal of Architectural and Planning Research, 7,* 114–131.

22. Barry, D. (1997, Sept. 7). Taxpayer-funded "art" need better labels. *The Columbus Dispatch.* 3D.

23. Basin, J. (1984). *Architectural competitions in nineteenth-century England.* Ann Arbor, MI: UMI Research Press.

24. Bechtel, R. B. (1972). The public housing environment: A few surprises. In W. J. Mitchell (Ed.). *Environmental Design: Research and Practice, Proceedings of the Environmental Design Research Association* (pp. 13–1–1 to 13–1–9). Los Angeles: University of California.

25. Bechtel, R. B. (1996). The paradigm of environmental psychology. *American Psychologist, 51,* 1187–1188.

26. Berlyne, D. E. (1971). *Aesthetics and psychobiology.* New York: Meredith.

27. Bilello, J. (1993). Deciding to build: University organization and the design of academic buildings. *Dissertation Abstracts International, 55* (04), 0767A. (University Microfilms, No. AAI9424999).

28. Bishop, J. (1984). Passing in the night: Public and professional views of Milton Keynes. *Places, 1,* 9–16.

29. Blake, P. (1974). *Form follows fiasco.* Boston: Atlantic Monthly Press.

30. Blau, J. R. (1984). *Architects and firms: A sociological perspective on architectural practice.* Cambridge, MA: MIT Press.

31. Boles, D. (1988). P/A reader poll competitions and awards programs, *Progressive Architecture, 69,* 15–17.

32. Bornstein, R. F. (1989). Exposure and affect. Overview and meta-analysis of research. 1968–1987. *Psychological Bulletin, 106,* 265–289.

33. BOSTI (Buffalo Organization for Sociological and Technical Innovation, Inc.) (1981). *The impact of office environment on productivity and quality of working life: Comprehensive findings.* Buffalo, New York: Author.

34. Box, S., Hale, C., & Andrews, G. (1988). Explaining fear of crime. *British Journal of Criminology, 28,* 340–356.

35. Boyer, E. L., & Mitgang, L. D. (1996). *Building community: A new future for architectural education and practice.* Princeton, New Jersey: The Carnegie Foundation for the Advancement of Teaching.

36. Brolin, B. (1976). *The failure of modern architecture.* New York. Van Nostrand.

37. Brower, S. (1988). *Design in familiar places: What makes home environments look good.* New York: Praeger.

38. Brush, R. O. 1976. Perceived quality of scenic and recreational environments: Some methodological issues. In Craik, K. H., & E. H. Zube (Eds).

*Perceiving environmental quality: research and applications* (pp. 47–58). New York: Plenum.

39. Brush, R. O., & J. F. Palmer (1979). Measuring the impact of urbanization on scenic quality. Land use change in the northeast. In G. Elsner, & R. S. Smardon (Eds.). *Our national landscape* (USDA-Forest Service General Tech. Rep. No PSW-35, pp. 358–364). Berkeley, CA: Pacific Southwest Forest and Range Experiment Station.

40. Building Research Board (1987). *Post-occupancy evaluation practices in the building process: Opportunities for improvement.* Washington, DC: National Academy Press.

41. Campbell, D. T., & Fiske, D. W. (1959). Convergent and discriminant validity by the multitrait-multimethod matrix. *Psychological Bulletin, 56,* 81–105.

42. Canter, D. (1969). An intergroup comparison of connotative dimensions in architecture. *Environment and Behavior, 1,* 37–48.

43. Canter, D., & Thorne, R. (1972). Attitudes to housing: A cross-cultural comparison. *Environment and Behavior, 4,* 3–32.

44. Carp, F. M., Zawadski, R. T., & Shokron, H. (1976). Dimensions of urban environmental quality. *Environment and Behavior, 8,* 239–264.

45. Carr, S., Francis, M., Rivlin, L. G., & Stone, A. M. (1992). *Public space.* New York: Cambridge.

46. Charles, Prince of Wales. (1989). *A vision of Britain: A personal view of architecture.* London: Doubleday.

47. Cherulnik, P. D. (1991). Reading restaurant facades: Environmental inference in finding the right place to eat. *Environment and Behavior, 22,* 150–170.

48. Cherulnik, P. D. (1993). *Applications of environment-behavior research: Case studies and analysis.* New York: Cambridge University Press.

49. Cherulnik, P. D., & Wilderman, S. K. (1986). Symbols of status in urban neighborhoods: Contemporary perceptions of nineteenth century Boston. *Environment and Behavior, 18,* 604–622.

50. Coastal Zone Management Act of 1972. 16 U.S.C.A. Section 1452 (2).

51. Cobb, H. N. (1984). Jury report. In Arnell, P., & T. Bickford (Eds). *A center for the visual arts: The Ohio State University competition* (pp. 24–27). New York: Rizzoli.

52. Construction Engineering Research Laboratory (CERL). (1982). *Information exchange bulletin,* R5:1, Urbana, IL.

53. Cooper, C. (1972). Resident dissatisfaction in multifamily housing. In W. M. Smith (Ed.), *Behavior, design and policy aspects of human habitats* (pp. 119–146). Green Bay: University of Wisconsin.

54. Craik, K. H. (1983). The psychology of the large scale environment. In N. R. Feimer & E. S. Geller (Eds.), *Environmental psychology: directions and perspectives* (pp. 67–105). New York: Praeger.

55. Craik, K. H., & G. E. McKechnie. (1974). *Perception of environmental quality: Preferential judgments versus comparative appraisals.* Unpublished manuscript, University of California at Berkeley.

56. Cronbach, L. J. (1951). Coefficient alpha and internal structure of tests. *Psychometrika, 16,* 297–334.

57. Cuff, D. (1989). Through the looking glass: Seven New York architects and their people. In R. Ellis, & D. Cuff (Eds.). *Architect's people* (pp. 64 102). New York: Oxford University Press.

58. Cuff, D. (1991). *Architecture: The story of practice.* Cambridge, MA: MIT Press.

59. de Haan, H, & Haagsma, I. (1988). *Architects in competition. International architectural competitions of the last 200 years.* London: Thames and Hudson.

60. Devlin, K., & Nasar, J. (1989). The beauty and the beast: Some preliminary comparisons of "high" versus "popular" residential architecture and public versus architect judgments of same. *Journal of Environmental Psychology,* 9, 333–344.

61. Duerk, D. P. (1993). *Architectural programming: Information management for design.* New York: Van Nostrand Reinhold.

62. Eley, J. (1990). Urban design competitions: A British Perspective. *Journal of Architectural and Planning Research,* 7, 132–141.

63. Espe, H. (1981). Differences in perception of national socialist and classicist architecture, *Journal of Environmental Psychology,* 1, 33–42.

64. Evans, G. W., & Wood, D. (1981). Assessment of environmental aesthetics in scenic highway corridors. *Environment and Behavior, 12,* 255–274.

65. Evenson, N. (1973). *Two Brazilian capitals: Architecture and urbanism in Rio de Janeiro and Brasilia.* New Haven: Yale University Press.

66. Evenson, N. (1979). *Paris, a century of change, 1887–1978.* New Haven: Yale University Press.

67. Fechner, G. T. (1876). *Vorschule der asthetik.* Leipzig: Breitopf & Hartel.

68. Fisher, B., & Nasar, J. L. (1992). Fear of crime in relation to three exterior site features: Prospect, refuge and escape. *Environment and Behavior, 24,* 35–56.

69. Fisher, T. (1985) An energy education. *Progressive Architecture, 66,* 74–77.

70. Fox, C. (1989, November 26). Peter Eisenman's powerful forms. *Atlanta Journal Constitution,* p. L1.

71. Francis, M. (1982, October 26–27). *Reflections on community design.* Paper presented at National Conference on Participatory Design in Low Income Communities. American Institute of Architects, Washington, D.C.

72. Frank Lloyd Wright Foundation (1977). *An autobiography: Frank Lloyd Wright.* New York Horizon Press.

73. Fried, M. (1963). Grieving for a lost home. In L. J. Duhl (Ed.) *The urban condition* (pp. 151–171). New York: Basic Books.

74. Friedman, A., Zimring, C., & Zube, E. H. (1978). *Environmental design evaluation.* New York: Plenum.

75. Gallup Poll. (1989). Most important problem. *The Gallup Report.* March/April.

76. Gans, H. (1974). *Popular culture and high culture: An analysis and evaluation of taste.* New York: Basic Books.

77. Gaver, W. W., & Mandler, G. (1987). Play it again Sam. *Cognition and Emotion, 1,* 259–282.

78. Geller, D. M., Cook, J. B., O'Connor, M. A., & Low, S. K. (1982). Perceptions of urban scenes by small town and urban residents: A multidimensional scaling analysis. In P. Bart, A. Chen, & G. Francescato (Eds.),

*Knowledge for design: Proceedings of the 13th international conference of the Environmental Design Research Association* (pp. 128–141). College Park, MD: Environmental Design Research Association.

79. Gibson, J. J. (1979). *The ecological approach to visual perception.* Boston: Houghton Mifflin.

80. Gifford, R. (1980). Environmental dispositions and the evaluation of architectural interiors. *Journal of Research in Personality, 14,* 386–399.

81. Gill, B. 1987. *Many masks: A life of Frank Lloyd Wright.* New York: Putnam.

82. Goldberger, P. (1989, November 5). The museum that theory built. New York Times, Sunday, Section 2, pp. 1, 38.

83. Goldblatt, D., & K. B. Jones. (1989). An interview with Eisenman. *Anfione Zeto: Quadrimestrale di Architettura e Arte, 4,* 278–292.

84. Good, D. et al. (Eds.) (1992) *Compton's encyclopedia and fact index.* Chicago, IL: Compton's Learning Co.

85. Gould, P., & R. White (1974). *Mental maps.* Middlesex, England: Penguin Books.

86. Gouldner, A., Pittman, D., Rainwater, L., & Stroberg, J. (1966). A preliminary report on housing and community experiences of Pruitt-Igoe residents. St. Louis, MO: Washington University.

87. Grabmeier, J. (1991, October 10). Budget, teaching, crime top a list of concerns. *On Campus,* p. 5.

88. Grannis, P. (1994). Postoccupancy Evaluation: An avenue for applied environment-behavior research in planning practice. *Journal of Planning Literature, 9,* 210–219.

89. Green, J. (1984). Architecture as logic, architecture as symbol. In Arnell, P., & T. Bickford (Eds). *A center for the visual arts: The Ohio State University competition* (pp. 18–20). New York: Rizzoli.

90. Groat, L. (1982). Meaning in Post-Modern architecture: An examination using the multiple sorting task. *Journal of Environmental Psychology, 2,* 3–22.

91. Groat, L. (1984, November). Public opinions of contextual fit. *Architecture, 73,* 72–75.

92. Groat, L. N., & Despres, C. (1990). The significance of architectural theory for environmental design research. In E. H. Zube, & G. T. Moore (Eds.). *Advances in environment, behavior, and design* (Vol. 3, pp. 3–53). New York: Plenum.

93. Gunn, S. (1983). *Eagle Ridge: An architectural design competition from inside the jury room.* Dallas: Inner Images, Inc.

94. Gutman, R. (1988). *Architectural practice: a critical view.* New York: Princeton Architectural Press.

95. Gutman, R. (1989). Human nature in architectural theory: The example of Louis Kahn. In R. Ellis, & D. Cuff (Eds.). *Architect's people* (pp. 105–129). New York: Oxford University Press.

96. Halsey, W. et al. (Eds.) (1991). *Collier's encyclopedia with bibliography and index.* New York: MacMillan Education Co.

97. Hanyu, K. (1993). The affective meaning of Tokyo: Verbal and non-verbal approaches. *Journal of Environmental Psychology, 13,* 161–172.

98. Hartig, T., Mang, M., & Evans, G. W. (1991). Restorative effects of natural environment experiences. *Environment and Behavior, 23*, 3–26.

99. Hekkert, P. (1996, August). *Assessment of aesthetic quality in art.* Paper Presented at the 104th annual convention of the American Psychological Association, Toronto, Canada.

100. Heise, D. R. (1970). The semantic differential and attitude research. In G. F. Summers (Ed.) *Attitude measurement* (pp. 235–253). Chicago: Rand McNally & Co.

101. Hershberger, R. G. (1969). A study of meaning and architecture. In H. Sanoff, & S. Cohn (Eds.), *EDRA 1: Proceedings of the first annual conference of the Environmental Design Research Association* (pp. 86–100). Raleigh, NC: North Carolina State University.

102. Hershberger, R. G., & Cass, R. C. (1974). Predicting user responses to buildings. In G. Davis (Ed.) *Man environment interaction: Evaluations and applications, the state of the art in environmental design research—field applications* (EDRA5, pp. 117–134). Milwaukee: Environmental Design Research Association.

103. Herzog, T. R., Kaplan, S., & Kaplan, R. (1976). The prediction of preference for familiar urban places. *Environment and Behavior, 8*, 627–645.

104. Herzog, T., Kaplan, S., & Kaplan, R. (1982). The prediction of preference for unfamiliar urban places. *Population and Environment, 5*, 43–59.

105. Herzog, T., & Smith, G. A. (1988). Danger, mystery, and environmental preference. *Environment and Behavior, 20*, 320–344.

106. Hesselgren, S. (1975). *Man's perception of man-made environment.* Stroudsburg, PA: Dowden, Hutchinson, & Ross.

107. Hitchcock, H-R., & Johnson, P. (1966). *The international style.* New York. Norton.

108. Holston, J. (1989). *The modernist city: An anthropological critique of Brasilia.* Chicago: University of Chicago Press.

109. Horayangkura, V. (1978). Semantic dimensional structures: A methodological approach. *Environment and Behavior, 10*, 555–584.

110. Hughes, R. (1995). *The shock of the new.* New York: Alfred A. Knopf.

111. Im, S-B. (1984). Visual preferences in enclosed urban spaces: An exploration of a scientific approach to environmental design. *Environment and Behavior, 16*, 235–262.

112. International Monetary Fund (1995). *International financial statistics yearbook.* Washington, DC: Author.

113. Jacobs, A. B. (1978). *Making city planning work.* Chicago: American Society of Planning Officials.

114. Jacobs, D. W. et al. (Eds.) (1993). *The world book encyclopedia.* Chicago, IL: World Book, Inc.

115. Jacobs, J. (1961). *The death and life of great American cities.* New York: Vintage.

116. Jockusch, P., Hegger, P., & Ettinger-Brinckmann, B. (1984, May). German Lesson 1: Just how successful in reality are the organization and results of the much praised German competition system. *The Architect's Journal, 180*, 39–46.

117. Judd, C. M., Smith, E. R., &, Kidder, L. H. (1995). *Research methods in social relations.* Fort Worth, TX: Holt, Rinehart & Winston.

118. Kamin, B. (1993, April 18). Wexner Center: A building that "shrieks" at visitors. *Chicago Tribune,* Section 13, 4.

119. Kang, J. (1990). Symbolic inferences and typicality in five taste cultures. *Dissertation Abstracts International, 51* (12), 3929A. (University Microfilms No. AAI 9105142).

120. Kaplan, R., & Kaplan, S. (1989). *The experience of nature: A psychological perspective.* New York: Cambridge University Press.

121. Kaplan, S. (1995). The restorative benefits of nature: Towards an integrative framework. *Journal of Environmental Psychology, 15,* 169–182.

122. Kaplan, S., Kaplan, R., & Wendt, J. S. (1972). Rated preference and complexity for natural and urban visual material. *Perception and Psychophysics, 12,* 354–56.

123. Kasmar, J. V. (1970). The development of a usable lexicon of environmental descriptors. *Environment and Behavior, 2,* 153–158.

124. Kasmar, J. V., Griffin, W. V., & Mauritzen, J. H. (1968). Effects of environmental surroundings on outpatients' mood and perception of psychiatrists. *Journal of Consulting and Clinical Psychology, 32,* 223–226.

125. Katakis, M. (1988). *The Vietnam Veterans Memorial.* New York: Crown.

126. Keeney, R., & Raiffa, H. (1976). *Decisions with multiple objectives: preferences and value tradeoffs.* New York: Wiley.

127. Kimmelman, M. (1990, March 8). A new arts complex that's hard on art. *The New York Times,* pp. C15, C21.

128. Kuller, R. (1975). Beyond semantic measurement. In B. Honikman (Ed.). *Responding to social change* (EDRA 16, pp. 181–197). Stroudsburg, PA.: Dowden Hutchinson and Ross.

129. Lang, J. (1987). *Creating architectural theory: the role of the behavioral sciences in environmental design.* New York: Van Nostrand Reinhold.

130. Lang, J. (1994). *Urban design: The American experience.* New York: Van Nostrand.

131. Lansing, J. B., Marans, R. W., & Zehner, R. B. (1970). *Planned residential environments.* Ann Arbor, MI: University of Michigan, Survey Research Center Institute for Social Research.

132. Lazarus, R. S. (1984). On the primacy of cognition. *American Psychologist, 39,* 124–129.

133. Lee, L-S. (1982). The image of city hall. In Bart, P., A. Chen, and G. Francescato (Eds.). *The knowledge for design* (EDRA 13, pp. 310–316). Washington, DC: Environmental Design Research Association.

134. Leff, H. L., Gordon, L. R., & Ferguson, J. G. (1974). Cognitive set and environmental awareness. *Environment and Behavior, 6,* 395–447.

135. Lethbridge, F. D. (1973). The honors awards program in retrospect. *American Institute of Architects Journal, 59,* 22.

136. Lewis, R. K. (1991). At the Wexner Center, the building is part of the exhibitry. *Museum News, 17,* 34–37.

137. Lightner, B. (1993, January). A survey of design review practice in local government. *MEMO: Planning Advisory Service.* Chicago: American Planning Association.

138. Lorimer, L. T. et al. (Eds) (1993) *The encyclopedia Americana*. Danbury, CT: Grolier.
139. Lynch, K. 1960. *The image of the city*. Cambridge, MA: MIT Press
140. Lynch, K. E., & Rivkin, M. (1959). A walk around the block. *Landscape, 8,* 24–34
141. Lynes, R. (1954). *The tastemakers*: New York: Harper.
142. Mandel, R. (1986, April 6). The beauties and the beasts. *San Francisco Examiner*, B1–B3.
143. Mandel, R. (1992, November 8). A question of taste – or lack of it. *San Francisco Examiner*, B1, B4.
144. Mandler, J. M. (1984). *Stories, scripts, and scenes: aspects of schema theory*. Hillsdale, New Jersey: Erlbaum.
145. Marans, R. W. (1976). Perceived quality of residential environments: Some methodological issues. In K. H. Craik, & E. H. Zube (Eds.), *Perceiving environmental quality: Research and applications* (pp. 123–147). New York: Plenum.
146. Marans, R. W., & K. F. Spreckelmeyer. (1982). Measuring overall architectural quality: A component of building evaluation. *Environment and Behavior, 14,* 652–669.
147. Martindale, C. (1990). *The clockwork muse: The predictability of artistic change*. New York: Basic Books.
148. McCue, G. (1973). $57,000,000 later. *Architectural Forum, 138,* 42–45.
149. McGuigan. C. (1989, November 20). Eisenman's gridlocked mind game. *Newsweek, 114,* 74–75.
150. McHenry, R. (Ed.) (1987). *The new encyclopedia Britannica* (15th ed.). Chicago, IL: Britannica.
151. Mehrabian, A., & Russell, J. A. (1974). *An approach to environmental psychology*. Cambridge, MA: MIT Press.
152. Michelson, W. (1987). Groups, aggregates, and the environment. In E. H. Zube, & G. T. Moore (Eds.). *Advances in environment, behavior, and design* (Vol. 1, pp. 161–185). New York: Plenum Press.
153. Miller, R. (1984). The competition process. In Arnell, P., & T. Bickford (Eds). *A center for the visual arts: The Ohio State University competition* (pp. 21–23). New York: Rizzoli.
154. Mills, J. S. (1961). Utilitarianism. In *The utilitarians* (1863 original edit.). New York: Doubleday.
155. Moore, E. (1982). A prison environment's effect on health care service demands. *Journal of Environmental Systems, 11,* 17–34.
156. Moore, G. T. (Ed.) (1982). *Environment and behavior. Vol. 14: Applied architectural research: Post-occupancy evaluation of buildings*. Beverly Hills: Sage.
157. Moore, G. T. (1989). Environment and behavior research in North America: History, developments, and unresolved issues. In. D. Stokols, & I. Altman (Eds). *Handbook of environmental psychology* (pp. 1359–1410). New York: Wiley.
158. Moreland, R. L., & Zajonc, R. B. (1977). Is stimulus recognition a necessary condition for the occurrence of exposure effects? *Journal of Personality and Social Psychology, 35,* 191–199.

159. Moreland, R. L., & Zajonc, R. B. (1979). Exposure effects may not depend on stimulus recognition. *Journal of Personality and Social Psychology, 37,* 1085–1089.

160. Musgrove, J. (Ed.) (1987). *Sir Banister Fletcher's History of Architecture* (19th ed.). London: Butterworth.

161. Nasar, J. L. (1974, May). *A Reinforcement Analysis of Design Behavior.* Paper presented at the fifth annual conference of the Environmental Design Research Association, Milwaukee.

162. Nasar J. L. (1980). Influence of familiarity on responses to visual qualities of neighborhoods. *Perceptual and Motor Skills, 51,* 635–642.

163. Nasar, J. L. (1983). Adult viewers' preferences in residential scenes: A study of the relationship of environmental attributes to preference. *Environment and Behavior, 15,* 589–614.

164. Nasar, J. L. (1984). Visual preference in urban street scenes: A cross-cultural comparison between Japan and the United States. *Journal of Cross-Cultural Psychology, 15,* 79–93.

165. Nasar, J. L. (1987a). Effects of signscape complexity and coherence on the perceived visual quality of retail scenes. *Journal of the American Planning Association, 53,* 499–509.

166. Nasar, J. L. (1987b). Environmental correlates of evaluative appraisals of central business district scenes. *Landscape and Planning Research, 14,* 117–130.

167. Nasar, J. L. (1987c). Physical correlates of perceived quality in lakeshore development. *Leisure Science, 9,* 259–279.

168. Nasar, J. L. (1988a). *Environmental aesthetics: Theory, research, and applications.* New York: Cambridge University Press.

169. Nasar, J. L. (1988b). Perception and evaluation of housing scenes. In J. L. Nasar (Ed.). *Environmental aesthetics. Research, theory and application* (pp. 275–288). New York: Cambridge University Press.

170. Nasar, J. L. (1988c). Urban scenes: Introduction. *In Environmental aesthetics: Theory, research, and applications* (pp. 257–259). New York: Cambridge University Press.

171. Nasar, J. L. (1989a). Perception, cognition, and evaluation of urban places. In I. Altman, & E. H. Zube (Eds.). *Public places and spaces: Human behavior and environment* (Vol. 10, pp. 31–56). New York: Plenum.

172. Nasar, J. L. (1989b). Symbolic meanings of house styles. *Environment and Behavior, 21,* 235–257.

173. Nasar, J. L. (1994). Urban design aesthetics: The evaluative qualities of building exteriors. *Environment and Behavior, 26,* 377–401.

174. Nasar, J. L. (1997). *The evaluative image of the city.* Beverly Hills, CA: Sage.

175. Nasar, J. L., Adam, K., Arroyo-Rodriguez, A, Buchanan, R., Chang S-L., Imeokparia, T., Nicholson, T. M., Popovich, S., & Vazquez, M. I. (1996). *Newman & Wolfrom Lab Building Post Occupancy Evaluation.* Report submitted to the university architect. The Ohio State University.

176. Nasar, J. L., Braam, S., Eom, J. Y., Kehlhem, D., Ramirez, S., Shrimplin, R., Sloan, R., Stansberry, S., York, K., Choo, C-J., Warsaw, S., & Petersen, P. J.

(1995). *Math Tower and Classroom Postoccupancy Evaluation.* Report submitted to the university architect. The Ohio State University.

177. Nasar, J. L., & de Nivia, C. (1987). A post-occupancy evaluation for the design of a light pre-fabricated housing system for low income groups in Colombia. *Journal of Architectural and Planning Research, 4,* 199–211.

178. Nasar, J. L., & Fisher, B. (1992). Design for vulnerability: Cues and reactions to fear of crime. *Sociology and Social Research, 76,* 48–58.

179. Nasar, J. L., & Fisher, B. (1993). "Hot spots" of fear of crime: A multiple-method investigation. *Journal of Environmental Psychology, 13,* 187–206.

180. Nasar, J. L., Fisher, B., & Grannis, M. (1993). Proximate physical cues to fear of crime. In J. L. Nasar (Ed.). *Landscape and Urban Planning: Special Issue on Urban Design Research, 26,* 161–178.

181. Nasar, J. L., & Jones, K. (1997). Landscapes of fear and stress. *Environment and Behavior, 29,* 291–323.

182. Nasar, J. L., & Kang, J-M. (1989a). A post-jury evaluation: The Ohio State University design competition for a center for the visual arts. *Environment and Behavior, 21,* 464–484.

183. Nasar, J. L., & Kang, J. (1989b). Symbolic meanings of building style in small suburban offices. In G. Hardie, R. Moore, & H. Sanoff (Eds.). *Changing paradigms* (EDRA 20, pp. 165–172). Oklahoma City: Environmental Design Research Association.

184. Nasar, J. L., & Kang, J. (1995). *Taste Cultures And House Styles.* City and Regional Planning Working Paper. The Ohio State University at Columbus.

185. Nasar, J. L., Pawley, J., & Zoller, L. (1994). Preferences for citation and non-citation architecture over time. In R. Feldman, & D. Saile (Eds.). *Power by design* (EDRA 24, pp. 46–50), Oklahoma City: Environmental Design Research Association.

186. National Endowment for the Arts (1981). *Design Competition Manual, Vision.* Cambridge, MA: National Endowment for the Arts, Design Arts Program.

187. National Environmental Policy Act of 1969, 42, U.S.C.A. Section 4321 *et seq.*

188. National Opinion Research Center. (1987). *General social survey (1972–1987). Cumulative codebook.* Chicago: Author.

189. Newman, O. (1972). *Defensible space.* New York: Macmillan.

190. Newman, O. (1995). Defensible space: A new physical planning tool for urban revitalization. *Journal of the American Planning Association, 61,* 149–156.

191. Norberg-Schulz, C. (1965). *Intentions in architecture.* Cambridge, MA: MIT Press.

192. Ohio State University (1983). *Program of Requirements Center for the Visual Arts Design Competition.* Office of Campus Planning and Space Utilization. Columbus, OH. Author.

193. Ohio State University (1989a). *The architectural competition for the Wexner Center.* Press Kit, Wexner Center for the Visual Arts: Author.

194. Ohio State University (1989b). *For immediate release. Major arts complex scheduled to open doors on November 17, 1989.* Press Kit, Wexner Center for the Visual Arts. Author.

195. Ohio State University (1989c). *An interview with Peter Eisenman.* Press Kit, Wexner Center for the Visual Arts. Columbus, OH: Author.

196. Ohio State University (1989d). *An interview with Robert Stearns. Director, Wexner Center for the Visual Arts.* Press Kit, Wexner Center for the Visual Arts. Columbus, OH: Author.

197. Ohio State University (1989e). *Peter Eisenman: Theory and practice.* Press Kit, Wexner Center for the Visual Arts. Columbus, OH: Author.

198. Ohio State University (1989f). *Statement by Edward H. Jennings.* Press Kit, Wexner Center for the Visual Arts. Columbus, OH: Author.

199. Ohio State University (1989g). *Statement by Leslie H. Wexner.* Press Kit, Wexner Center for the Visual Arts. Columbus, OH: Author.

200. Ohio State University (1991). *Wexner Center for the Arts: 1991 Annual Report.* Columbus, OH: Author.

201. Ollswang, J. E. (1990). Successful competitions: Planning for quality, equity and useful results, *Journal of Architectural and Planning Research, 7,* 105–113.

202. Ollswang, J., & Witzling, J. (1986). *The Planning and Administration of Design Competitions.* Milwaukee, WI: Midwest Institute for Design Research.

203. Oostendorp, A. (1978). The identification and interpretation of dimensions underlying aesthetic behaviour in the daily urban environment. *Dissertation Abstracts International, 40* (02), 0990B. (University Microfilms No. AAI0531007).

204. Oostendorp, A., & Berlyne, D. E. (1978). Dimensions in the perception of architecture: Measures of exploratory behavior. *Scandinavian Journal of Psychology, 19,* 83–89.

205. Ornstein, R. (1991). *The evolution of consciousness: Of Darwin, Freud, and cranial fire – the origins of the way we think.* New York: Prentice Hall Press.

206. Osgood, C. E., Suci, G. J., & Tannenbaum, P. H. (1957). *The measurement of meaning.* Urbana, IL: University of Illinois Press.

207. Palmer, M (Ed.). (1981). *The architects' guide to facility programming.* Washington, DC: Architectural Record Books.

208. Palmer, J. (1983, April). *Residential Greenspace Visual Quality.* Paper presented at the 14th annual conference of the Environmental Design Research Association, Lincoln, Nebraska.

209. Pearlman, K. T. (1988). Aesthetic regulation and the courts. In J. L. Nasar (Ed.). *Environmental aesthetics: theory, research, and applications* (pp. 476–92). New York: Cambridge University Press.

210. Pegrum, R., & Bycroft, P. (1989). Quality down under: Building evaluation in Australia. In W. F. E. Preiser (Ed.) *Building evaluation* (pp. 221–47). New York: Plenum.

211. Pena, W., Parshall, S., & Kelly, K. (1987). *Problem seeking: An architectural programming primer.* Washington, DC: American Institute of Architects Press.

212. Physical Facilities, Equipment and Library Committee. (1986). *A study of the relationship between the physical environment of the college campus and the quality of academic life.* Columbus, OH: The Ohio State University.

213. Pitt, D. G. (1988). The attractiveness and use of aquatic environments as outdoor recreation places. In I. Altman, & E. H. Zube (Eds.). *Public places and spaces: human behavior and environment* (Vol. 10, pp. 217–254). New York: Plenum.

214. Plato (1951). *Symposium* (trans. W. Hamilton). Baldmore: Penguin Books.

215. Prak, N. L. (1984). *Architects: The noted and the ignored.* New York: Wiley.

216. Preiser, W. F. E. (Ed.) (1978). *Facility programming: methods and applications.* Stroudsburg, PA: Dowden, Hutchinson and Ross.

217. Preisier, W. F. E. (Ed.) (1993). *Professional practice in facility programming.* New York, Van Nostrand Reinhold.

218. Preiser, W. F. E., Rabinowitz, H. Z., & White, E. T. (1988). *Post occupancy evaluation.* New York: Van Nostrand Reinhold.

219. *Progressive Architecture.* (1957, August). P/A news survey: Why Utzon won Sydney Competition, 38, 95–97.

220. *Progressive Architecture* (1985). 66, 1, 98–100.

221. *Progressive Architecture* (1991). Readers respond. Architecture's survey reveals how practitioners envision their profession, 81, 91–95.

222. Purcell, A. T. (1986). Environmental perception and affect: A schema discrepancy model. *Environment and Behavior, 18,* 3–30.

223. Purcell, A. T. (1995). Experiencing American and Australian high- and popular-style houses. *Environment and Behavior, 27,* 771–800.

224. Purcell, A. T., & Nasar, J. L. (1992). Experiencing other peoples houses: A model of similarities and differences in environmental experience. *Journal of Environmental Psychology, 12,* 199–211.

225. Rabinowitz, H. Z. (1989). The uses and boundaries of post-occupancy evaluation: An overview. In W. F. E. Preiser (Ed.) *Building evaluation* (pp. 9–18). New York: Plenum.

226. Rainwater, L. (1966). Fear and house as haven in the lower class. *Journal of the American Institute of Planners, 32,* 23–31.

227. Rapoport, A. (1990a). *History and precedence in environmental design.* New York: Plenum.

228. Rapoport, A. (1990b). *The meaning of the built environment: A non-verbal communication approach* (Updated Edition). Tucson: University of Arizona Press.

229. Rapoport, A. (1995, June). *Comments on environmental aesthetics.* Symposium presentation at the 27th annual conference of the Environmental Design Research Association, Salt Lake City, UT.

230. Rapoport, A., & Hawkes, R. (1970). The perception of urban complexity. *Journal of the American Institute of Planners, 36,* 106–111.

231. Reizenstein, J. E., & C. M. Zimring (Eds.) (1980). *Environment and behavior, 12. Evaluating occupied environments.* Beverly Hills, CA: Sage.

232. Riger, S. (1985), Crime as an environmental stressor. *Journal of Community Psychology, 13,* 270–281.

233. Rittell, H. (1976, March 7–9). Evaluating evaluators. In papers published from the accreditation Evaluation Conference of the National Architectural Accrediting Board, New Orleans.

234. Ross, C. E. (1993). Fear of victimization and health. *Journal of Quantitative Criminology, 9,* 159–175.

235. Royal Institute of British Architects (1986). *Architectural competitions: RIBA code of practice.* London: Author.

236. Russell, J. A., & Snodgrass, J. (1989). Emotion and environment. In D. Stokols, & I. Altman (Eds.). *Handbook of Environmental Psychology* (Vol. 1, pp. 245–280). New York: Wiley.

237. Russell, J. A., & Ward, L. M. (1981). The psychological representation of molar physical environments. *Journal of Experimental Psychology: General, 110,* 121–152.

238. Russell, J. A., Ward, L. M., & Pratt, G. (1981). Affective quality attributed to environments: a factor analytic study. *Environment and Behavior, 13,* 259–288.

239. Sadalla, E. K., Verschure, B., & Burroughs, J. (1987). Identity symbolism in housing. *Environment and Behavior, 19,* 569–587.

240. Sagan, C. (1996). *The demon haunted world.* New York: Ballantine Books.

241. Saint, A. (1983). *The image of the architect.* New Haven: Yale University Press.

242. Sanoff, H. (1977). *Methods of architectural programming.* Stroudsburg, PA: Dowden, Hutchinson & Ross.

243. Sanoff, H. (1989). Facility programming. In E. H. Zube and G. M. Moore (Eds.). *Advances in environment, behavior, and design* (Vol. 2, pp. 239–286). New York: Plenum.

244. Sauer, L. (1972). The architect and user needs. In W. M. Smith (Ed.). *Behavior, design and policy aspects of human habitats* (147–170). Green Bay: University of Wisconsin Press.

245. School of Architecture. (1985, Summer). A school of architecture alumni newsletter. Columbus, OH: The Ohio State University.

246. Scruggs, J. C., & Swerdlow, J. L. (1985). *To heal a nation: The Vietnam Veterans Memorial.* New York: Harper & Row.

247. Seaton, R. W., & Collins, J. B. (1970). Validity and reliability of ratings of simulated buildings. In W. S. Mitchell (Ed.). *Environmental design: Research and practice* (EDRA 2, pp. 6-10-1–6-10-12). Los Angeles: University of California Press.

248. Seidel, A. D. (1990). Design competitions receive mixed reviews. *Journal of Architectural and Planning Research, 7,* 172–180.

249. Shafer, E. L. Jr., & Richards, T. A. (1974). A comparison of viewer reactions to outdoor scenes and photographs of those scenes. (United States Department of Agriculture, Forest Service Research Paper NE 302) Upper Darby, PA: Northeast Forest Experiment Station.

250. Shaftsbury, A. A. Cooper., Earl of (1964). *Characteristics of men, manners, opinions, times* (Vol. 2). J. M. Robertson (Ed). Indianapolis: Bobbs-Merrill. (Original work published 1708)

251. Shelly, M. (1969). *Analysis of satisfaction* (Vol. 1). New York: MSS Educational Publishing Co.

252. Shirvani, H. (1985). *The urban design process.* New York: Van Nostrand Reinhold.

253. Simonton, D. K. (1984). *Genius, creativity, and leadership: Historiometric inquiries.* New York: Cambridge University Press.

254. Simonton, D. K. (1990). *Psychology, science and history: An introduction to historiometry.* New Haven: Yale University Press.

255. Skogan, W. G., & Maxfield, M. (1981). *Coping with crime: Individual and neighborhood reactions.* Beverly Hills, CA: Sage.

256. Smets, G. (1973). *Aesthetic judgment and arousal: An experimental contribution to psychoaesthetics.* Leuven, Belgium: Leuven Universitiy Press.

257. Smithson, P., & Smithson, A. (1967). *Urban structuring.* New York: Reinhold/Studio Vista.

258. Sommer, R. (1983). *Social design: Creating buildings with people in mind.* Englewood Cliffs, NJ: Prentice-Hall.

259. Sonnenfeld, J. (1966). Variable values in the space and landscape: An inquiry into the nature of environmental necessity. *Journal of Social Issues, 22,* 71–82.

260. Spreiregen, P. D. (1979), *Design competitions.* New York: McGraw-Hill.

261. Stamps, A. E. (1992). Bootstrap investigation of respondent sample size for environmental preferences. *Perceptual and Motor Skills, 7,* 220–222.

262. Stamps, A. E. (1995). Beauty is in . . .? In J. L. Nasar, P. Grannis, & K. Hanyu (Eds.), *EDRA26/1995* (pp. 48–53). Edmond, OK: Environmental Design Research Association.

263. Stamps, A. E. (1997a) Meta-analysis in environmental research. In. M. S. Amiel & J. C. Vischer (Eds.) *Space Design and Management for Place Making. Proceedings of the 28th Annual Conference of the Environmental Design Research Association* (pp. 114–124). Edmond, OK: Environmental Design Research Association.

264. Stamps, A. E. (1997b). Of time and preference: Temporal stability of environmental preferences. *Perceptual and Motor Skills, 85,* 883–896.

265. Stamps, A. E., & Nasar, J. L. (1997). Design review and public preferences: Effects of geographic location, public consensus, sensation seeking, and architectural styles. *Journal of Environmental Psychology, 17,* 11–32.

266. Starbuck, J. C. (undated a). *The most depicted buildings erected in the U.S.A. between the wars.* Vance Bibliographies, Architecture Series, A34.

267. Starbuck, J. C. (undated b). *The most depicted buildings erected in the U.S.A. since 1945.* Vance Bibliographies, Architecture Series, A34.

268. Stiny, G. (1981). The language of the prairie: Frank Lloyd Wright's prairie houses. *Environment and Planning B, 8,* 295–323.

269. Stoks, F. G. (1983). Assessing urban public space environments for danger of violent Crime especially rape. In D. Joiner, G. Brimikombe, J. Daish, J. Gray, & D. Kernohan (Eds.), *PAPER: Proceedings of the Conference on People and Physical Environment Research* (pp. 331–342). Wellington: New Zealand. Ministry of Public Works and Development.

270. Storr, R. (1985). "Tilted Arc": Enemy of the people? *Art in America, 73,* 90–97.

271. Strong, J. (1996). *Winning by design: architectural competitions.* Oxford: Butterworth–Heineman Architecture.

272. Sudman, S. (1976). *Applied sampling.* New York: Academic Press.

273. Swift, J. (1726). *Gulliver's Travels* (Reprinted, 1992). Philadelphia, PA: Courage books.

274. Taschen, B. (1994). *Architectural Competitions* (Volume 1, 1792–1949). Naarden, The Netherlands: Cees de Jong.

275. Taschen, B. (1994). *Architectural Competitions* (Volume 2, 1950-Today). Naarden, The Netherlands: Cees de Jong.

276. Taylor, R. B. (1989). Towards an environmental psychology of disorder: Delinquency, crime, and fear of crime. In D. Stokols, & I. Altman (Eds.), *Handbook of Environmental Psychology* (Vol. 2, pp. 952–986). New York: Wiley.

277. Thayer, R. L. Jr., & Atwood, B. G. (1978). Plant complexity, and pleasure in urban and suburban environments. *Environmental Psychology and Nonverbal Behavior, 3*, 67–76.

278. Thelen, L. (1996, June). *Correlates of Preferences for Urban Parks and Plazas.* Paper presented at the 27th annual conference of the Environmental Design Research Association, Salt Lake City.

279. Trites, D., Galbraith, F., Sturdavant, M., & Leckwert, J. (1970). Influences of nursing unit design on the activities and subjective feelings of nursing personnel. *Environment and Behavior, 3*, 303–334.

280. Tversky, A. (1977). On the elicitation of preferences: Descriptive and prescriptive considerations. In D. E. Bell, R. L. Keeney, & H. Raiffa (Eds.). *Conflicting objectives in decisions* (pp. 209–222). New York: Wiley.

281. Tversky, B., & Hemenway, K. (1983). Categories of environmental scenes. *Cognitive Psychology, 15*, 121–149.

282. Ulrich, R. S. (1974). Scenery and the Shopping Trip: The Roadside Environment as a Factor in Route Choice. *Dissertation Abstracts International 35* (1), 0346A. (University Microfilms No. AAI 7415878).

283. Ulrich, R. S. (1983). Aesthetic and affective response to natural environment. In I. Altman, & J. F. Wohlwill (Eds.). *Behavior and the natural environment: Human behavior and environment, advances in theory and research* (Vol. 6, pp. 85–125). New York: Plenum.

284. Ulrich, R. S. (1984). View through the window may influence recovery from surgery. *Science, 224*, 420–4221.

285. Ulrich, R. S., Simons, R. F., Losito, B. D., Fiorito, E., Miles, M., & Zelson, M. (1991). Stress recovery during exposure to natural and urban environments. *Journal of Environmental Psychology, 11*, 201–230.

286. United States Bureau of The Census (1993). *Statistical abstract of the United States: 1993* (113th edition.). Washington, DC: Department of Commerce.

287. Van Tuyl, L. (1989, December 11). A building waiting to be a building. *The Christian Science Monitor*, p. 10.

288. Verderber, S., & Moore, G. T. (1979). Building imagery: A comparative study of environmental cognition. *Man-Environment Systems, 7*, 332–341.

289. Villecco, M., & Brill, M. (1981). *Environmental design research: Concepts, methods and values.* Washington, DC: National Endowment of the Arts.

290. Vining, J., & Orland, B. (1989). The video advantage: A comparison of two environmental representation techniques. *Journal of Environmental Management, 29*, 275–283.

291. Vischer, J. C., & Cooper Marcus, C. (1986). Evaluating evaluation: Analysis of a housing design awards program, *Places, 3*, 66–85.

292. Vitruvius, P. (1960). Vitruvius: The ten books of architecture (M. H. Morgan, Trans. 1914). New York: Dover.

293. Vitz, P. (1966). Preference for different amounts of visual complexity. *Behavioral Science, 11*, 105–114.

294. Warr, M. (1985). Fear of rape among urban women. *Social Problems, 32*, 238–50.

295. Weidemann, S., & Anderson, J. R. (1985). A conceptual framework for residential satisfaction. In I. Altman, & C. Werner (Eds.) *Home environments*. New York: Plenum.

296. Wener, R., Frazier, W., & Farbstein, J. (1985). Three generations of evaluation and design of correctional facilities. *Environment and Behavior, 17*, 71–95.

297. Whitaker, C. (1996). *Architecture and the American dream*. New York: Clarkson N. Potter.

298. White, E. T. (1972). *Introduction to architectural programming*. Tucson, AZ: Architectural Media.

299. White, E. T. (1982). *Project programming: A growing architectural service*. Tallahassee: Florida A & M University, School of Architecture.

300. Whitfield, T. W. A. (1983). Predicting preference for everyday objects: An experimental confrontation between two theories of aesthetic behavior. *Journal of Environmental Psychology, 3*, 221–237.

301. Whyte, W. (1980). *The social life of small urban spaces*. Washington, DC: Conservation Foundation.

302. Wilson, M. A., & Canter, D. V. (1990). The development of central concepts during professional education: An example of a multivariate model of the concept of architectural style. *Applied Psychology: An International Review, 39*, 431–455.

303. Wineman, J., & Zimring, C. (1986). Energy past and future. *Progressive Architecture, 67*, 115–117.

304. Winkel, G., Malek, R., & Thiel, P. (1970). A study of human response to selected roadside environments. In H. Sanoff, & S. Cohn (Eds.), *EDRA 1: Proceedings of the 1st annual conference of the Environmental Design Research Association* (pp. 224–240). Stroudsburg, PA: Dowden, Hutchinson, & Ross.

305. Witzling, L., & Farmer, P. (1982). *Anatomy of a competition*. Milwaukee: University of Wisconsin-Milwaukee, Center for Architecture and Urban Planning Research,

306. Wohlwill, J. F., (1974, July). *The place of aesthetics in studies of the environment*. Paper presented at the Symposium on Experimental Aesthetics and Psychology of the Environment at the International Congress of Applied Psychology, Montreal, Canada.

307. Wohlwill, J. F. (1976). Environmental aesthetics: The environment as a source of affect. In I. Altman, & J. F. Wohlwill (Eds.). *Human behavior and the environment: Advances in theory and research* (Vol. 1, pp. 37–86). New York: Plenum.

308. Wohlwill, J. F. (1982). The visual impact of development in coastal zone areas. *Coastal Zone Management Journal, 9*, 225–248.

309. Wohlwill, J. F. (1983). The concept of nature: A psychologist's view. In I. Altman, & J. F. Wohlwill (Eds.). *Behavior and the Natural Environment: Human Behavior and Environment, Advances in Theory and Research* (Vol. 6, pp. 5–37). New York: Plenum.

310. Wohlwill, J. F., & Kohn, I. (1973). The environment as experienced by the migrant: An adaptation-level view. *Representative Research in Social Psychology, 4*, 135–164.

311. Wolfe, T. (1981). *From Bauhaus to our house.* New York: Farrar, Straus Giroux.

312. Wrigley, M. (1988). Deconstructivist architecture. In P. Johnson & M. Wrigley (Eds.), *Deconstructivist architecture* (pp. 10–20). New York: Museum of Modern Art.

313. Wyngaard, S. (1996). Living in Peter Eisenman's library, or, managing the mundane in postmodern paradise. *Art Documentation, 15*, 37–39.

314. Wynne, G. G. (Ed.) (1981). *Winning designs: The competitions renaissance.* New Brunswick, NJ: Transaction Books.

315. Zajonc, R. B. (1984). On the primacy of affect. *American Psychologist, 39*, 117–123.

316. Zeisel, J. (1981). *Inquiry by design.* Belmont, CA: Brooks/Cole.

317. Zimring, C. (1989). *Post occpuancy evaluation: Contra Costa County Main Detention Facility.* Atlanta: Environment/Behavior Inquiry.

318. Zube, E. H., Sell, J. L., & Taylor, G. (1982). Landscape perception: Research, application and theory. *Landscape Planning, 9*, 1–33.

# INDEX

The designation f in the index stands for figure and t stands for table